Vygotsky and Special Needs Education

Also available from Continuum

Justice and Equality in Education, Lorella Terzi
Lev Vygotsky, René van der Veer

Vygotsky and Special Needs Education

Rethinking Support for Children and Schools

Edited by

Harry Daniels and Mariane Hedegaard

continuum

Continuum International Publishing Group

The Tower Building	80 Maiden Lane
11 York Road	Suite 704
London SE1 7NX	New York, NY 10038

www.continuumbooks.com

© Harry Daniels, Mariane Hedegaard and Contributors 2011

The names of subjects in this book have been changed to protect their identities.

Harry Daniels, Mariane Hedegaard and Contributors have asserted their right under the Copyright, Designs and Patents Act, 1988, to be identified as Authors of this work.

British Library Cataloguing-in-Publication Data
A catalogue record for this book is available from the British Library.

ISBN: 978-1-4411-9858-7 (hardcover)
       978-1-4411-9172-4 (paperback)

Library of Congress Cataloging-in-Publication Data
Vygotsky and special needs education : rethinking support for children and schools / edited by Harry Daniels and Mariane Hedegaard.
    p. cm.
  Includes index.
  ISBN: 978-1-4411-9858-7 (hardcover)
  ISBN: 978-1-4411-9172-4 (pbk.)
  1. Vygotsky, L. S. (Lev Semenovich), 1896–1934–Criticism and interpretation. 2. Special education–Philosophy. 3. Early childhood education–Philosophy. I. Daniels, Harry. II. Hedegaard, Mariane. III. Title.

  LB880.V94V94 2011
  371.901–dc22
                                                2010025026

Typeset by Newgen Imaging Systems Pvt Ltd, Chennai, India
Printed and bound in India

Contents

Part III SUPPORT THAT TRANSCENDS BORDERS

8 Support for Children and Schools through Cultural Intervention

Harry Daniels

9 Relational Agency in Collaborations for the Well-Being of Children and Young People

Anne Edwards

Notes on Contributors

Louise Bøttcher

Louise Bøttcher is Cand. Psych, PhD and employed as assistant professor at Department of learning, DPU Aarhus University, where she is associated with the research program Inclusive Education and Social Pedagogy. Her research departs in cultural-historical activity theory, special pedagogy and developmental neuropsychology and is aimed at the investigation and theoretical understanding of children with disabilities and neurobiologically based impairments. In her research, she focuses on the enhancement of learning and development among children with cerebral palsy. She has combined quantitative studies of cognitive functions in children with cerebral palsy and qualitative case studies of learning and social participation of children with cerebral palsy in mainstream schools or special classes.

Her research received Vanfoerefondens [The foundation for people with motor disabilities] Research Award in 2009.

Seth Chaiklin

Seth Chaiklin is a Reader in the Department of Education at University of Bath, UK. His research interests include cultural-historical science (i.e. analysis of practice), psychology of subject-matter teaching and learning, strategies for the development of professional practice ('practice-developing research') and conceptual roots of cultural-historical theory.

Harry Daniels

Professor Harry Daniels is Professor and Director of The Centre for Sociocultural and Activity Theory Research at the Department of Education at the University of Bath and has been Professor of Educational Psychology and Special Educational Needs at the University of Birmingham for nine years. He draws on post Vygotskian and Bernsteinian theory to study processes of marginalization, exclusion and collaboration.

He is the author of *Vygotsky and Research*, *Vygotsky and Pedagogy*, and editor of *An Introduction to Vygotsky* and *Charting the Agenda: Educational activity after Vygotsky* (Psychology Press). He also edited *The Cambridge Companion* to *Vygotsky* (Cambridge University Press) with James V Wertsch and Michael Cole. He is also Adjunct Professor, Centre for Learning Research, Griffith University, Brisbane, Australia, Research Professor, Centre for Human Activity Theory, Kansai University, Osaka, Japan and Research Professor in Cultural-Historical Psychology, Moscow State University of Psychology and Education.

Anne Edwards

Anne Edwards is Professor of Education and Director of the Department of Education at the University of Oxford, where she also co-convenes the Oxford Centre for Sociocultural and Activity Theory Research (OSAT). She is a former President of the British Educational Research Association and holds a visiting Professorship at the University of Oslo. She has written extensively in the area of professional learning in educational settings and lately has focused on inter-professional practices when working with vulnerable children and families and, in particular, the expertise needed to work with others on complex problems. Her book on the relational turn in expertise is published by Springer in 2010 as *Being an Expert Professional Practitioner: The Relational Turn in Expertise* and in 2009 with Harry Daniels and others she produced *Improving Inter-Professional Collaborations: Multi-Agency Working for Children's Wellbeing* and *Activity Theory in Practice: Promoting Learning across Boundaries and Agencies*, both with Routledge.

Ros Fisher

Ros Fisher is Associate Professor in the Graduate School of Education at the University of Exeter. She moved into initial teacher training and educational research following several years as a primary school teacher in England and USA. She writes widely about classroom interaction and the teaching of literacy from a socio-cultural perspective. Books include *Inside the Literacy Hour* (Routledge, 2002), and edited the collection of papers from an ESRC funded research seminar series *Raising Standards in Literacy* (Falmer, 2002), and the recently published *Using Talk to Support Writing* (Sage 2010) with Debra Myhill, Susan Jones and Shirley Larkin. She is currently involved in projects to evaluate the DCSF pilot Every Child a Writer programme and an Esmée Fairbairn funded project investigating the impact of dialogic talk on young children's understanding of arithmetic. She is particularly interested in the use of Cultural-Historical Activity Theory to explore classroom contexts.

Jan Georgeson

Dr Jan Georgeson is Senior Lecturer in Early Years Professional Studies at University of Chichester.

Jan's background is in teaching children with special educational needs across a wide age range, specialising in working with young children with speech and language difficulties both in the home and in schools, nurseries and playgroups. After training as registered nursery inspector, she developed an interest in the variety of early years settings outside the state-maintained sector, and the resilience and ingenuity of the practitioners who work there. This interest provided the impetus for her doctoral study into organizational structure and interactional style in day nurseries and pre-school playgroups, which used sociocultural theory and functional linguistics to analyse the connections between culture and discourse in individual settings. She has also been involved in several research projects on disability and children's voice, remodelling the social workforce and supporting parents as educators of very young children. Jan currently teaches on the Early Years Professional Status programme at the University of Chichester, and has a particular interest in practitioners taking vocational pathways into work in early years settings.

Geoff Hayward

Dr Geoff Hayward is Reader and Director of Research in Education at Oxford University's Department for Education. He is the Associate Director of the ESRC Research Centre on Skills, Knowledge and Organisational Performance (SKOPE), a director of the Nuffield 14–19 Review, co-director of the Oxford Centre for Sociocultural and Activity Theory (OSAT), co-convenor of the Higher Education and Professional Learning research group, and a Governor of Oxford and Cherwell Valley College. His research interests include the economics and politics of education and training, transitions into the labour market and Higher Education, national qualification frameworks, and the relationship between Higher Education and the economy.

Initially trained as a research biologist, Geoff subsequently became a Further Education lecturer, his research interest in vocational education and training stemming from this experience. During this time and subsequently at the Liverpool Institute of Higher Education he became actively involved in working with young people at risk of social exclusion. This was developed further through the Engaging Youth Enquiry, part of the Nuffield 14–19 Review.

Mariane Hedegaard

Mariane Hedegaard is Professor and Convenor of the Centre for Practice, Person, Development, Culture (PPUK at Department of Psychology, Copenhagen University.

Research interests: (1) studying children in their everyday life across different institutions. The focus is children's activities across different institutional practices, home, school and after school activities, and to follow how children's activities in families influence their activities in school and after school and vice versa. (2) Formulating a cultural-historical methodology for studying children's development in everyday settings drawing on the cultural-historical approach of L. S. Vygotsky and the phenomenology approach of Alfred Schutz, where both institutional practice and children's motives and engagement is in-cooperated.

Charlotte Højholt

Charlotte Højholt completed her master degree in Psychology and PhD at the University of Copenhagen and is now an Associate Professor at the Department of Psychology and Educational Studies, Roskilde University. She is doing research in the field of children, working with theoretical development through 'Practice Research' – a unity of empirical research and developmental work. She takes her point of reference in children's participation in social practice, going across different life contexts as family, school, kindergarten recreation centres and special help arrangements. This has given a focus on the cooperation between the grown-ups (parents, teachers, pedagogues, psychologists) and on the communities of children. In this way she emphasizes the meanings of others to the personal development of a child. She has published books and articles in the areas of development, learning, professionalism, interdisciplinary work and methodology.

She is also Leader of the Ph.D. program 'Social Psychology of Everyday life', Roskilde University.

Jane Leadbetter

Dr Jane Leadbetter is a Tutor in educational psychology and is Director of the doctoral programme for practising educational psychologists in the School of Education, University of Birmingham. She is a member of the University's Centre for Research in Organizations and Pedagogy. Her doctoral research utilized activity theory to investigate and conceptualize professional practices of psychologists and teachers and she contributes to doctoral programmes at the university, where she introduces sociocultural activity and theoretical approaches to understanding organizations. Her current interests centre on learning in the workplace, using activity theory within educational psychology practice and supporting change processes within organizations. She is also interested in the profession and practice of educational psychology particularly from a cultural-historical perspective. She continues to work a day a week as a Senior Educational Psychologist for Birmingham Children's Services with a range of children, families and schools. She was one of the research team on the four-year ESRC funded Learning in and for Interagency Working project, which was assessed as outstanding by independent reviewers. Jane has contributed to books and written a range of articles on educational psychology and activity theoretical approaches. She has presented at key national and international conferences on her own research and joint research, including presentations at the last three International Society for Cultural and Activity Research (ISCAR) conferences.

Jill Porter

Dr Jill Porter is Director of Studies for research students at the Department of Education, University of Bath. She is also Adjunct Professor at the Department of Special Psychology, Faculty of Special and Clinical Psychology Moscow Department of Education, State Educational Institution of Higher Professional Education, Moscow State University of Psychology and Education. She has written extensively in the field of special education with particular interest and expertise in teaching pupils with severe and profound learning difficulties. Her book on *Researching Learning Difficulties* looks critically at previous research and sets an agenda for developing research practice in the field and in particular giving voice to children and young people who are often marginalized by the research process.

A series of recently funded research projects on developing Disability Data Collection methods for Children's Services has resulted in a consistent way of identifying disability through foregrounding the importance of the subjective experience of the child and their family and providing a means by which schools can respond to and understand the needs of disabled children and their families.

Christine Vassing

Christine Vassing is a Doctoral Student at the Department of Psychology, University of Copenhagen. She is a member of the PPUK (Practice, Person,

Development, Culture) centre in the Department of Education. She is studying how educational psychological consultation in schools influences children's participation in school. The study is framed within the cultural-historical theory of child development including the child's perspective inspired by L. S. Vygotsky and Mariane Hedegaard as well as within ideas derived from practice developing research as outlined by Seth Chaiklin.

Before embarking on her studies she worked as an educational psychologist in schools from 2002–2007.

Introduction

Mariane Hedegaard and Harry Daniels

Reframing problems in schools

Our intention is to offer a way of thinking about problems in schools without pathologizing those who work and study within them. We believe that there is much to be gained from theory that guides intervention towards the person in a situation rather than towards a feature that lies within the person alone. The work of theory is to direct the gaze, reformulate challenges and redesign intervention. Vygotsky's theory of development gives a possibility to meet these challenges. We build our understanding of children's learning and development in school on Vygotsky's (1993, 1998) theory of multiple pathways for children's development. This theory takes departure in the conception that there is a wide diversity of biological and social conditions for children's development but development through educational support always can be forward directed towards realizing children to appropriate motives and competences appreciated in the societal institutions that the child is part of.

The differences between medical and social models of disability give rise to profound differences in the understandings that professionals use to formulate their actions. A reformulation of the relation between biological and social features of a situation could provide new ways of thinking about pedagogic approaches to conditions such as Cerebral Palsy.

In the school today there is a political agenda that challenge teachers to include children with disabilities or learning problems in the classroom – a challenge teachers often have to meet without the necessary educational support and theoretical understandings of how to accomplish the special education that are needed.

Many teachers work in schools in which there is very little collaboration between them and their colleagues. They become isolated and often anxious about the extent to which they can respond to the many demands that teaching makes of them as professionals. This division of labour denies the possibility of sharing knowledge, skills and understanding that can be brought to bear on the multitude of challenging problems that are presented in classrooms and schools. Professional isolation can result in a retreat from engagement with problem solving and the adoption of survival strategies which are not necessarily aligned with pedagogic intentions. In situations such as these, interventions can be designed, in our view often mistakenly, to influence individuals when they should be geared toward transforming patterns of staff collaboration.

We will introduce the chapters in this book through an outline of the sorts of problems that people face in school. We do so because our intention is to offer possibilities for thinking of these problems through frameworks and theories that do not conform to those that seem to predominate in education at the present time.

Problems that the chapters take departure in are: How and when should children with problems for instance cerebral palsy be included in classroom teaching? (Bøttcher, Chapter 1). How can teachers and psychologist become more conscious of how children, when they enter school or special education, have different ways of understanding the tasks and demands they meet and what is meaningful for them? (Porter, Chapter 2; Fisher, Chapter 3). How can teachers support each other in an inclusive classroom politics? (Daniels, Chapter 8). How do professional support children's relation to caregivers so they develop resilience toward for instance social conditions of poverty, broken families, and other social difficult conditions (Edwards, Chapter 9; Højholt, Chapter 4).

Educational psychologists also meet the demands of an inclusive politics. This can create a dilemma between support for the school and the child. How do the educational psychologist and professional connected with schools develop new practices to handle this dilemma? (Højholt, Chapter 4; Hedegaard and Chaiklin, Chapter 5; Vassing, Chapter 6). What are the ideals for professionals' cooperation and communication to realize support to children and schools? (Leadbetter, Chapter 7; Daniels, Chapter 8; Edwards, Chapter 9). How can practice research become a tool for developing practice in schools? (Hedegaard and Chaiklin, Chapter 5; Porter, Chapter 2). How should one look at the societal conditions for changing practice with children and schools with problems? (Hayward, Chapter 10; Gorgeson, Chapter 11).

The chapters in this book take up the challenge that we regard as lying within the cultural-historical tradition for specific aspects of practice of support for individuals and institutions within education. This perspective seeks to forge a connection between societal, institutional and individual analyses. According to this theoretical standpoint, developmental psychology and childhood research has to embrace the child as an individual person and at the same time as a participant in a societal collective interacting with other persons in different institutional practices. A child develops both as an individual with a unique distinctiveness and as a member of a society where different institutional practices are evident (Hedegaard and Chaiklin, Chapter 5).

Developmental pathways

In Chapters 1, 3, 4, 5 and 6 (Bøttcher, Ross, Højholt, Hedegaard and Chaiklin, Vassing) children's social situation of development is in focus. Vygotsky points to the importance of taking the child's social situation of development into consideration. A child's social situation of development changes in relation to different periods in a child's development. The social situation of development indicates that the relation between the child's personality and his social environment at each age level are mobile.

The relation of the whole to the part such as how the relation between language development and the child's general development change at each age level is important. Vygotsky points to developmental lines (that is the child's development of language, memory, thinking and reflection) becoming central or peripheral according to their relations to the child's developmental age. For example, at the age of two, speech development is a central line of development. During school age, the continuing development of child's speech has a completely different relation to the central neo-formation of this age and, consequently, must be considered as one of peripheral lines of development (Vygotsky, 1998, p. 197).

In Vygotsky's terminology developmental lines cannot be separated into biological, environmental and psychological lines but they are woven together. The environment in this relation must not be conceived as something outside the child, as an aggregate of objective conditions without reference to the child and how they are affecting him by their very existence (Vygotsky, 1998, p. 198). Vygotsky writes that the child's chronological age cannot serve as a reliable criterion for establishing the actual level of development. To determine the actual level of development requires studies to diagnose the child's development. To do this one has to focus on reliable traits or functions which can be used to identify each developmental age in the process of a child's development. It means that one has to formulate ideals of child development, ideals that interweave biological lines as well as cultural-historical lines of development, so that caregivers and educators have to formulate ideals of cultural development that are specific for a cultural tradition in an institution for instance in the different grades in school.

Instead of using developmental lines we will take a more holistic approach that Vygotsky's conception of the social situation of development gives possibility for and use the concept developmental pathways both to highlight how a pathway can be recognized by the involved persons and to highlight that there are several pathways for the development of each child. Here it is important to combine the concept of institutional practice as well as person's activity with the concept of developmental pathways. This is in line with Vygotsky's conception of how the child's social situation of development is created.

The social environment as it is realized in institutional practice is the source for the appearance of all specific human properties that has been gradually acquired by the child. A child currently participates in several institutional settings and arenas in his or her everyday life, for instance home, day-care and extended family, or home, school and community peer group or after school activities. In Western industrialised/information societies, the child's participation in different institutions can be seen as a developmental pathway where the dominant institutions in a child's life change from being home, to day care/infant school, to school.

Learning and development through entering institutional practices

The children's daily life can be seen from three perspectives: a societal perspective, an institutional perspective and a person's perspective. The societal perspective is a macro perspective that gives conditions for the practices children can participate in, in home, education and work. Changes in children's relation to the world are first and foremost connected to qualitative changes in what are the dominant institutional practices in a child's life. Entering a new institutional practice such as going to school is from a societal perspective viewed as important for a child's development. How children's participation and learning in different institutional practices lead to developmental changes for a child has to be analysed in relation to the child's social situation of development.

Children's activity takes place in different activity settings within different practices where their motivation and engagements are directed towards participating or creating activities in these specific activity settings. The setting is the cultural-material conditions in the form of the material characteristic of the institutions, room size, furniture, all sorts of material including books, TV, computers etc. available to the child. Practice and activity are related concepts. *Practice* we will use when the institutional perspective is taken, *activity* when the person's perspective is taken (an overview of the conceptual relations can be seen in Table 0.1). Children develop through participation in institutionalized practice that are characterised by communication and shared activities. These forms of practice initiate but also restrict children's activities and thereby become conditions for their development. A child's participation in activity settings in kindergarten practice such as meals and play lead to different activities for the child in kindergarten than in home since the kindergarten setting and its practice traditions gives different conditions than home settings and traditions for these activities.

In school, learning activities such as mathematics, eating lunch and playing are done within the practice tradition of schools. The institutional practice traditions contribute as well as the child's actions to the concrete activities that can be found within the school practice.

Table 0.1 Relations between entity, process and dynamic

Entity	Process	Dynamic
Society	Tradition	Conditions
Institution	Practice	Object motives
Activity setting	Social situation	Motivation/Engagement
Person	Activity	Motives/Interests/Projects

Revised from Hedegaard, 2008, p. 17

To describe and understand the conditions for development, one has to ask what kind of institutional practices do children in modern society participate in, what activities dominates the institutional practices of modern society, what demands do they put on children, and what possibilities for activities and how do children act in these activities. Also what kind of crises will children meet through conflicting demands and motives (i.e. moving from one institution to the next [from home to school, or from school to special institutions]) appropriating the orientation and competence required by these institutions.

How practice may be understood in institutions

In the Chapters 7, 8, 9, 10 and 10 (written by Leadbetter, Daniels, Edwards and Georgeson respectively) there is a focus on patterns of communication within institutions. For example, in Chapter 8 Daniels considers shifts in patterns of communication as practices become progressively more collaborative. In Chapter 10 Georgeson examines the relationship between patterns of pedagogic communication and modalities of institutional structure. Both these and other chapters call for a theoretical tool which will enable researchers to consider patterns of communication as features of the character of institution and then to examine the implications for development. Bernstein's (2000) model is one that is designed to relate macro-institutional forms to micro-interactional levels and the underlying rules of communicative competence. He provides a semiotic account of cultural transmission which is avowedly sociological in its conception. His analysis of the school, as an institution, shows his continuous engagement with the inter-relations between changes in organizational form, changes in modes of control and changes in principles of communication.

Bernstein's (2000; 1981) analysis and description focuses upon two levels: a structural level and an interactional level. *The structural level* is analysed in terms of *the social division of labour* it creates and *the interactional level* with the form of *social relation* it creates. The social division of labour is analysed in terms of strength of the boundary of its divisions, that is, with respect to the degree of specialization. The interactional level emerges as the regulation of the transmission/acquisition relation between teachers and taught: that is, the interactional level comes to refer to the pedagogic context and the social relations of the classroom or its equivalent. Bernstein uses the concept of *classification* to determine the underlying principle of a social division of labour and the concept of *framing* to determine the principle of its social relations. This enables him to analyse the structural and interactional levels in such a way that they can be analytically separated from each other and yet be considered as a whole.

He also proposes an analytical distinction between two kinds of knowledge: knowledge pertaining to abstract concepts and skills and knowledge pertaining to moral conduct. He argued that these two modes of knowledge are related through specialized pedagogic discourses. For him pedagogic discourse is a single discourse, created by the embedding of an *instructional* (i.e. knowledge and skills and their relations to each other) into a *regulative* discourse (principles of social order, relation and identity). Both these aspects of pedagogic discourse may be described in terms of classification and framing concepts, a variety of pedagogic structures may be generated according to their organizing principle, that is, in terms of their underlying code. The form of the code contains principles for distinguishing between contexts *and* the creation and production of specialized communication within contexts.

Bernstein (1993) suggests that much of the work that has followed Vygotsky 'does not include in its description how the discourse itself is constituted and recontextualised'. He argues that the code of a specific practice is formed through the institutional recontextualization of social practices that are external to it. Pedagogic discourse is constructed by a principle which selectively appropriates, relocates, refocuses, and relates other discourses to constitute its own order. In the same way that Vygotsky (1987) talked of the relation between the internal and the external as not being a copy, so Bernstein argues that a pedagogic discourse can never be identified with any of the discourses it has recontextualized. Schools appropriate and transform the dominant pedagogic activities of society and make them their own.

Mariane Hedegaard suggested (1999) that 'institutions stand between society and persons'. Bernstein provides an account of the possible details of this relation as shown in Figure 0.1 below.

The language that Bernstein has developed, uniquely, allows researchers to take measures of institutional codes. That is to describe and position the discursive, organizational and interactional practice that has resulted from the institutional recontextualization of societal motives. Research may then seek to investigate the connections between the rules that people use to make sense of their pedagogic world and the code of that world.

Taken together the post Vygotskian cultural-historical tradition as represented in the work of Mariane Hedegaard and the more sociological account

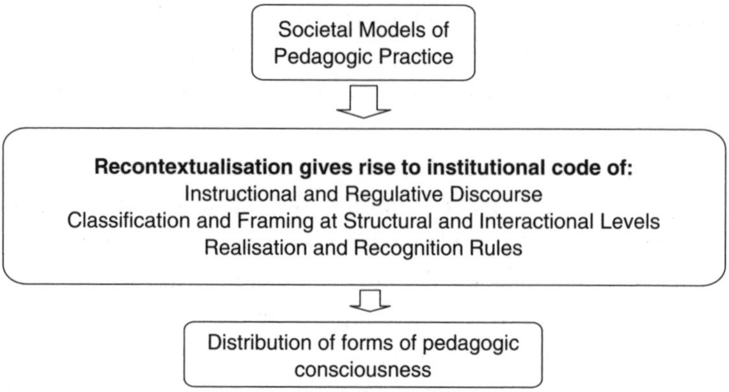

Figure 0.1 Bernstein's approach to the society, institution, individual relation.

of cultural transmission that has been developed from Bernstein's work for researching child development, communication and institutional practice as interrelated features of the way in which societal motives are locally transformed and enacted. As such they can be deployed in the consideration of issues such as support which by its very nature plays between the institution and the individual.

References

Bernstein, B. (2000). Pedagogy, Symbolic Control and Identity: Theory, Research, Critique (revised edition). Lanham, Maryland: Rowman & Littlefield Publishers Inc.

Hedegaard, M. (1999). Institutional Practice, Cultural Positions and Personal Motives: Immigrant Turkish Parents' Conceptions about their Children's School Life, in: S. Chaiklin, M. Hedegaard, J. Juul Jensen, (eds), Activity Theory and Social Practice (pp. 276–301). Aarhus: Aarhus University Press.

Vygotsky, L. S. (1993). The Collected Works of L. S. Vygotsky. Volume 2. Problems of General Psychology. New York: Plenum Press.

—(1998). The Collected Works of L. S. Vygotsky. Volume 5. Child Psychology. New York: Plenum Press.

Part I
Children with Special Needs

Cognitive Impairments and Cultural-Historical Practices for Learning: Children with Cerebral Palsy in School

1

Louise Bøttcher

Chapter Outline

Children with Cerebral Palsy (CP) are often placed in mainstream schools. Although some of these children function similarly to their peers, a substantial amount of them experience learning problems (Frampton et al., 1998), problems in social relations (Yude et al., 1998), or both. Often, these problems are approached and understood from the perspective of cognitive psychology and neuropsychology. Within this perspective, cognitive functions are considered in an individualized way as processes in a symbol-processing system. Through the various cognitive processes, symbols are manipulated and transformed into other symbols, which ultimately relate to the external world. The mind is seen as a limited-capacity processor, which depends on a neurological substrate, but is not wholly constrained by it (Pinker, 1994; Gazzaniga, 2000).

From a cultural-historical perspective this approach fails to notice how the so-called external world shapes cognitive processes in general:

Memory and thinking in daily life are not separate from, but part of, doing. We understand cognitive tasks, not merely as ends in themselves, but as means for achieving larger objectives and goals; and we carry out these tasks in constant interaction with social and material resources and constraints. (Scribner, 1997 p. 297)

Studies in situated cognition emphasize how cognitive processes depend on situated structures and processes including the person, the activity, the tools and the socio-cultural practices (Wortham, 2001). Beginning in the concept of mediation Vygotsky and Luria formulated a theory of how cultural means like tools and signs transformed human cognition (Cole and Engeström, 1993). The cognitive symbol manipulation is culturally mediated and the cultural means are learned by children and adults through their activities in practices. Salomon (1993) proposes a reciprocal relation between individual's cognitions and distributed cognition within activities.

The relation between cognitive functioning and the world in which cognition is taking place is described as interactive, because individuals' cognition is constrained by the institutional practices for cognitive activity, by which is meant knowledge domains, skill systems, technologies and practices for using them. In a spiral-like dialectic, individuals' cognition and the practice framework of the distributed cognitions develop each other. This implies an approach to human cognitive functioning, in which cognition is neither located exclusively in the individual, nor in the situated activity systems of particular groups of people alone, but requires individuals and activity systems together (Salomon, 1993). This chapter examines children with CP as individuals acting in learning practices and demonstrate how their learning and learning impairments can be understood as activity constrained by both biological and social frameworks. It will be done through an examination of the dialectical dynamic between school practices and the learning activities of children with CP, with a focus on how to understand cognition as constrained by neurobiology and cultural-historical practices at the same time, both of which are mutually interacting and potentially movable.

Vygotsky's idea of developmental disontogenesis

The medical model of disability assumes that a direct relationship exists between the biological defect and the disability: The child with CP has a brain lesion, which gives rise to learning impairments. From the cultural-historical point of view, this understanding of disability fails to notice how a child with a biological defect has to act in social institutions first and foremost adapted to children with normal psychophysical constitutions. For typical children, the biological and psychological lines of development are interwoven and the child meets relevant expectations and demands in its different institutional settings. In contrast, the often problematic development of children with biological defects is the result of a mismatch between the two developmental lines (Vygotsky, 1993). The primary defects such as sensory, organic or neurological impairments have an impact on the development of perceptual and higher cognitive functions and through this impact influences on the development of the child as a whole, including social development and the learning of cultural tools, which often result in secondary defects (1993, p. 35 f.). This process of *disontogenesis* implicates that the presence of a defect or disability in a child *reorganizes the development of that particular child as a whole.*

However, the learning of higher mental functions can transform more primary functions. Through mastering of cultural tools, learned through compensatory techniques, children with disabilities should be able to overcome both primary and secondary defects and develop mental skills equivalent of their peers, although by different learning trajectories (Vygotsky, 1993). Taken together, this cultural-historical perspective emphasizes the dialectical nature of the relation between a biological defect and the development of the child and offers a new way of thinking about pedagogic approaches to children with conditions such as CP.

The brain lesion functions as neurobiological constraints on cognitive processes

Above, the relation between the child's cognitive functioning and the environment of the child was described as a dynamic, in which individuals' cognition is constrained by practice framework of cognition. In order to incorporate the dynamic nature of the biological defect in this understanding of the development of a child, the brain lesion can be considered a *neurobiologically* based regulator of the developing child in its environment. Following recent research in neural plasticity (Stiles, 2000; Stiles et al., 2005; Juenger et al., 2007), the

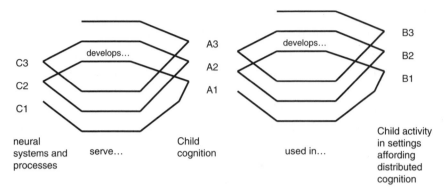

Figure 1.1 The double spiral showing the mutual impact of neural and social processes on individual cognition.

biological base is no longer regarded as stable, but seen as changeable in response to the activity of the child. Especially synaptic connections have been shown to be mouldable in response to the activity of the child. This biological dynamic can be visualized as a doubling of the spiral from Salomon (1993).

The brain lesion (C1) impacts on the left spiral as neurobiological constraints on the ability of the neural systems and processes to serve the individual cognition (A1) and, through the feedback process, the possibilities for further development of the neural systems and processes in the brain (C2, C3, Cx). The neurobiological constraints denote the dialectic processes in the left spiral. However, the development of both cognitive functions and neural processes are dependent on the right spiral, where the child's participation in different activities affords and develops particular cognitive activities and processes. The child's activities in activities (B) in the right spiral create developmental possibilities or social constraints that feedback on the individual cognitive activity of the child (A) and further back to the development of neural systems and processes (C) in the left spiral. The two spirals represent different processes, much in common with Vygotsky's two lines of development mentioned earlier, and are not mirror images of each other. The problematic mismatch, which arises when the child with a significant brain lesion have to act in practices cultivated for typically developing children, might constrain cognitive *and* neural development through its impact on the possibilities of the child to participate in activities.

The developmental processes in the two spirals can be approached from different perspectives (Hedegaard and Chaiklin, this book). From the institutional perspective, the analysis will focus on the organization of the learning practice and the teacher remediation in relation to the identified learning difficulties of different children. The interest becomes how to organize learning activities that afford the desired kind of learning and cognitive development in individual children.

However, in order to understand the way the child participates in different activities, it becomes necessary to include the perspective of the child in the analyses (Hedegaard and Fleer, 2008; Hedegaard and Chaiklin, this book). Analyses of individual children's perspectives focus on the personal and engaged relation between that child and the different practices, it participates in. The specific motives of a particular child arise from former experiences, development in interests and ideas about what he or she would like to do in the near future. Motives develop and change as the cognitive and emotional abilities of the child grows, leading the child to new forms of acting (Hedegaard, 2002). Through a focus on the motives of the child, it becomes possible to relate the analysis of cognitive remediation to the activity of a particular child.

Executive dysfunction as a particular neurobiological constraint

Vygotsky stated that the particular primary and secondary defects can be remediated through the use of compensatory techniques, which enable the child to master psychological tools and use them to acquire cultural forms of behaviour. This point of view focuses on the right side of the model. However, if we include the left side of the double-spiral in Figure 1.1, it becomes apparent that the learning and use of strategies is much more difficult, if the primary neurobiological defect affects the ability of the child to learn the psychological tools aimed at remediation. Recent research implies that this might be the case in children with brain lesions in the prefrontal cortex or in neural systems serving prefrontal cortex functioning; the so-called executive functions.

From the perspective of neuropsychology and cognitive psychology, there is general agreement that executive functions are several higher-order functions aimed at self-regulation in cognitive, behavioural and emotional domains (Powell and Voeller, 2004). Several approximately similar definitions stress different aspects. The definitions by Welsh & Pennington (1988) and Alexander and Stuss (2000) each mention planning and mental flexibility. Baddeley (1986) stresses the role of executive functions in situations, which require the simultaneous operation of different cognitive processes; meta-cognition. Baron (2004) links the whole complex of different domains to the ability to act in a common sense way towards a purposive goal.

From a cultural-historical situated cognition perspective, executive functions are comparable with the concept of higher mental functions in the sense that both enable us to acquire and use cultural tools such as mental strategies to utilize our natural cognitive functions in new ways. Executive functions such as meta-cognition, planning and mental flexibility are also essential, when we engage in social activities and for example try to follow personal motives in particular practices or weigh different personal motives against each other.

Compensation for impairments in natural functions are often accomplished through the use of psychological tools mastered through higher mental functions (Kozulin and Gindis, 2007). However, impairments in executive domains decrease the ability to learn mental strategies and the ability to reflect on one's own cognition (Powell and Voeller, 2004). This can compromise the appropriation of psychological tools. A blind child might learn Braille and become able to read and learn similar to typical children although by different means. A child with a brain lesion affecting visual perception might need to learn to read by different means too, but if the brain lesion also affected his executive control of attention, the executive dysfunction might impede learning how to compensate for the visual impairment. Compensation for the executive impairment might also be required.

Empirical study

In order to explore how learning activities and the individual cognitive activity of children with brain lesions are dynamically related, a study was done with children with cerebral palsy and their learning activities in school. CP is a group of developmental disorders most recognizable by their disturbances of movement and posture. The disorders are due to an early non-progressive lesion of the central nervous system and the main symptoms are disorders of movement and posture, but other symptoms are often seen in addition; disturbances of sensation (vision or hearing) and perception (understood as the capacity to incorporate and interpret sensory information), global or specific cognitive difficulties, communication disorders, and seizures (Bax et al., 2005). Studies have pointed to children with spastic CP (the largest group constituting between 66 and 82 % of children with CP [Blondis, 2004]) as having social and learning problems more often than typical children (Frampton et al., 1998;

Yude et al., 1998). A recent study showed that executive impairments are present in one third of children with spastic CP and with a general verbal cognitive functioning within the average range of typically developing children (Bottcher et al., 2009).

In order to explore the dialectical dynamic between neural systems and processes, the development of executive functioning and activity in cultural-historical practices, a small number of children ($n = 4$) from a larger study were chosen to participate in a case study. All four children were tested with a neuropsychological test battery. In addition, the primary teacher completed a questionnaire about executive functions (Behaviour Rating Inventory of Executive Function [BRIEF]). Knowledge about lesions is inferred from the CP diagnosis and the neuropsychological assessment. Participant observation was chosen as the preferred method to gain knowledge about the child's everyday life at school (Hedegaard & Fleer, 2008). Each child was observed for one week during school. Two children would not allow class observations and separate interviews with the children and their teachers were done as alternative.

First, both observations and interviews were analysed by identification of repeated sequences of interactions, defined as shared activity in practice involving two or more persons. Child intentions were identified as engagements and intentional focus in particular situations. Child capacities were identified as knowledge and abilities apparent in situations, both in the class room and in the neuropsychological assessment.

In the second level of interpretation, the interpretation moved beyond particular situations and the identified sequences of interactions were used to characterize the learning practices of each of the children. Often repeated intentions were assumed to characterize child motives.

Two cases are reported here. First, the cognitive functioning of one child (Donna) is analysed in two different learning activities; math and English, within the same institutional setting in order to show how variations within the same setting can create learning opportunities for a child. Second, Donna's learning activity is contrasted with another child's learning activity within a different setting (Peter) to illustrate how different organizations of learning practices have an impact on the learning of the children that participate in the practice. Together, the two cases illustrate different instances of mismatch between biological and social aspects of development and how they affect the developmental possibilities of particular children. Even though the cases represent unique examples of children in their everyday practices, the similarity of social institutions such as schools and the learning practices in them and the high incidence of executive impairments of children with spastic CP give reason to suspect that the patterns of difficulties described in relation to the two children are not exceptional.

Donna

Donna is a 11-year-old girl with cerebral palsy. Both of her legs are affected, it is strenuous for her to move around and most of the time she uses a walker or a wheelchair. She writes large and it is clumsy. Donna is in fifth grade in a special class.

The neuropsychological examination points to problems with focused attention, divided attention, visual perception, visuo-construction and certain domains of executive functioning such as working memory and mental flexibility. Her performance in timed measures is generally slow and can be interpreted as slow information processing.

Donna was observed for one week in her school during lessons and recesses. In the observations, she recurrently appears as cheerful and as one who tries her best during classes despite several learning difficulties (described later), which is interpreted as a result of both a learning motive and a motive for receiving positive attention from the teacher. She usually spends breaks with a couple of best friends; mostly from her own class. In their social interactions, Donna often assumes an organizing position. Donna's activities are often impeded by her motor impairment, even though her teachers and friends help her with practicalities.

Peter

Peter is 13-years-old with cerebral palsy; the hand, arm and leg of one side of his body is affected. He moves around without need of remedies and even plays basketball, a big interest of his. Peter is mainstreamed in a seventh grade class. He was identified as having learning impairments and difficulties in social relations at school start, so a full-time assistant teacher was assigned to him.

The neuropsychological examination of Peter points to problems with abstract verbal reasoning, focused attention, visuo-construction and domains of executive functioning such as mental flexibility and working memory.

Peter and his assistant teacher (Anna) were interviewed about Peter's learning practice. From Peter's perspective, most activities are either interesting or confusing. He expresses motives for both social relations and learning, but his activities are characterized by increasing passiveness and withdrawal, according to both Peter and Anna. Either he withdraws from the activity and waits for Anna to come by and tell him what to do. Or he refuses to participate despite Anna's assistance; another kind of withdrawal from the learning activity.

Different learning activities within the same setting

Donna participates in a learning practice where all the children present are identified with special needs. There is a high number of teachers and a low number of pupils and the teachers have extensive knowledge of each pupil's strengths and difficulties. Most of the time, the learning activities are organized in small groups or individually. Often, the teacher (e.g. Nan in the observation further down) moves between two or three children, who work individually, helping and supporting them in their work.

For Donna, the cognitive impairments identified in the neuropsychological examination were apparent in her learning practice too. The lesions associated with bilateral cerebral palsy often affect brain areas supporting visual processes. These areas are among the less plastic, probably because the neurons and neural connections in these areas are highly specialized plus the bilateral nature of Donna's neural lesion further impairs the possibility of other areas taking over (Stiles, 2000). The visuo-perceptual problem impedes Donna's decoding of printed letters and words and the process of making spatial representations of math problems; for example which number to take from what other number. In math, Donna has trouble reading and writing numbers and often reverses numbers, either the number itself or the sequence of the number, e.g. writes '51' instead of '15'. She has trouble adding or subtracting numbers larger than ten. Donna has difficulties understanding the description of math exercises and needs her teacher to explain what she is supposed to do. In addition, she needs help from the teacher to devise a procedure of calculation; which numbers and mathematical operations to use and how. Many of Donna's problems are commonly seen in children in first and second grade. However, the extent and persistence of Donna's problems into fifth grade convert them into learning impairments in math, possibly due to a combination of reading problems, impairments in processing of visuo-spatial relations and problems with planning such as identifying a goal and devising a sequence of operations in order to reach the goal.

To circumvent her learning impairments in math, Donna has been given remedies; an abacus and a table of the numbers from 1 to 100. In the learning practice, Donna's teacher encourages Donna to use them:

> *Observation day 3. Math*
> *Donna has finished her exercise, Nan, her teacher, is leafing through the exercise book to find a new exercise, [. . .] Nan finds a new exercise. '"What's it about?" Donna asks'. 'Backwards, subtracting', Nan explains. She shows Donna how to use her abacus to solve the exercise. Donna begins, but adds instead of taking away. Nan monitors and corrects Donna right away, so she starts taking pieces away and ends up with the correct answer. Next calculation, Nan supports Donna with questions; 'How many did you have from the start?' and this time Donna gets it right.*

In her assistance of Donna, Donna's teacher Nan gives her concrete instructions about procedures for calculation and how to perform them with different remedies. In line with Vygotsky's idea of disontogenesis and the double-spiral model (Figure 1.1), Donna has an impairment in the neural system, which impacts on her development of cognitive functions, both basic visuo-spatial processes such as determining direction and higher cognitive processes such as mental manipulation of spatial properties through rules for calculation, both of which causes learning impairments in the math activities. However, the learning practice, Donna participates in, is organized with a focus on cognitive remediation; the learning of alternative cultural tools and compensatory techniques, which can help Donna overcome her cognitive difficulties. Through the assistance from Nan and the use of the abacus, Donna manages to solve the math exercise. When Nan diminishes her support during the second, third and following similar exercises, Donna is able to proceed independently.

The remediation of Donna's visuo-spatial problems is impeded by her trouble remembering or switching procedures or keeping information in mind during work:

> *Observation day 3. Math*
> *New exercise. Donna asks Nan how to solve the exercise. First, Nan explains the exercise. Donna needs to find the difference between the scores of two children. Second, she asks Donna how she is going to solve the problem. Donna wants to use the abacus again. Ah, Nan says, and Donna suggests the table of numbers. Donna uses the table of numbers with the first exercise, counts. Nan must help Donna remember, which number to start with, which direction to count and the number to end with. By the next, similar exercises, Donna still relies heavily on Nan.*

Donna has to rely on her teacher to remember both information and procedure not only in the first, but also in the following exercises too. Her mastering of cultural tools in math, both arithmetical procedures and remedies like the table of numbers, is compromised by her different learning impairment and the question arises as to how to circumvent the difficulty with using and keeping information in mind, which present an obstacle to the movability of Donna's other neurobiological constraint, the processing of visual-spatial relations. How to add one further level of cognitive remediation?

To answer that question, it is interesting to consider how Donna functions in other learning activities. Looking at Donna's English lesson later the same day, it appears that her neurobiological constraints in the executive domain are related to the specific learning activity of math. In English, a foreign language to Donna, a different picture emerges:

> Observation, day 3, English lesson
> Nan sits down with Donna and two other children at the large, oval table in the middle of the class room. The children are given exercise sheets with drawings of places to live, which must be paired with the English words for them. The English words to use are on a list in the upper corner of the exercise sheet. What does 'castle' mean? Nan asks. Donna raises her hand, knows 'Castle' means 'Slot' [The Danish word for castle]. Should we erase it from the list of words? Donna asks and Nan agrees that it would be a good strategy. 'House'? Again Donna raises her hand; knows the word means 'hus'[Danish for house]. On the sheet are two different drawings of houses and Donna suggests they wait to write the word house until they know for sure which one is correct, to which Nan agrees that it sounds like a good idea.

In the excerpt, Donna is suddenly the one to suggest procedures for solving the exercise. To understand the difference between those two situations, the idea from cognitive psychology about cognition as dependent on a limited capacity system seems useful. Due to Donna's neurobiological constraint in the visuo-spatial areas, the math exercise puts a much larger strain on Donna than the English exercise, leaving less capacity for higher cognitive processes. As long as Donna has to focus a substantial amount of attention on reading and writing numbers and doing calculations, she lacks the capacity to structure the information into a computational approach or consider appropriate remedies. The exercise in English does not involve the same requirements to reading and spatial processing and leaves Donna with cognitive capacity to make metacognitive reflections on how to solve the exercise.

The interaction between Donna's cognition and different learning activities makes it possible to move the neurobiological constraints of executive dysfunctions in math activity also. In the preceding excerpt, Donna was taught the use of different remedies while working on a difficult exercise. In the following excerpt from another math lesson, Donna has been allowed to work on easier math exercises.

> Observation day 2, math
> Donna and her best friend Penny are doing math exercises in the common room outside class. It is very quiet. Donna is doing simple calculations. She counts on her fingers, finds the solution and wants to write it down, but is uncertain whether she writes the number five correctly. She borrows Penny's calculator and compares the number five on the calculator to how she has written it on the page.

During work on the undemanding exercise with a straight-forward procedure, Donna is able to compensate on her own. She counts on her fingers and acts on her uncertainty about the spatial direction of the number five and finds a way to check whether she has written the number correctly or not.

In her practice of learning, it is possible for Donna to get varied experiences of what she can do, both on her own and with help from her teachers. Donna's learning practice encourages physical and cognitive remediation, but it is Donna's learning activity with the (too) easy math exercise, which enables her to make reflections about her learning of learning and her use of remedies that she can use to facilitate her work with more difficult exercises. If we accept an approach to cognition as always embedded in activity, 'cognition-in-practice', it enables us to understand how variations in pressure on cognitive capacity and in the organization of learning activity, the right spiral in Figure 1.1, are both important for new levels of cognitive functioning to emerge and feed into the left spiral of the model. The encouragement of cognitive remediation and activities in which Donna can make independent reflections on her use of remedies provides an additional level of cognitive remediation.

Learning activities in two different school settings

The preceding section illustrated how the same child can function very different cognitively depending on the particular activity in the same institutional setting. The neurobiological constraints in the left spiral (Figure 1.1) are not stable, but emerge and change along with the mismatch between cognitive impairments and activity in practices in the right spiral. In this section, the aim is to unfold the dynamic interaction between the organization of learning practices and the development of cognition and motives of children participating in the practices.

In contrast to Donna, Peter participates in a learning practice, which is founded on the premise that all children in the class can participate in the same learning activity. The ratio of children per teacher (23:1) in the class does not allow individual organization of learning activities.

Like Donna, Peter needs an explanation of what to do in an exercise, before he is able to start work. Also, both of them need continuous attention, and assistance when changing from one type of exercise or type of arithmetical operation to another. However, the purpose of Peter's assistant teacher is first and foremost to support his acquisition of the general curriculum and with a substantial amount of help, Peter has been able to follow the same curriculum as his class to some extent, although he is experiencing rising difficulties:

> (From interview with Peter's full time assistant teacher)
> Anne: 'He cannot, not now anyway, maybe he could when he was smaller, when the level of reading was less difficult, the curriculum was easier for him to read back then, but now it has become too difficult. [. . .] So I read it to him and interpret it and explain what the text says and ask him questions, so he is able to learn.'

Peter's acquisition of the same curriculum as his peers has become more difficult during the last couple of years and in order to compensate, Peter's assistant teacher has taken over more and more of the metacognitive activity such as identifying a goal, planning the steps towards the goal and monitoring progress. While the other children in Peter's class are practising to work more independently and on more complex assignments, Peter has become increasingly dependent on Anne's support. The learning of cognitive remedies, which is so central in Donna's learning activities, is missing from Peter's learning activities in the right spiral of the model. Peter's biological disadvantage, his early brain lesion, has developed into a major neurobiological constraint on his cognitive activity through his participation in a learning practice, which lacks activities organized around his special need for explicit cognitive remediation. This organization of his learning practice often makes the learning activities seem confusing to Peter:

(From interview with Peter)
Interviewer: 'Are there things in school you find difficult'?
Peter: 'Yes, it is like . . . History, Christianity, and sometimes, most of the time biology and sometimes science'.
I: 'What is difficult about these subjects?'
P: 'It is because the teacher, we got, says a lot of different things, I don't understand, and then Anna [the assistant teacher] explains them to me.'

Peter's executive dysfunctions and the lack of cognitive remedies in his learning practice make it difficult for him to handle the confusing situations. He has no idea about how to approach the activity, the instructions and assignments and make sense of them. Passivity and withdrawal seem to be Peter's choice when the activity in a practice becomes too confusing for him.

Motives in relation to learning practices and learning impairments

As stated in the introduction of this book, motives are an integrated part of development. Donna's and Peter's motives for participation in social activities are affected by their particular practices and in turn affect their learning activities and the movability of their neurobiological constraints. Donna's cultivation of social relations is impeded by the extensive use of individual learning activities, leaving social activities to recesses, and by the fact that Donna often has to take care of practicalities during recess, such as switching remedies or moving from one part of the school to another. Donna has become adept at organizing combinations of social activities and management of her remedies and belongings and organizes activities in which she gets her friends to join her and help her. The remediation practice taught in class; find a way to negotiate what is difficult, goes for the activities during recess too and ensures Donna plenty of practice with developing executive skills. She has to weigh several motives against each other and against the organization in the practice. For example, Donna wants to improve the functionality of her legs by using her walker and she wants to spend recess having fun with her friends. The recess offers a limited amount of time, in which she has to move to the particular area of the school, where remedies are allowed to be parked, to switch from her wheelchair to her walker, and back to her class again to be ready for the next lesson. On her own, she could spend most of recess just going back and forth, but when she gets her friends to help her, the switch can be made much quicker and time is left for games and fun. Donna's management skills are supported by an integrated practice among her friends and teachers for helping her compensate for her motor impairments.

Peter experiences rising problems in his ability to participate in the social activities during recess and after school. Earlier, Peter has participated in an organized after-school practice together with his friends from class. Now in seventh grade, the practice of organized after-school activities has been replaced by a new practice of ad hoc meetings of friends and a free choice between a wide range of leisure-time activities such as soccer or break dance. All children in the class have had to learn to negotiate this transformation from one type of after-school practice to another. They need to develop new ways to participate in their friendship groups after school. Peter seems to be motivated for participation in the social activities and the new teenage life. He brings his basket ball to school and he likes to watch the movie 'High School Musical'. However, due to his executive dysfunctions, the learning of how to navigate in the new social situation might be a greater challenge for Peter compared to his peers. The increasing dependence of Peter on Anne to structure activities for him rather than teaching him strategies for structuring himself makes him further disadvantaged. So instead of participating, he goes home alone after school and watches television or plays basketball at his Playstation. During recess, changes in Peter's participation are seen too. Often, he withdraws and watches his class mates from a distance. Peter's brain lesion and its impact on his cognitive functions has put him at a disadvantage from the beginning of the change of practices and the beginning of teenage life, but it is his passivity and withdrawal which maintains and extends the brain lesion as a neurobiological constraint, keeping him away from many of the activities his friends participate in, thereby disqualifying him further compared to his peers.

Conclusion

Throughout the chapter, cognition has been approached not as an abstract concept, but as an activity constrained by both practice frameworks and by neurobiology. It has been argued that the impairments of a particular child is neither caused by biology, nor socially constructed, but something which arises in the interaction between two developmental spirals; one between neural structures and processes, and cognition; and another one between cognition and activities that afford different types of child (cognitive) activities. Because cognition figures in both spirals, they become parts in the same developmental dialectic. Many of the learning problems of children with CP are biologically based, but in line with Vygotsky's theoretical approach they must always be seen and analysed through their social moderation and mediation. The developmental dynamic depicted in the double spiral needs to be anchored in relation to concrete perspectives on the practice. From an institutional perspective, the analysis focus on the organization of the learning activities within the setting and how the teachers organize the remediation. The analysis of Donna's cognition in practice showed how small variations within a particular learning practice enabled her to learn both math and strategies for solving math problems through cognitive remediation, both of which are important for the movability of Donna's neurobiologically based constraints. The analysis of the two different school practices revealed a dialectical dynamic between practices for learning and the development of cognition and learning. The organization of Peter's learning practice was aimed at the acquisition of curriculum, while the learning of learning strategies was more implicit in the learning practice. The pressure put on Peter (and his assistant teacher) to acquire the same curriculum as his peers had increased his dependence on external structure and support, at the same time as the practice during and after school is decreasing in structure and support.

Taking the perspective of the child, the analysis move to a focus on the motives of the particular child and how the child acts in particular settings affording different types of activity. Both Donna and Peter come with motives for participation in social relations with peers, but their practices and development of cognitive functioning in practice present them with different opportunities for following their motives. Donna's practice offers her good opportunities to follow her leading motives. In contrast, Peter experiences shrinking opportunities to follow his leading motives, possibly due to the lack of remediational activities that could help him find ways to move his neurobiological constraint. Instead, he has become increasingly dependent on his assistant teacher during lessons. During leisure time, he is left to manage on his own and finds alternative ways such as watching a movie about a group of adolescents having fun together rather than joining one himself, which only enhances the neurobiological constraint of his executive impairments.

The analyses from the perspective of the child enabled an understanding of how the child's motivated activity feeds back on the cognitive processes of the child and possibly on the development of the child's neural system also.

The cases illustrated an understanding of cognitive remediation, not as the repair of an isolated, impaired cognitive function, but as the reshaping of cognition in practice through learning. This understanding is based in Vygotsky's theory of inter-functional relationships in mental development and the possibility of overcoming primary and secondary defects through mastering of cultural tools learned through compensatory techniques. The movability of particular neurobiological constraints is necessarily embedded in concrete practices and needs to be analysed as part of the activities within social practices. On the other hand, the mental ability to learn and apply compensatory strategies is served by a biological base too as was seen in the case of children with executive impairments. The executive impairments undermine the learning and use of alternative cognitive strategies aimed at overcoming impairments in for example, motor function or visual perception. Another level of remediation is called for. Often compensation for impairments in executive function is accomplished by placing the child in a highly structured environment. Environmental structuring can be helpful as long as it is regarded as an intermediate strategy, run in parallel with explicit learning of strategies for structuring. Unless the child is so disabled that independent living as an adult is out of the question, a long-term goal need to be the gradual learning of cognitive functions and activity necessary for independent living.

Explicit learning of structuring and learning of learning need to be included in the organization of the learning practice and in the learning activity of children with impairments in executive functions, perhaps the way it is in Donna's learning practice, perhaps some other form. Otherwise there is a danger of the child's continuous reliance on pedagogical support, as in the situation with Peter, which enhances his problems instead of diminishing them. A practice that values and teaches the independent use of cognitive remedies, such as Donna's, put the child in a much better position for developing executive functions than a practice with a main focus on learning curriculum and where the learning of strategies for learning remains much more implicit.

The cultural-historical approach of situated cognition and the understanding of cognitive functions and impairments as they develop in practice present an alternative to interventions aimed at influencing individual children and isolated cognitive functions only. Consideration of impairments in practice involves linkages of cultural-historical practices and the concrete activities of children with impairments in for example, cognition or perception. The activity of the child is an expression of what the child is able to do within this particular practice. Through explicit manipulations of conditions for solving different tasks, it becomes possible to assist the child in moving its neuro-biologically based constraints and improving its cognition in practice.

References

Alexander, M. P. and Stuss, D. T. (2000). Disorders of Frontal Lobe Functioning. *Seminars in Neurology*, 20, 427–437.

Baddeley, A. D. (1986). *Working Memory*. New York: Oxford University Press.

Baron, I. S. (2004). *Neuropsychological Evaluation of the Child*. New York: Oxford University Press.

Bax, M., Goldstein, M., Rosenbaum, P., Leviton, A. and Paneth, N. (2005). Proposed Definition and Classification of Cerebral Palsy, April 2005 – Introduction. *Developmental Medicine and Child Neurology*, 47, 571–576.

Blondis, T. A. (2004). 'Neurodevelopmental Motor Disorders: Cerebral Palsy and Neuromuscular Diseases', in D. Dewey and D. E. Tupper (eds), *Developmental Motor Disorders: A Neuropsychological Perspective* (1st edn.). New York: Guilford Press, pp. 113–136.

Bottcher, L., Flachs, E. M. and Uldall, P. (2009). Attentional and Executive Dysfunctions in Children with Spastic Cerebral Palsy. *Developmental Medicine and Child Neurology*, 52(2), e42–e47.

Cole, M. and Engeström, Y. (1993). 'A Cultural-Historical Approach to Distributed Cognition', in G. Salomon (ed.), *Distributed Cognitions. Psychological and Educational Considerations*. New York: Cambridge University Press, pp. 1–46.

Frampton, I., Yude, C., and Goodman, R. (1998). The Prevalence and Correlates of Specific Learning Difficulties in A Representative Sample of Children with Hemiplegia. *British Journal of Educational Psychology*, 68, 39–51.

Gazzaniga, M. S. S. (2000). *The New Cognitive Neurosciences*. (2nd edn.) Cambridge, Mass: MIT Press.

Hedegaard, M. (2002). *Learning and Child Development*. Aarhus: Aarhus University Press.

Hedegaard, M. and Fleer, M. (2008). *Studying Children. A Cultural-Historical Approach*. Berkshire: Open University Press.

Juenger, H., Linder-Lucht, M., Walther, M., Berweck, S., Mall, V., and Staudt, M. (2007). Cortical Neuromodulation by Constraint-Induced Movement Therapy in Congenital Hemiparesis: An fMRI Study. *Neuropediatrics*, 38, 130–136.

Kozulin, A. and Gindis, B. (2007). 'Sociocultural Thinking and Education of Children with Special Needs. From Defectology to Remedial Pedagogy', in H. Daniels, M. Cole, and J. V. Wertsch (eds), *The Cambridge Companion to Vygotsky*. New York: Cambridge University Press, pp. 332–362.

Pinker, S. (1994). *The Language Instinct*. New York: Morrow.

Powell, K. B. and Voeller, K. K. S. (2004). Prefrontal Executive Function Syndromes in Children. *Journal of Child Neurology*, 19, 785–797.

Salomon, G. (1993). 'No Distribution without Individuals' Cognition: A Dynamic Interactional View', in G. Salomon (ed.), *Distributed Cognitions: Psychological and Educational Considerations*. New York: Cambridge University Press, pp. 111–138.

Stiles, J. (2000). Neural Plasticity and Cognitive Development. *Developmental Neuropsychology*, 18, 237–272.

Stiles, J., Reilly, J., Paul, B., and Moses, P. (2005). Cognitive Development following Early Brain Injury: Evidence for Neural Adaptation. *Trends in Cognitive Sciences*, 9, 136–143.

Vygotsky, L. S. (1993). *The Collected Works of L.S. Vygotsky. Vol 2. The Fundamentals of Defectology.* (vols. 2) New York: Plenum Press.

Welsh, M. C. and Pennington, B. F. (1988). Assessing Frontal Lobe Functioning in Children: Views from Developmental Psychology. *Developmental Neuropsychology*, 4, 199–230.

Wortham, S. (2001). Interactionally Situated Cognition: A Classroom Example. *Cognitive Science*, 25, 37–66.

Yude, C., Goodman, R. and McConachie, H. (1998). Peer Problems of Children with Hemiplegia in Mainstream Primary Schools. *Journal of Child Psychology and Psychiatry and Allied Disciplines*, 39, 533–541.

2

The Challenge of Using Multiple Methods to Gather the Views of Children

Jill Porter

Introduction

Children are an important source of information about the ways in which schools can best support their learning and collecting their views is arguably an essential requirement in the development of school provision. As a result there is a burgeoning array of literature that describes and illustrates the use of non-traditional and often creative methods (e.g. Punch, 2002; Curtis et al., 2004; Flutter and Ruddock, 2004; Kirova, 2006; Ravet, 2007; Bragg, 2007). Although driven by different positions and values (Robinson and Taylor, 2007; Noyes, 2005) they often have a shared assumption that pupil views are central to improving teaching and learning (Flutter and Ruddock, 2004). There are however a number of tensions that underlie their collection which may go some way to explaining the gap between the commitment to the statement of rights articulated in the United Nations Declaration, and the development of practice in educational decision-making (Lewis, 2004; Lundy, 2007). The declaration sets out the importance of not only ensuring that the child has the right to express themselves with the attendant importance of being provided with both the opportunity and support to do so, but just as fundamentally, that their opinions are given due weight, namely that they are truly listened to and acted upon (Lundy, 2007). The intention therefore is that the process is transformative, an aspect that has been keenly interrogated elsewhere (Fielding, 2004; 2009). Key questions for schools concern how they collect this data, how they ensure that all voices are heard and how they recognize and respond to contrasting or conflicting views.

Characteristically medical professionals have played a decisive role in identifying disabled children, usually to provide access to specialized services and thereby often deploying resource driven definitions. More recently in the UK a common definition of disability linked to the Disability Discrimination Act has been employed and this places due emphasis on the impact of the impairment on everyday life (DfES/DRC, 2006). The Disability Discrimination Act (DDA) (2005) widens the meaning of disability far beyond definitions previously used within the general population and to some extent by professionals in welfare services. This new definition includes individuals with impairment where the difficulty may be largely invisible to schools (e.g. mental health difficulties). The definition foregrounds four important aspects: that disability arises from an impairment; that the condition is one that has lasted a year or more (or is expected to); that it has an impact on everyday activities; and that the effect is substantial (i.e. not trivial). As the central element of the DDA definition concerns the impact of disability, finding out about the lived experience of the child and their family is vital. The extension by the DDA definition to include issues of mental health and medical conditions such as HIV and facial disfigurements highlights the importance of recognizing that 'impairment' can only be viewed within the context of its impact. It therefore recognizes the contribution played by the supports that are in place.

The foregrounding of the subjective experience of an individual highlights the ways in which social and cultural factors mediate the experience of an impairment (see Chapter 6 by Hedegaard and Chaiklin). Inevitably this may result in home and schools having slightly different views about the ways in which a child's difficulties impact on daily life and the sharing of information about different contexts provides a key element in enabling schools to make adjustments to the provision that is generally available. The focus of the chapter concerns *how* we collect those views and the challenge to schools to recognize that the methods they use can influence the views that are surfaced. Rather than overlook differences that arise from using different methods or dismiss seemingly paradoxical data we can view discrepancies as indicative of the contextualized nature of data collection.

Choosing methods

Rarely are the views of all students collected, and therefore there is often an expectation that children will speak on behalf of others. It is likely that some voices might be more easily or readily listened to than others (Ruddock and Fielding, 2006) with those who are least articulate or have difficulties communicating being seen as having less to contribute. Some research suggests that while high achievers may be more insightful about learning and more able to adopt the perspectives of others (Pedder and McIntyre, 2006) lower achievers may be less forthcoming in their views. This may reflect a number of factors. They may be less articulate, have less faith in their views being listened to and/or have nothing much to say about a learning agenda that is seen to have little relevance in their lives. It is important that the methods we adopt don't reinforce these notions.

More generally the use of flexible methods dominates the field of pupil voice. A brief look at the special edition of Educational Review in 2006, for example, illustrates the way in which researchers use qualitative unstructured approaches, typically interviews, in either individual or group settings. These methods usually rely on a dialogue, and potentially facilitate a better adult understanding of the meaning of the views expressed by young people. The role of unstructured versus structured approaches has been keenly debated within the learning difficulties field with concern that structured approaches can constrain or pre-empt the topics that children feel they can 'talk about' or the range of responses they can make (Porter and Lacey, 2005; Lewis and Porter, 2007). There is recognition however that open and unstructured methods can also be problematic where students are less articulate and where facilitation can ultimately result in greater suggestibility as the interviewer provides 'a supportive cradle' (Antaki et al., 2002) to elicit a response, often referring to something that they explicitly know (Porter, 2009). As a result the pupil eventually produces the 'right' answer and previous responses are forgotten. Booth and Booth (1996) remind us about the place of closed questions and the importance of listening to silence, 'being attentive to what goes unsaid' (p. 64). They make a distinction between an 'expressive silence (waiting to be broken) and a closed silence (waiting to be passed over)'. In the pursuit of children's right to be heard, their right to silence, privacy and non-response can be ignored (Lewis and Porter, 2007). This can be a challenge to schools as they aim to make appropriate adjustments to provision.

Of equal importance to the format of the data collection is finding the right language to use to elicit children's views on the barriers to learning. Research on children's experiences of disability is not extensive, although a recent series of studies funded by the Disability Rights Commission have given some important insights into approaching this complex area. The particular language sensitivities around labelling have been highlighted, notably for children in secondary mainstream settings (Lewis et al., 2005) together with the importance of not portraying disability as a 'single signifier of identity', a view re-iterated by Kelly (2005) in a study of the experiences of learning disabled children. Studies by Connors and Stalker (2002; 2007) suggest that many children see their disability in medical terms and speak about the effects of an impairment rather than the barriers that are presented to them although they talk about other people's behaviour and being made to feel different which the authors describe with reference to Thomas (1999) as 'barriers to being'. The research of Lewis et al. (2005) suggests that children may rather talk about their difficulties than disabilities and Connors and Stalker's study (2002) note that some children may find it hard to talk in general about difficulties but instead can identify one off concrete examples.

One conclusion of the Disability Rights Commission study (Lewis et al., 2005) into collecting pupil views was that

> Children with diverse physical/sensory impairments or special needs can be included in meaningful and valid ways in sharing their views. However one fixed approach will not work for all children and young people . . . (p. 73)

In addition to exploring multiple methods the study also suggested that there is a need to leave room within methods for schools and others to make choices and adaptations.

Using multiple methods

In the field of pupil voice multiple methods has been seen as a way of gaining a more authentic picture of what pupils really think (Flutter and Ruddock, 2004). In choosing to use more than one method we may be adopting what has been termed a 'mixed method approach'. This term is more readily applied when there is a planned relationship between the data, often when the findings from one method are used to inform the subsequent collection of data using a different method, but in some instances the data may be collected in parallel (Johnson and Onwegbuzie, 2005). For those adopting a pragmatic approach, guided by the need to find the best way to answer a specific question, the use of one method to inform another appears to be logical and unquestionable (Gorard and Taylor, 2004). Others however have raised concerns about the different theoretical and philosophical assumptions and values that underpin different types of research (Yanchar and Williams, 2006; Kushner, 2002). We might ask ourselves if we see the collection of children's views as something that is measurable and that can be meaningfully aggregated, or as a phenomenon that is socially constructed and needing to be contextualized. Although these might be seen as irrresolvable positions (Sale et al., 2002) a dialectical stance has been suggested by Greene (2008) that recognizes the legitimacy of different ways of

> making sense of the social world, and multiple standpoints on what is important to be valued and cherished. (p. 20)

Despite the long history of using mixed methods in applied fields (Greene 2008) there are still a number of unanswered questions, not least with respect to how and when we integrate the data, described by Teddlie and Tashakkori (2009) as the 'most unchartered area'. A recent paper by Darbyshire et al. (2005) suggests with respect to comparing methods in qualitative research with children, that there are important and subtle differences that provide complementary insights. However there are a whole variety of additional reasons for using mixed methods including convergence and elaboration of the data but also the potential for paradox (Green et al., 1989; Greene, 2008). Recognizing differences between groups of children in their experience of learning plays an important role in understanding the impact (and non-impact) of a disability or difficulty and making appropriate adjustments.

In the research reported here, we were as others have indicated, driven by the pragmatic need to use mixed methods (Gorard and Taylor, 2004; Johnson and Onwuegbuzie, 2004) but not without reservations about the potential for developing research that crossed paradigm boundaries with the attendant difficulties of shifting perspectives and value systems (Kushner, 2002; Grocott et al., 2002; Porter and Lacey, 2005). Arguably different methods answer different research questions (Kushner 2002) which has important implications for how we portray the data.

The following sections of this chapter draw on data generated through developmental work with schools as part of a larger project designed to develop data collection methods that would enable both mainstream and special schools to identify who their disabled pupils were and what barriers to learning they encountered (Porter et al., 2008). Data was gathered from all children, recognizing that schools have incomplete data on disabled children. Many schools tried out a single method or conversely multiple methods but with different groups of children, however one secondary school chose two methods which it used with overlapping pupil groups. It therefore provided an opportunity to examine the strengths and limitations of these two methods and to explore the process of aggregating and disaggregating the data in order to gain a picture of the views of an entire year group, and that of some sub-groups, including disabled pupils.

Details of the study

The school was in a large inner city with around 30% of pupils identified as having a special educational need. The school was offered a choice of five methods (talking mats, interviews, 'point to point activity', focus groups and an online questionnaire, more details of these can be found in Porter et al., 2008). They chose to try out the focus groups and the questionnaire with a total of 30 pupils in year 7. The latter was used with all 142 children in year 7 which for timetabling reasons they administered offline.

Focus groups

The focus groups drew on nominal group technique, a structured method for group-work that encourages contributions from everyone which through discussion are narrowed down prior to every member of the group ranking them through a voting system (Van de Ven and Delbecq, 1972). This method is seen to have the advantage over interviews where people's responses 'are often continuously tailored to the reactions of the interviewer' (p. 388) and where language barriers may intrude as researchers fail to find the argot of the interviewees – both particular issues for school-based studies. The following procedures were adopted, adapting slightly those outlined by Van de Ven et al. (1972). Each child was asked to silently think of and write down (or represent in some way) as many ideas as possible in five minutes. In turn they then each stated aloud one idea in a round-robin with the researcher keeping a record on the flipchart. Each idea was accepted with no comment or discussion allowed at this point. Ideas given did not need to be from the team member's written list. A child could 'pass' on his or her turn, and then add an idea on a subsequent turn.

This was continued around the group until all members had provided their ideas. Each idea was then discussed in turn and the wording changed only when the idea's originator agreed. Ideas could also be removed from the list but only by unanimous agreement. Discussion served to clarify meaning, explain the logic or analysis, raise and answer questions or state agreement or disagreement. The sessions lasted 35 minutes once the children had settled.

These ideas were then prioritized using anonymous multi-voting on prepared voting slips. Working individually, each member selected up to three items he or she considered most important and ranked them with the first choice ranking highest (i.e. 3). The group then discussed what emerged from the voting.

Design and result of focus group research

The pupils in the focus groups had been wihdrawn from at a time when subjects were taught in sets. The first group was described to the research team as a 'bottom set' in which the majority of children experienced difficulty in reading. The second group was drawn from a 'middle set'. In the first group the broad question posed was: *What gets in the way of getting on in school?*

As Table 2.1 reveals the 'getting on' phrase clearly triggered responses referring to the social life of school rather than focusing on lessons and learning although the top item 'bunking off' is revealing of what they see as inhibiting 'getting on'. The other top responses largely refer to aspects of interaction with their peers. Notably teachers feature little in their analysis. This appears to

Table 2.1 Response of the first focus group to *What gets in the way of getting on in school?*

Rank order of Ideas		Votes
1	Bunking off	22
2	Stealing	18
3	Blackmail	13
4	Fighting	13
5	Time wasters forgetting equipment	9
6	Bullying	8
8	People who don't word as a team	5
8	People who don't concentrate	5
8	Teachers threatening people	5
10	People not participating	4
11.5	Name calling	3
11.5	Disturbing classes	3

Other items named but not receiving any votes: Physical attacking, Silly people, Trouble makers, Arguing, Noisy people, People not listening, People threaten teachers.

reflect the observation of Flutter and Ruddock (2004) that the social life of the school can be more important than the academic.

Because of the possibility that the phrasing of the question had inadvertently pre-disposed the group to highlight social aspects, the question was changed for the second group into a more neutral question: *What do you find difficult in school?* Their responses are set out in Table 2.2.

With this group the responses were more orientated to school work and in particular more concerned with teachers and teaching, although bullying featured more highly than in the previous group. Interestingly, both friends and other people were equally rated as sources of interference.

Despite the differences between the responses of the two groups, the use of nominal group technique within a focus group had a number of advantages. In effect the children code their own data – reaching agreement on categories and rating them accordingly. There was therefore less interference from the teacher/researcher and less opportunity for imposing a view. The presence of adult's co-ordinating this process may however influence how pupils view the task and respond. The method did allow pupils the 'right to silence' and to opt out but the group process may have inhibited some individuals more than others. Notably in both groups the girls were less forthcoming with ideas

Table 2.2 Response of the second focus group to *What do you find difficult in school?*

Rank order of Ideas		Votes
1	Teachers not being fair	32
2	Teachers not listening	26
3	Bullying	16
4	Teachers pick on you	16
5.5	Long lessons	11
5.5	Getting the blame unfairly	11
7.5	Friends talking and distracting	9
7.5	People who are annoying	9
9	Talking behind backs	8
10	Atmosphere	7
11	Being taught by teachers who aren't subject specialists	6
12	Lessons on the board – copying	4
13.5	Touching girls	3
13.5	Punishments	3
16	The space we work in for example Small classrooms are claustrophobic	2
16	People turning off computers	2
16	Firewall blocking things	2

Other items: Fighting, Throwing equipment, Abusive language, Computers (arguments caused over wrong use)

than the boys and, as we can see from the scores, not all pupils used their full range of votes.

The question however remains about the extent to which differences between the two groups represented differing attitudes toward schools, was a response to being asked a question in a different way or was in some way an interaction between these elements and the way the group responded to the activity as a whole. For further insights we turn to examine the data from the questionnaire.

Questionnaire

This was developed as an online tool (which the school chose to use in hard copy) and designed to be inclusive recognizing that children may encounter difficulties in school for a whole variety of reasons which could arise in a range of different contexts. Following a brief introductory explanation of the purpose of the questionnaire a series of simple questions were presented asking children to rate their experiences during lessons, during break, during lunch times and on special event days using a five-point smiley face scale.

Following the rating questions children were invited to 'tell us a bit more, what helps at different times' and 'what makes things more difficult'. In a similar way information was sought about different types of lesson, and different ways of working again using the rating system but with an open question in each section for children to tell us what helped and what made things difficult. It also asked them whether they experienced difficulties getting on with others, learning in class, joining in activities.

Findings

As the questionnaires were all administered during lesson time unsurprisingly returns were received from all 142 pupils in the relevant year group. Rating questions were more likely to be answered than those asking for qualitative data with the average percentage of children who skipped rating questions 7% (range 1–13%) whereas for the questions requiring a qualitative response the average was 33% (range 26–37%) with later questions more likely to be skipped than earlier. Twenty seven children indicated on the form that they had a disability, difficulty or health condition.

As the children who took part in the nominal group work completed the questionnaire with the rest of their year it provides us with an opportunity to compare the types of responses elicited by two different research tools, although as the questionnaire was anonymous we cannot match their specific responses. Neither of the two questions posed to the focus groups appeared in precisely the same way in the questionnaire but after the first four rating questions on different aspects of school life, children were asked if they could tell us a little more about 'what helps at different times? What makes things more difficult?' Appearing early in the questionnaire and taking a very open form it tapped into the spontaneous ideas of the pupils about the barriers in school. Ninety-nine children provided qualitative responses to this question of varying lengths, including 20 disabled pupils. Data from this sub-group is too small to report separately in relation to this single question. Both groups gave more comments in relation to what helps than what makes things more difficult.

To facilitate the comparison between data sets we generated codes for *all* the data incorporating categories from the focus groups into broader groupings from the questionnaire. Table 2.3 shows the result of this process.

Table 2.3 Pupil responses from the questionnaire and focus groups.

% of pupil responses	Questionnaire N = 142	Focus grp 1 Focus grp 2 N = 14 +15
Teacher behaviour	16/68 (24%)	Grp 1 = 5% (5)
		Grp 2 = 55% (91)
Behaviour of peers	16/68 (24%)	Grp 1 = 75% (81)
		Grp 2 = 26% (44)
Behaviour of self	6/68 (9%)	Grp 1 = 20% (22)
Lesson Content/characteristics	19/68 (28%)	Grp 2 = 9% (15)
Other school activities		Grp 2 = 2% (3)
Aspects of the environment- noise, space, temperature	2/68 (3%)	Grp 2 = 1% (2)
Resources	1 (1%)	Grp 2 = 1% (2)
Moving around the school	2 (3%)	
Total number of comments	68	Grp 1 = 108
		Grp 2 = 167

This revealed that the highest proportion of questionnaire comments detailing what children found difficult related to lesson content or characteristics. These did not feature in the responses of focus group 1 and relatively little in focus group 2. Teacher behaviour was also prominent in the questionnaire returns and included 'being picked on for no reason', teachers 'peering over your shoulder', being a bad or 'rubbish teacher' and finding it difficult 'when teachers shout at you'. Peers also contributed to the difficulties experienced although this included not 'being with one's mates' as well as people 'messing around' 'talking and shouting', 'being noisy and acting all silly'.

A number of comments were self-reflective with pupils recognizing aspects of their own behaviour that constituted a barrier (6) 'during the day im normally tired' 'if its at the end of school you might be impatient' but also included behaviours that were helpful (5) such as 'thinking before doing'.

Perhaps surprisingly, given the focus group responses, there was only one mention of bullying ('bally's kick you in different sessions' and conversely for the same child it helps when there is 'no ballying or teasing') and only nine mentioned the behaviour of others in lessons being a barrier because, for example, they were 'noisy', 'distracting' or 'disrupting' or 'talking or shouting', 'acting silly' or 'not listening' or simply 'refusing to work with you'. The responses of the questionnaire therefore appeared to highlight the difficulties of teachers and lessons rather than difficult social interaction. To explore this anomaly further we looked specifically at a later question which asked about '*getting on with others. What do you find difficult?*' Of the 81 responses to this question only two mentioned bullying. There were also no reference to blackmail, stealing or fighting which had featured so highly in the first focus group raising the issue of the context shaping the result.

The responses of the children who indicated that they had a disability or health condition to being asked 'What makes things more difficult' were consistent with the larger group. However the transformation of the data for comparison purposes had in many ways concealed the nuances of meaning in the returns, not least through splitting up positive and negative elements of the children's responses. Indeed both groups, those children with and without a disability answered more fully on what they found helpful than on what they found difficult. One of the most notable aspects was that taking both the helpful and difficult aspects together friends featured in just over a third of the responses ($n = 35$). For example, friends 'help me cheer up when im bored', 'help me through things' (from a disabled child) 'help me in my work' and conversely not being with them is a difficulty.

> at break time and lunch I am happy because I am with my friend cause they are in none of my classes
>
> to eat dinner and see my friends (from a disabled child)
>
> **and its difficult**
>
> when I have no one to talk to in my class and have no fun.
>
> My friends help me at different times. It would be harder for me if I was on my own. I'm not very independent . . .

Taking the total responses to questions rather than focusing narrowly on what was directly comparable supported an analysis that social aspects of schooling are an important element for children. As others have argued it may well take precedence over academic aspects (Flutter and Ruddock, 2004). Moreover friendships in particular contribute to pupils' confidence and self-esteem and for those who are experiencing difficulties may well provide the most valued kind of support.

Making sense of diverse views

A comparison across methods reveals a mixed canvas of diverse views with a different range of responses characterizing different approaches as well as the impact of asking questions in slightly different ways. The challenge for both the researcher and the school is how one strives to make sense of this diversity: how does one analyse the data and how does one seek to combine views? It also raises questions about the relative strengths and limitations of different methods and what is to be gained by mixing approaches.

The pursuit of different methods arose from the pragmatic need to ensure that the views of some pupils were not inadvertently marginalized through the use of an inappropriate data collection tool. Equally it was important to provide teachers with a choice of methods that were usable in the classroom, so they could select whether to adopt a group or an individual activity, one that could be provided in class-time or not. The two approaches the school chose resulted in a range of views being surfaced. Rather than serving as a kind of triangulation, producing corroboration, convergence, elaboration or clarification around pupil views, contradictions and paradoxes surfaced (Greene et al., 1989).

This raised the challenge of whether and how to combine the data. Johnson and Onwuegbuzie (2004) argue that combining data analysis is an underdeveloped aspect of mixed methods designs. Although they with others (Greene, 2008) have suggested possible models there is less discussion of how it works in practice, in part because many see it as essentially unproblematic (Gorard and Taylor, 2004). Comparing two sets of data requires some form of transformation in the portrayal of one set, to foreground differences and similarities with another. At a simple level, key words from one set can be looked for in another. However while key words may adequately portray quantitative data it does not do justice to the meanings conveyed in qualitative data. For example we looked for evidence of 'bullying' which featured in the focus groups to see if it appeared in the qualitative comments in the questionnaire. It didn't, although notably two of the disabled children mentioned it elsewhere on the questionnaire. Did this mean that in some way the focus group context had made this a more prominent issue? Children may choose to describe negative behaviour of their peers in a variety of ways or allude to times that they feel vulnerable by writing that they don't like lunch-times. Starting from the qualitative data to compare with the quantitative highlighted that friends were an important feature of children's written comments but were largely absent from the focus group ratings. Again does this reflect contextual sensitivity in the collection of data (Yanchar and Williams, 2006)? It could therefore be argued that, while using mixed methods provide a richness of data, its combination can be problematic and requires careful thought.

It was useful to reflect back on the beliefs and purposes of the study in order to further consider what would be an appropriate strategy for combining the data. The adoption of a social model of disability suggests that we need to provide data at the level of a school in order that organizational structures that constitute barriers can be identified. However we also need to ensure that we don't marginalize the views of groups of pupils whose voices might be less readily heard either because they are less articulate or because what they have to say is viewed as inappropriate. We therefore need to portray the data in a way that identifies group differences. We can extend this argument to acknowledge the importance of ensuring that individual voices are also heard – disability is a field where there can be as many differences within a group as between groups. In analysing the data therefore we need to be able to move between individual, group and whole school and to recognize the contribution of different methods in shaping the outcome. Inevitably the unit of analysis will lead to the surfacing of different views. The focus group captured a consensus, but did not surface individual differences. The questionnaire enabled the aggregation of data across the year group, yet the qualitative comments provided insights into the perspective of the individual. It is also possible to look specifically at the responses of those pupils who indicate they have a disability.

Contextualizing the findings

The differences between the two methods reinforce the importance of recognizing the contextual nature of the data collection process. It is perhaps unsurprising if the questionnaire surfaced views concerning work as the context of its presentation and the decision by the school to administer it offline effectively made it indistinguishable from a lesson where work is carried out individually without interaction with others.

In contrast the corner stone of the focus group is discussion, and while the teachers' role in the dialogue is more about providing a structure to the activity, as scribe they do play an overtly listening role. The manner in which group discussion or debate takes place may however, make this a gendered activity. It may also be a context where aspects of interaction (particularly difficulties) come more naturally to the fore as children jostle to put their ideas forward. In contrast the questionnaire provides an asocial context where the presence of others, including adults, are less intrusive and in this sense it cannot be argued as a dialogic format. That may however be an advantage in some circumstances. Roose and John (2003) found that children of a similar age were 'wary about confiding in teachers' with respect to mental health issues and turned to friends and family for support. On the same theme, Davies and Wright (2008) recognize the ambivalence children may have towards intervention by professionals rather than someone with whom they have a special relationship. A dialogue with a teacher is not necessarily wanted, or at least not in the first instance, peers and family are seen as the main people to provide support. It may be that for sensitive topics this format has particular applicability providing that, as with the one used here, there is an invitation to follow this up and the opportunity for a fuller dialogue over which the child has control.

In addition to focusing on dialogue in the traditional sense, there is a second important element to these activities that may also have a transformative quality. This is the extent to which they prompt self-reflection. Children's comments in the questionnaire were in some instances particularly insightful about the ways in which their own behaviour could on occasions create difficulties. The provision of an activity that prompts self-reflection has the potential to enable pupils to take control and change their situation, and also may help them reflect on the kinds of support that is appropriate to seek. For sensitive aspects, the questionnaire also had the advantage of providing anonymity and the right to silence.

Conclusion

Children provide important insights on the barriers they encounter in school. The data from this study has highlighted how social aspects frame the way many children view their experiences in school. This has important implications for the organization of learning, an aspect that can be overlooked when the focus is on specialist pedagogies and the viewpoint is largely that of professionals. Collecting the views of children is however by no means straightforward and often calls for the use of more than one method. The data from this research has revealed the 'complications and tensions' that arise from using different methods (Yanchar and Williams, 2006). If we ignore these differences we ignore important contextual information that situates and extends our understanding of the views of pupils. At the same time that this is a methodological issue, it is also one which is integral to our understanding of disability where there is both concern for adopting an inclusive whole school approach and recognition of the need to ensure that each voice is heard (Barnes and Sheldon, 2007). It is perhaps unsurprising that the dichotomies apparent in the subject area are played out in the methodological.

In making choices of methods professionals need to be mindful of the ways in which the format and organization of the activity impact on the responses and responsiveness of pupils. Slight differences in the phrasing of questions can result in cueing a different range of response. Methods differ in the extent to which they ensure the child's right to both anonymity and silence. Adopting research methods that support self-reflection has the potential to bring about changes at both the organizational and individual level, and together will enhance the experience of schooling of pupils with a disability.

References

Antaki C., Young N. and Finlay M. (2002). Shaping Clients' Answers: Departures from Neutrality in Care-Staff Interviews with People with a Learning Disability. *Disability & Society*, 17(4), 435–455.

Barnes C., and Sheldon A. (2007). '"Emancipatory" Disability Research and Special Educational Needs', in L. Florian Sage *Handbook of Special Education.* London: Sage, Chapter 17.

Bragg, S. (2007). *Consulting Young People: A Review Of The Literature* London: Creative Partnerships.

Booth, T. and Booth W. (1996). Sounds of Silence: Narrative Research with Inarticulate Subjects. *Disability & Society,* 11(1), 55–69.

Connors, C. and Stalker K. (2002). *Children's Experiences of Disability: A Positive Outlook.* Interchange 75. Edinburgh: Scottish Executive.

—(2007). Children's Experiences of Disability, *Disability and Society,* 22(1), 19–33.

Curtis K., Roberts H., Copperman J., Downie A. and Liabo K. (2004) How Come I Don't Get Asked No Questions? Researching 'Hard to Reach' Children and Teenagers. *Children and Family Social Work,* 9, 167–175.

Darbyshire P., Macdougall C. and Schiller W. (2005). Multiple Methods in Qualitative Research with Children: More Insight or Just More? *Qualitative Research,* 5(4), 417–436.

Davies J. and Wright J. (2008). Children's Voices: A Review of the Literature Pertinent to Looked-After Children's Views of Mental Health Services. *Child and Adolescent Mental Health,* 13(1), 26–31.

Department for Education and Skill / Disability Rights Commission (2006). *Implementing the Disability Discrimination Act in Schools and Early Years Settings.* Nottingham: DfES.

Fielding, Michael (2004). Transformative Approaches to Student Voice: Theoretical Underpinnings, Recalcitrant Realities, *British Educational Research Journal,* 30(2), 295–311.

—(2009). 'Interrogating Student Voice: Pre-Occupations, Purposes and Possibilities', in H. Daniels, H. Lauder and J. Porter (eds) *Educational Theories, Cultures and Learning. A Critical Perspective.* London: Routle

Flutter J. and Ruddock J. (2004). *Consulting Pupils: What's In it for Schools?* London: Routledge.

Gorard S. and Taylor C. (2004). *Combining Methods in Educational and Social Research.* Maidenhead: Open University Press.

Green H., McGinnity A., Meltzer H., Ford T. and Goodman R. (2004). *Mental Health of Children and Young People in Britain.* Office for National Statistics.

Greene, J. C. (2008). Is Mixed Methods Social Inquiry a Distinctive Methodology? *Journal of Mixed Methods Research*, 2(1), 7–22.

Greene J. C., Caracelli V. J. and Graham W. F. (1989). Toward a Conceptual Framework for Mixed Methods Evaluation Designs. *Educational Evaluation and Policy Analysis*, 11, 255–274.

Grocott, P., Cowley, S. and Richardson, A. (2002). Solving Methodological Challenges Using a Theory-Driven Evaluation in the Study of Complex Patient Care. *Evaluation*, 8(3), 306–321.

Johnson R. B. and Onwuegbuzie A. J. (2004). Mixed Methods Research: A Research Paradigm Whose Time has Come. *Educational Researcher*, 33(7), 14–26.

Kelly, B. (2005). Chocolate . . . Makes You Autism: Impairment, Disability and Childhood. *Disability and Society*, 20(3) 261–275.

Kirova A. (2006). A Game-Playing Approach to Interviewing Children about Loneliness: Negotiating Meaning, Distributing Power and Establishing Trust. *Alberta Journal of Educational Research*, 52(3), 127–147.

Kushner, S. (2002). I'll Take Mine Neat: Multiple Methods but a Single Methodology. Evaluation, 8(2), 249–258.

Lewis A. (2004). And When Did You Last See Your Father? Exploring the Views of Children with Learning Difficulties/Disabilities. *British Journal of Special Education*, 13(1), 4–10.

Lewis A. and Porter J. (2007). 'Research and Pupil Voice', in L. Florian (ed.) *Handbook of Special Education* London: Sage.

Lewis, A., Robertson, C. and Parsons S. (2005). *Experiences of Disabled Students and their Families. Phase 1,* Research report to Disability Rights Commission, The University of Birmingham, School of Education.

Lundy L. (2007). 'Voice' is Not Enough: Conceptualising Article 12 of the United Nations Convention on the Rights of the Child. *British Educational Research Journal*, 33(6), 927–942.

Noyes, A. (2005). Pupil Voice: Purpose, Power and the Possibilities for Democratic Schooling. Thematic review. *British Educational Research Journal* 31(4), 533–540.

Pedder D. and McIntyre D. (2006). Pupil Consultation: The Importance of Social Capital. *Education Review*, 58(2), 145–157.

Porter J. (2009). Missing out? Challenges to Hearing the Views of All Children on the Barriers and Supports to Learning *Education 3–13,* 37(4), 349–360.

Porter J., Daniels H., Georgeson J., Hacker J. and Gallop V. (2008). *Disability Data Collection for Children's Services.* Research report No DCSF-RR062. Nottingham: DCSF.

Porter J. and Lacey, P. (2005). *Researching Learning Difficulties.* London: Sage.

Punch S. (2002). Interviewing Strategies with Young People: The 'Secret Box', Stimulus Material and Task-Based Activities. *Children & Society*, 16, 45–56.

Ravet J. (2007). Enabling Pupil Participation in a Study of Perceptions of Disengagement: Methodological Matters. *British Journal of Special Education*, 34(4), 234–242.

Robinson C. and Taylor C. (2007). Theorizing Student Voice: Values and Perspectives. *Improving Schools*, 10(5), 5–17.

Roose G. A. and John, A. M. (2003). A Focus Group Investigating into Young Children's Understanding of Mental Health and their Views on Appropriate Services for their Age Group. *Child Care Health and Development*, 29(6), 545–550.

Ruddock J. and Fielding, M. (2006). Student Voice and the Perils of Popularity. *Educational Review*, 58(2), 219–231.

Sale, J., Lohfeld, L and Brazil K., (2002). Revisiting the Quantitative-Qualitative Debate: Implications for Mixed-Methods Research. *Quality and Quantity*, 36, 43–53.

Teddlie, C. and Tashakkori, A. (2009). *Foundations of Mixed Methods Research: Integrating Quantitative and Qualitative Techniques in the Social and Behavioral Sciences.* London: Sage.

Thomas C. (1999). *Female Forms: Experiencing and Understanding Disability.* Buckingham: Open University.

Van de Ven A. H. and Delbecq A. L. (1972). The Nominal Group as a Research Instrument for Exploratory Health Studies. A. J. P. H February 1972, pp. 337–342.

Yanchar S. C. and Williams D. D. (2006). Reconsidering the Compatibility Thesis and Eclecticism: Five Proposed Guidelines for Method Use. *Educational Researcher*, 35(9), 3–12.

3 Failing to Learn or Learning to Fail? The Case of Young Writers

Ros Fisher

Introduction

This chapter explores patterns of participation of young children (age 5–7) in classroom writing tasks. It draws on data from 'Talk to Text', an Esmée Fairbairn funded research collaboration between university based researchers and teachers that explored how talk supports writing with young children. Data include paired interviews with children and video data of classroom activity. The question posed in this chapter is, 'How do young children judged by their teachers as having low attainment in writing participate in writing activities in the classroom?' It draws on a Cultural-Historical Activity Theory (CHAT) perspective to argue that these children's low achievement is partly the result of their difficulty in negotiating a productive role as learner in the writing classroom. Their intentional choices reflect underlying motives that direct their actions as learners. This raises the question as to the extent to which these children have a 'learning problem' or a problem in identifying the appropriate strategies to thrive within the classroom setting.

In recent years, particularly in UK, concern about literacy standards has shifted from standards of reading to standards of writing with some children falling well below expected standards of achievement from the earliest stages (OFSTED, 2003). Reasons given to explain some young children's poor performance in writing have tended to focus on perceived shortcomings in the teaching, the supposed lack of innate capacity of the child, the lack of support provided by parents and the difficulty of writing itself. Although initiatives to improve the teaching of writing have shown some success in raising test scores (Earl et al., 2003), high stakes assessment strategies have failed to raise young writers' performance in national tests. Various initiatives have been put in place to address low attainment (e.g. Developing Early Writing, DfEE, 2001; Every Child a Writer, DCSF, 2009) but tend to treat those children who do not reach the required standard as an homogeneous group who require more of what they have already received. Seeing the problem as within the child or the home background can give rise to reductive remedial measures that locate blame rather than trying to understand the nature of the problem by considering the perspective of the learner within the learning context. However, beyond the tangible, and therefore measurable, skills of early writing, lies the way in which children negotiate their ways to act in the world of the classroom.

Literacy learning from a socio-cultural perspective

Learning to write presents multiple challenges for children. Psychological perspectives on the development of writing highlight that writers have to juggle with various constraints imposed on them by the writing task (Sharples, 1999) and by the limited capacity of working memory which means that cognitive attention cannot be simultaneously addressed to composition, transcription and revision (Hayes and Flower, 1980). It is argued that for children, who have to concentrate on the secretarial aspects of writing at the same time as composing, the demands on working memory may significantly hamper their ability to compose continuous prose. (Latham, 2002). Such views take literacy learning as something intrapersonal and linear. They focus on instruction in the early technical skills as the route to success in learning to write. From a linguistic perspective, the difference in conventions between spoken and written language also presents a challenge to the young writer (Perera, 1984). As Kress (2000) argues, the focus of research into literacy development 'has been to see how, or to demonstrate that children "move into" the adult system'. (p. 88). From this theoretical perspective, the child's task is to master a complex abstract system and failure is the inability to cope with such a system.

However studies of children learning literacy that draw on socio-cultural theories have argued that learning cannot be understood separately from the context within which it is located (Mercer and Littleton, 2007) or from a culture's history and values (Razfar and Guttierez, 2003). Literacy learning takes place within the institution of school and to understand children's learning we need to look at the child within the practice (Hedegaard and Fleer, 2008) and the child's understanding of that practice.

Vygotsky (1978) argued that human action on an object is guided not by instinct, as with animals, but by 'motives, socially rooted and intense' (p. 37) that provide direction. It is mediated action in which 'a complex psychological process through which inner motivation and intentions, postponed in time, stimulate their own development and realisation' (p. 26). Leontiev (1978) further developed the idea of object motive, arguing that there is no such thing as objectless activity. Leontiev discusses how the objects of activity are formed. He argues that human activity is formed not from within the individual but as a result of the reinforcement of the external environment; 'Society produces the activity of the individuals forming it' (p. 51). Moreover, activity is not static. It is dynamic and evolving across institutions. To understand the performance of children in school it is necessary to look at the object of the activity within the institution and beyond and how children's individual intentions and goals support or hinder them as participants in the social context of the classroom.

Activity as described by Leontiev is manifested in actions with goal-directed purposes. Their purposes are given in objective circumstances and cannot be abstracted from the situation nor contrived or created by the subject arbitrarily. Both goals and actions relate to an ideal image of the object – psychic reflection of reality which is mediated by the subject comparing it to an image of the ideal. Leontiev proposes that the object of the activity is perceived at two levels: one in independent existence and the other as an image of the object in the mind of the subject (p. 51). It is this second existence that is of interest here. How do young writers see their role in the classroom? How do they make personal meaning to guide their actions?

Children do derive personal meanings from the context of their learning. Wing (1995) examined young children's perceptions of work and play in their early years of schooling. She argues that it is classroom activities and routines that indicate to children what school is all about. In her study children expressed clearly different interpretations of 'work' and 'play' and these seemed largely to be a result of the behaviour of their teachers which in turn revealed different approaches to the two kinds of activity. It was these contextual cues that appeared more influential than the actual activity. In particular, in relation to writing, children appeared not to consider writing to be playing unless they chose to write. The fact that children were normally required to produce a particular product during writing time seemed important to children as an indication of the nature of the task as work or play. They also expressed concern over neatness and spelling when they were doing writing work which was not apparent when it was a chosen activity. Here children seem to respond to the institutional context of the task more than the practice of writing itself. Similarly Howard's (2002) research into young children's perceptions of play showed how children responded to more than obvious clues of play activity. They interpreted signals such as teacher proximity and choice as signs that an activity constituted play. She argues, Perceptions of play are not only specific to situations and contexts . . . but are also based on experience and are modified or elaborated over time (p. 499).

It is this active engagement of the learner with the often apparently incidental routines of the classroom that lead to the child's understanding of classroom activity and thus their modes of participation. Bourne (2002) examines the construction of 8- and 9-year old writers' identities though analysis of their classroom discourse around writing. She found that children who did well were better able to interpret the teacher's signals about their writing. She argues that children in classrooms cannot be seen solely as writers or only as learners positioned by 'the teacher in a discourse of academic achievement' (p. 243). They are people with other histories, other experiences who act within and upon classroom activity. She shows that despite whole class teaching sessions, certain children seemed restricted in their access to different identities as learners. She shows 'how children are active in taking up positions within the multiplicity of discourses they are given access to' (p. 252). Here, in the classroom, writing is shown to be far more a social than developmental process.

Thus it is the child's interpretation of what matters that orients their actions. Hedegaard (2009) gives the example of Jens, a 5-year-old boy in kindergarten. Jens appeared unwilling to read with the kindergarten teacher. Close observation indicated that he seemed unhappy with the 'cosy' nature of a story-reading session. When the book was changed to one about whales, he settled down and listened. Hedgaard speculates that Jens' dominant orientation was to learning and thus rejected the teacher's intentions of providing a settling and nurturing context for the young child whom she saw as unruly. Hedegaard argues that educators need to find a way to characterize crises such as the one described above so that they 'are included in a child's social situation of development without charactersing the children as mentally ill or obstructive' (p. 67).

Fleer (2008) compares the activity of two siblings as the older starts formal schooling and the younger attends with his mother. She compares their motivation. While the younger sibling Nathan's orientation is towards books and reading, his brother Andrew devoted his energy to learning how to behave in school rather than to the curriculum content. Fleer proposes that Nathan's interest in books and print seem likely to help him develop productively as a reader. However, she speculates that for Andrew, when school tasks became more demanding, he will be less well equipped than his brother to keep pace with curriculum.

These two examples illustrate the importance of considering children's understandings of the activity in which they are involved. I want to argue in this paper that in order to understand the nature of underachievement in young writers, researchers need to look at young children's participation in the institutional practices associated with writing in school. Although the data presented here relate to children learning to write, it is likely that the implications drawn go beyond writing to other curriculum areas where under-achievement is a problem.

Talk to text

The children who are the focus of this chapter were part of a research project that was a collaboration between the teachers of six classes with children aged between 5 and 7 years in the south of England and researchers at Exeter University. The overall aim of the project was to explore the relationship between talk and text in young writers. The data from which the following examples are drawn consist of video recordings of literacy lessons and interviews with pairs of focus children. A boy and a girl from each class were chosen by their teacher for each of three achievement levels. The focus children were identified by their teachers as being of high, average or low achievement in writing.

Video recordings were made of 24, hour-long lessons focusing on teacher input and children's paired talk before and while writing. Eight of the 24 videotaped lessons were of the 12 children who had been identified as undera-chieving in writing. The video data were analysed and coded for content of the talk using Atlas Ti software and further analysis of critical episodes.

Semi-structured interviews were conducted at the beginning and end of the year of study. Interviews were with the focus children and conducted in pairs to reduce the possible tension of individual interviews. This had the disadvantage that one child may have been influenced by the response of the other. Accessing children's attitude is always a problematic activity. Their desire to please or, at least, say the right thing; the unformed nature of their understanding at this early age; as well as the slipperiness of language itself means that only general trends can be identified. Interviews were transcribed and coded inductively. The purpose of the interviews was to find out about children's attitudes towards writing before and after the project; to investigate what children considered to be good writing; and to explore their understanding of how people learn to write.

Video data

The video data were coded for the main study in order to explore the relationship between talk and writing in general. Each of the 24, hour-long videos was watched in its entirety to get a sense of the whole lesson. Then the video was sectioned into small clips and coded. New codes were added to the code list as they occurred in different videos until no new codes emerged. In all 37 codes were allocated to the 24 lesson videos. Frequency counts of the behaviour corresponding to each code were made. Six of the 37 codes were teacher codes and 31 were child codes. The distribution of the eight most common pupil codes can be seen in Table 3.1.

In order to study the distribution of these codes for those children who had been identified by their teacher as underachieving in writing, the percentage of these codes as distributed between achievement pairs was calculated (See Table 3.2).

Table 3.1 Eight most common talk behaviours

Code	Total
Children manage or talk about the task	69
Children talk about writing, spelling or scribing	69
Child writes or works silently	66
Child says sentence as they write	52
Child sounds out spelling	51
Children share ideas together	45
Social talk	44
Ignores other child's idea or suggestion	10

Table 3.2 Most common talk behaviours by achievement

Code	HA (%)	AA (%)	LA (%)
Children manage or talk about the task	32	37	31
Children talk about writing, spelling or scribing	40	15	45
Child writes or works silently	18	47	35
Child says sentence as they write	43	35	22
Child sounds out spelling	22	31	47
Children share ideas together	63	34	3
Social talk	2	58	40
Ignores other child's idea or suggestion	11	11	78

Although some of the activities identified in the coding show little difference between achievement pairs, one or two aspects are worthy of comment. The focus of the research project was on children's talk and the teachers had worked hard to develop activities that would encourage talk. However the coding shows that, although those children identified as being high achieving shared ideas the most, of all the examples of children sharing ideas only 3% were the lower-achieving children. This distribution is almost reversed when the code is for social talk: the high achievers were recorded doing very little and the others quite a lot. It is also interesting to note that the low-achieving pairs were much more likely to ignore their partner's idea or suggestion. The distribution of these codes indicate that these low achieving children were not using talk in the way the teacher had planned or, apparently, in the way that those children who were judged to be higher achievers were using the talk.

Observation of these children during the writing lessons show that they appear to be concentrating on the task mainly and are rarely reprimanded by their teacher for inappropriate behaviour. However, the videos show incidents where these children are clearly concerned to behave as a school child should behave. The types of action that seem to show these children trying to do the right thing as pupils in a writing lesson included the way in which they used the artefacts provided to support their writing and incidents where they seemed to be motivated by pleasing the teacher. Also selected were episodes where there seemed to be some crisis of motivation: either where motives other than doing the right thing prevailed or when the actions appeared to have no motive beyond the activity itself.

Chloe

Chloe and Luke are both six years old. Both were identified by their teacher as underachieving in writing, although in the video data, Luke appears much better oriented to the expectations of the classroom. The samples of writing arising from the observed activity confirm the teacher's judgement of his level of achievement. In one of the video lessons, they have a complicated task in which they have to choose an animal, talk about and write where it lives and why it is threatened with extinction. They have been working on wild animals for a few days in class and at home. They are quite clear about which animals are threatened and know some of the reasons for this. Throughout the time that they are doing the talking and writing tasks, their main motivation seems to be getting the task right. First of all the teacher introduced a role play with children as the animals under threat of extinction.

Chloe:	I'm a seal
Luke [irritated]:	I've got to say, 'What are you?' first. What are you?
Chloe:	A seal
Luke:	Where do you live?
Chloe:	In the water
Luke [irritated]:	Ocean
Chloe:	Ocean
Luke:	Why are you becoming extinct?
Chloe:	They are draining the water away.
Luke [correcting her]:	No, wrong one. Wrong one. It's the fishing one!
Chloe:	The fisherman are taking the fish out so they can have dinner and are making the water dirty.
Luke:	Now it's me
Chloe:	What are you?
Luke:	Snow leopard
Chloe:	What do you eat? Why are you becoming extinct?
Luke [irritated]:	You mean where do I live? Because all the farmers are taking the grass and bits I need to survive.

When they start to write, Chloe is anxious about what to do. She asks Luke whether she should put her name on the back and whether they have to draw the animals. She fiddles with her pencil, sings quietly, pricks herself with her pencil and moves her paper around. She makes all the moves of a busy writer but does not write. Luke settles down quickly and writes. Half way through they stop and discuss whether they should write in columns like the teacher did or across the page. Later they argue about the position of the paper on the table. Finally, the teacher's voice is heard warning that the lesson will soon end.

> Teacher: There's two minutes left so finish your writing quickly.
> Chloe: Let's not talk [they write] two minutes. Oh I'm never going to . . . I've only got that space . . .
> Luke: I've only got to there.
> Chloe: Ah – look at this. [picks up pencil] I need to tell Mrs. M. Mrs. M I've found . . . [unclear]
> Luke: Come on stop messing about.
> Chloe: Oh I'm not going to make it. [Fiddles with T-shirt.]
> Luke: Stop getting undressed and get on with it.
> Chloe: Oh I've done that 'suh' wrong. Now what am I going to do?

This is not the dialogue of two children trying to be difficult. They are clearly concerned to be seen to do the right thing in the eyes of their teacher. Yet there is no clear progression from the object of pleasing the teacher to the object of the activity of school: learning to write.

Ben

Ben is in his first full year of formal schooling and became six years old during the year of the project. The first video recording of Ben shows him working on a piece of writing about healthy eating. His teacher, although relatively recently qualified, had an excellent relationship with her class and had recently won an award for her teaching skill. She had already done other work about healthy eating and the purpose of the writing task was to write what they had learned. The lesson started with the teacher reviewing what they had learned and then modelling the writing. After this the children went to their tables and worked as pairs talking and then writing about what they knew about healthy eating.

On several occasions during the video recording, Ben can be seen staring blankly into space. On other occasions he rocks back and forth, pulls faces and sings quietly to himself. For most of the time there is little or no expression on his face. The video only shows him writing when his teacher comes over to his table. Only on two occasions does he show animation. In the first the children have just been sent to start work at their tables. Ben and his partner are sitting and waiting quietly. Ben is sucking his fingers and staring into space. The video shows a child (off screen) putting one hand on the table in front of Ben and his partner, another child places their hand on top and others on the table follow. Slowly Ben's face changes and he tentatively puts his hand on top of those already there. The game speeds up and Ben leans forward eagerly, smiling; both hands now in the game. Without saying anything he changes his flat hand to a fist and others follow his lead. They play in this way for perhaps half a minute and then Ben slumps, puts his elbows on the table, his head in his hands and looks down. An adult appears on screen.

Much later in the lesson, he is rocking quietly back and forth, again staring into space when another child on his table puts her pencil forward and says, 'I've got the tallest pencil'. Her neighbour places her pencil alongside to check. Slowly Ben sits forward, alert, and puts his pencil alongside the other two. 'Oh no you have not', he says with a broad grin. The game stops when the teacher reminds them to carry on writing. At the end of the year of the project, Ben talked about being annoyed by the other people on his table, he said, 'they annoy me sometimes, when I'm trying to write they keep laughing and I'm trying not to join in'.

Although simple games such as these clearly motivate Ben, he also seems keen to please his teacher. Not only does he stop the play, immediately there is a reminder of the adult in the classroom, but also at the end of the lesson when the teacher stops the class by saying, 'stop writing and show me your hands', he jumps up quickly and waves his hands in the air. It appears that, when he knows the action is required, he is willing to do it. Fleer (2008) writes of how the children in her study watched others as a way of deciding on the appropriate way to act in the new situation of school. Ben also seems to have learned how to act from watching others. However, like Andrew in Fleer's study, what he has imitated does not help his school learning. The video shows Ben, when he does put his pencil onto the paper in front of him to be making very small marks. They are not letters or lines on a picture but just small dots on the work he has done while the teacher was at his side. To an uninformed observer he would appear to be working.

Further evidence of Ben acting the part of the good pupil is in his use of the artefacts that are an essential part of the writing classroom. As already observed above, his use of a pencil was not only to produce writing when supported closely by the teacher but also that it enabled him to look like he was doing what was required of him. There is an interesting episode about 30 minutes into the lesson. Ben is swinging back and forth on his chair and yawning. The teacher asks him if he would like an alphabet card. He says yes. This card has the letters of the alphabet written on it in upper and lower case and has pictures of objects that begin with the letter shown. His partner asks him, 'Ben, why do we need an alphabet card?' he replies, 'Because it helps you. If you forget how to write stuff you can look for the letters.' When the alphabet card arrives, he looks at it carefully and says 'tuh for tree' and points at the letter T. He then points at each letter in turn and says the alphabet (albeit incorrectly). He leans over the alphabet card and scribbles on the pictures. He then points to each letter in turn and runs his pencil along the line of letters. Then he resumes swinging and yawning. Although he can tell another child the purpose of the alphabet card, it is not at all clear that he understands how the card can help in his production of written script. Again, however, he looks as though he is using it correctly.

Other videos have similar examples of those children who have been described as underachieving in writing, showing concern to be seen as good pupils. Their efforts seem to be directed towards the peripheral but observable aspects of writing classroom practice. The cultural setting and relational activity within and beyond the classroom generate the motives that individuals adopt. These children are developing as pupils at the same time they are developing as writers. They act within the classroom setting according to a range of personal, social and societal influences. They have choices to make about how they will respond to the learning opportunities offered to them. The interaction between their own understanding of the activity of writing and how they interpret the goals of the classroom are likely to influence how they engage with and within the writing activities provided.

The children's voices

While the video data provide opportunities for the researcher to interpret the children's motives, it is also important to hear the voice of the child. The first interview began with children being shown a picture of children writing. These pictures showed three children writing and the focus children were asked to write or dictate to the researcher words to fill thought bubbles for each of the writers. The researcher then asked which of the three was a good writer and how could they tell. Later in the interview, children were asked whether they were good at writing and also who was a good writer in their class. For each of these questions, they were also asked how they knew.

Ben was interviewed twice; once at the beginning of the year and once at the end. He said that he thought he was a good writer. When asked why he said so, he said it was because he wrote small. This theme of the importance of small writing comes throughout both his interviews. At the end of the year, he thought his writing was better as it was smaller. To Ben it seems that thinking is an important part of what happens in writing lessons. When asked to comment on the picture of children writing he said:

Ben: I think they are thinking about writing and how they are going to write.

Researcher: OK, well I need to write in the thought bubble what each one is thinking, so you tell me what each one is thinking and I'll write it in for you.

Ben: I think she's thinking what should she write. I think you should write, 'I am thinking about how I am going to write.'

Ben: I think he's thinking, trying to read what he's writ[ten]. I think you should write 'I am thinking about what I am supposed to write.'

Researcher: OK, if you look at all those children on the paper, are any of the children good writers.

Ben: I think the one with the hand up is the best writer

Researcher: Why is that one a good writer?

Ben: Because I think that he is the best in the class.

Researcher: Why is he the best in the class?

Ben: Because he listens to the teacher and never talks.

From this initial interchange we can see a possible explanation for his demeanour on the video where he often appeared to be staring into space or swinging on his chair. It is interesting that this thinking does not seem to be related to writing composition but to do the right thing. Ben says that the boy is thinking about what he is *supposed to* write. These interview responses raise the question as to whether Ben's blank looks show a lack of motivation or arise from the need to look as though he is thinking.

When asked what helps him write, Ben didn't mention the alphabet cards even on one occasion. At the start of the project he said, 'what helps me is if someone's telling me what letters I have to do and then I can just write it.' A similar reliance on happenstance is evident at the end of the project year. He explained, 'well if the teacher leaves it [a model sentence] up on this big board then I find it easier.' And a bit later, 'I quite like it when people say that they are not going to leave anything up but they just forget it so that I can copy it.' These comments refer to the teacher's practice of modelling writing one or two sentences before children go to write independently. Usually the teacher would remove her sentences to encourage children to write on their own.

Chloe also demonstrated her anxiety about getting things right in the interviews. When asked who was the best writer in the class, she named a boy and explained, 'he's a very good writer and when I look at his writing it's really neat and he always gets it the right way.' The section in which she responded to a question about what she doesn't like about writing is revealing.

Researcher: OK what don't you like about writing?
Chloe: I don't like when I get really stuck in my writing I don't like that bit.
Researcher: What kinds of times do you get stuck, what makes you get stuck?
Chloe: My stuck bit is when I can't think of words to write and I try to think of it.
Researcher: Anything else?
Chloe: Getting in trouble doing writing

These responses seem to show these children's desire to do the right thing: to avoid trouble. Ben prioritizes looking right: thinking or not talking. Chloe is concerned to get the procedure right. Yet when asked what helps them write Chloe said that she relies on the teacher to give her the right answer and Ben hopes that something helpful will be left out by mistake.

Discussion

These data give some insight into how young writers who have not made a strong start as writers act in the writing classroom. These children are learning to write within the institution of school. The object of the activity of school as an institution is the education of children: that they become literate members of society. However, the choices for action made by the participants in the activity will influence their trajectory as learners. As educators we need to look beyond the performance of young writers to understand and influence the intentions that guide their participation.

Although the identification of intentions is problematic and there is not always a simple relationship between the motive and the action, there are instances in the video data where a change in the demeanour of these children gives a sense of sheer enjoyment in the activity. While their actions while at 'work' in the classroom indicate them working out new orientations, there are critical instances where their motivation seems to lie more in the doing of the action than in the result. As Leontiev describes, 'play is character-ised by its motive lying in the process itself rather than in the result of the action' (1978, p. 331).

These young children are relatively new to the more formal world of the school classroom. Whereas play was a more central feature of their pre-school experience, they now need to appropriate new motives and competencies in relation to the practice traditions of the writing classroom. Let us take the small example of Ben playing a game of piling up hands with his friends. This game in itself is completely acceptable in the home, the playground or the pre-school setting. It is not acceptable in the middle of a writing lesson. From looking at Ben's demeanour during the game, he appears to have found it stimulating and enjoyable. In order to thrive in the school situation he will need to find other motivation. He has already been labelled as a 'poor writer'.

The interview with Ben provides some insight into a crisis in his motivation. Whereas he finds it hard to resist the lure of his friend's play, he is aware that this is not what is required in the context of the writing classroom. His efforts with the alphabet card and his actions with his pencil indicate that he is making an attempt to be a 'good pupil'. His interpretation of what is expected seems to be based, as Fleer's Andrew, on watching what the others do. He has also clearly listened to his teacher. He was able to use the appropriate words to tell his partner why they needed an alphabet card. Yet these words and his actions did not appear to help him write.

Hedegaard and Fleer (2008) argue that 'children's efforts and motives are usually directed towards successfully participating in the practice traditions of particular institutions' (p. 15). While Ben appeared to imitate the behaviour of others, some children from this group seemed to focus on getting the product right. Chloe's session writing about animals becoming extinct seems fraught with anxiety. Had she presented the lines in the required way? A letter has been written the wrong way round. A pencil was in the wrong place. How could she finish on time? None of these anxieties are related to the main feature of writing: the expression of meaning. Only one is related to the secretarial aspects in the writing of the letter 'S'. Although her anxieties are about getting things right in the eyes of the teacher, the focus of her attention is mostly on those aspects of classroom activity that will ensure a safe response from the teacher but are less likely to help her become a more accomplished writer.

Leontiev's proposition that both goals and actions of the subject relate to an ideal image of the object seems relevant here. If, as Leontiev argues, activity exists at two levels; one in independent existence and the other as an image of the object in the mind of the subject, learners' understandings of the object are crucial to how they participate in activity. These children's understanding arise both from the practice of the particular institution and their interpretation of this. Thus to understand reasons for underachievement we need to focus on the child's activity within the institution rather than on institutional practice.

The data described here suggest two possible reasons for some children's failure to develop the writing skills they need to advance within the school system. First, children start formal schooling very early in England. They are required to make the transition from the self-initiated and play-oriented activity of family and pre-school to the more curriculum-driven activity of formal schooling. The description of the writing tasks that these five and six year olds were required to do may seem overly prescriptive and demanding to those more used to a less formal curriculum in the early years. They have to move to a context where the object of the activity is more directed and externally imposed at a very early age. They need to negotiate different motives within the new institution.

Elkonin (1972) saw institutional practice as the main source of intellectual development. His work shifted the focus from general characteristics of psychological development to understanding diversity of human development as it related to practice traditions in societal institutions (Hedegaard et al., 1999). As children develop, new modes of activity and forms of interaction become available to them. The place they occupy in 'the system of human relationships also changes' (Zaphorozhets et al., 1972, p. 208). They argue that 'the progress in development in the preschooler's thinking presupposes extensive changes in the character of his activity, which is associated with the appearance of new cognitive motives different from the motives of play and practical activity' (p. 236). Nevertheless, as argued by Fleer (2008), changes in practice that lead to a child appropriating new motives can sometimes result in the motive connected to the new activity not being the one intended by the practitioner. She gives the specific example of the demands of the practice being too high so that the child cannot participate as intended.

This leads to my second point, how children participate in the writing practices of the school will be linked to their conception of the ideal student; to what their interpretation of their experience of schooling has led them to focus their attention upon. This will orientate their actions as they develop as school pupils. Thus the object of action as perceived by young learners is crucial for how they develop within the activity of school. Many of the children in this project, wrote eagerly and willingly. They made good attempts to produce the writing required. However, one feature of the statistical evidence of test results is that England has a long tail of underachievement. In literacy, our best readers and writers achieve as good scores as anywhere else in the world. However, there are too many who fail to learn to read or write to the standard required to make good progress in the later stages of their education.

In order to help these young writers develop, it is necessary to look beyond the writing curriculum to the children themselves. This does not imply that the answer lies in providing more and improved intervention but in supporting children in their understanding of classroom activity and the way that they appropriate motives and participate in writing activities. Too often explanations of low attainment focus on children's failure to learn. Yet the data discussed here do not show children failing to learn; they show that they fail to focus on those aspects of classroom practice that will contribute to their development as writers.

References

Bourne, J. (2002). 'Oh, What will Miss Say!': Constructing Texts and Identities in the Discursive Processes of Classroom Writing. *Language and Education*, 16(4), 241–259.

DCFS (2009). *Every Child a Writer*, London: Department for Children, Schools and Families.

DfEE (2001). *Developing Early Writing*, London: Department for Education and Employment.

Earl, L., Watson, N., Levin, B., Leithwood, K., Fullan, M., and Torrance, N. (2003). *Watching and Learning 3: Final Report of the External Evaluation of England's National Literacy and Numeracy Strategies*: Ontario Institute for Studies in Education, University of Toronto.

Elkonin, D. B. (1972). Toward the Problem of Stages in the Mental Development of the Child. *Soviet Psychology*, 10, 225–251.

Fleer, M. (2008). The Significance of Practice Traditions in Schools for Shaping Activities and Generating Motives in Children's Development, ISCAR Pre-Conference Workshop on Cultural-Historical Approaches to Children's Development Section Meeting, 8th September 2008, San Diego: California, Unpublished.

Hayes, J. R. and Flower, L. S. (1980). 'Identifying the Organisation of Writing Processes', in L. W. Gregg and E. R. Steinberg (eds), *Cognitive Processes in Writing*. Hillsdale, New Jersey: Lawrence Erlbaum Associates, pp. 3–30.

Hedegaard, M. (2009). Children's Development from a Cultural-Historical Approach: Children's Activity in Everyday Local Settings as Foundation for Their Development. *Mind, Culture and Activity*, 16(1), 64–82.

Hedegaard, M. and Fleer, M. (2008). *Studying Children: A Cultural-Historical Approach*. Maidenhead: Open University Press.

Howard, J. (2002). Eliciting Young Children's Perceptions of Play, Work and Learning Using the Activity Apperception Story Procedure. *Early Child Development and Care*, 172(5), 489–502.

Kress, G. (1994). *Learning to Write*. London: Routledge.

Latham, D. (2002). How Children Learn to Write: Supporting and Developing Children's Writing in Schools. London: Paul Chapman.

Leont'ev, A. N. (1978). *Activity, Consciousness and Personality* (M. J. Hall, Trans.). Englewood Cliffs, NJ: Prentice Hall.

Mercer, N. and Littleton, K. (2007). Dialogue and the Development of Children's Thinking: A Sociocultural Perspective. London: Routledge.

OFSTED (2003). Annual Report London: Office for Standards in Education.

Perera, K. (1987). *Understanding Language.* Sheffeld: NAAE.

Razfar, A. and Guttierrez, K. (2003). 'Reconceptualising Early Childhood Literacy: The Sociocultural Influence', in N. Hall, J. Larson and J. Marsh (eds), *Handbook of Early Childhood Literacy,* London: Sage, pp. 34–48.

Sharples, M. (1999). *How We Write: Writing as Creative Design.* London: Routledge.

Wing, L. (1995). Play is Not the Work of the Child: Young Children's Perceptions of Work and Play. *Early Childhood Research Quarterly,* 10, 223–247.

Vygotsky, L. (1978). *Mind and Society: The Development of Higher Psychological Processes.* Cambridge, Massachusetts: Harvard University Press.

Zaporezhets, A. V., Zinchenko, V. P. and Elkonin, D. B. (1971). 'Development of Thinking' (J. Shybut and S. Simon, Trans.), in A. V. Zaporezhets and D. B. Elkonin (eds), *The Psychology of Preschool Children.* Cambridge, Massachusetts: MIT Press, pp. 186–254.

Part II
Educational Psychological Pedagogical Practice

Cooperation between Professionals in Educational Psychology – Children's Specific Problems are Connected to General Dilemmas in Relation to Taking Part

4

Charlotte Højholt

Chapter Outline

Introduction

Children live their lives *together* with other children and across different kinds of social contexts. In this chapter it will be discussed how rethinking support for children and schools must be aimed at the interplay between children and the possibilities of participation among them *as well as* at the relations between their different life contexts. Further, it will be argued that this involves cooperation between the grown-ups supporting the development of the children (e.g. parents, teachers, pedagogues and special teachers). The psychologist has an important role to play in these processes.

The paradox seems to be that while children live their lives across different contexts and together with other children, the professional help aimed at supporting children in trouble, is organized and understood in relation to individualized problems related to special functions in one place. To overcome this dilemma we have to work for changes in our understandings of children's possibilities for learning and development as well as in the way we organize our support for children and schools. How may we conceptualize the connections between children's personal and specific problems and the general social practice in which they take part? And how may we direct psychological interventions directly into *social possibilities* for the child to take part, engage itself and learn?

The chapter will take its point of reference in a research project: 'Across family work and inclusion in school' and thereby in empirical material from interventions related to inclusion of children in some kind of difficulties – these might be categorized as educational problems as well as behavioural problems.

The practical support for children will be discussed in the light of a theoretical discussion about the inner connection between the perspectives, intentions and engagements of a single child and the concrete social practices where the child takes part. In this way the chapter will also treat the importance of the concept of 'social practice' in a cultural theory approach (in continuation of the discussions by Hedegaard et al. 1999).

One main point will be to understand and investigate personal perspectives and social conditions in relation to one another – and through one another. Methodologically it will be argued that personal statements and engagements represent knowledge about concrete social practices and that we cannot understand the intentions of a child without studying the social interplay that these intentions somehow are aimed at, related to and part of. In this way participation becomes a key concept, and children's personal and specific problems are seen connected to *general* dilemmas in relation to taking part in contradictory social practice.

This is not just meant as a theoretical question but is indeed challenged from practical dilemmas in relation to how we may organize our professional support in relation to improving children's life conditions. In practice the support for children becomes detached from the contexts of the children's daily life – or you could say: Detached from the contexts of the problems.

This is why I find the theoretical clarification of the social basis of children's development and difficulties – or you could say: the relation between children and their social conditions – of great importance for the *practical possibilities* for creating changes in the developmental possibilities and for supporting children. If we conceptualize development as a kind of solo project, it becomes irrelevant to involve other persons in the understanding of developmental problems, as well as in the interventions in relation to overcoming the problems. Especially the practical support for children is in need of very concrete and situated approaches to the conditions relevant to children in their actual daily life at different places.

The discussions will start up with the theoretical challenges, leading into methodological considerations and thereafter different examples, questions and results from the research will follow.

Theoretical challenges in relation to practical support

Children's problems take place in an everyday and common life and no matter how special children's difficulties may be, children seem directed towards other children, and they seem engaged with – *general* – social dilemmas in relation to being part of relevant communities and being acknowledged here (e.g. Højholt, 2006, 2008; Morin, 2008; Schwartz, in prep). Still the helping system is organized in different more or less isolated contexts where different professionals are working with individual and *specific* problems.

Children live a compound life – what happens in one place has consequences for their possibilities in other places. Furthermore children's engagements as well as dilemmas and problems seem to be connected with their possibilities for participating in activities with other children. This points to theoretical challenges in relation to understanding specific and personal problems in the context of general dilemmas in the societal life of children.

To grasp these connections the chapter will take a point of reference in the theoretical concept of participation in social practice as a main concept in order to understand the relation between human beings and their social possibilities (Dreier, 2008; Hedegaard, 2008; Højholt, 1999, 2005; Lave and Wenger, 1991; Rogoff, 2003). In this understanding children learn and develop *through their participation* in social practice together with others, and they make up important developmental possibilities of each other.

In a discussion of the historical account as well as perspectives for further development of Activity Theory and the Cultural Historical Approaches, Hedegaard et al. elaborate on the meaning of social practice in relation to these traditions (1999).[1] They state that the concept of social practice lies in the heart of the theory's conceptual structure, but it is only in recent decades that it has started to receive the attention that it deserves – and the notion of social practice, as an analytical concept, needs to be developed further on (Hedegaard et al., 1999, p. 19). The concept of practice gives a possibility to focus on the dynamic between collective activity and a subject's actions and to understand persons as participating in several different activities in different institutions (ibid. p. 23). In relation to this debate the authors connect social practice to *structured* human activities around specific tasks and goals (ibid. p. 19), and I think we have to elaborate theoretically in relation to the structuring characteristic of social practice.

In my interpretation the great productivity of the concept of social practice connects to the emphasis on activities as *collective* and *historical*. This has consequences for the design of my empirical work, the focus for observations as well as interviews – and for the analytical work with the empirical material: I try to pay attention to the way participants make up the conditions for the possibilities for each other's actions, to *the inner connectedness* between different actions. When subjects relate to each other they do not just relate to accidental 'others' but to structured social arrangements – and through this situated interplay they take part in the reproducing and changing of the arrangements. When persons live and act together they participate in the structuring of the conditions for the acting and development of each other. Furthermore the contexts where they are acting together are structured in *historical* ways.

But I find that we have difficulties in connecting personal problems and social possibilities in a concrete way that will enable us to organize intervention *in the social possibilities*, and among other things this seem to be grounded in the way we work with the concept of structure. In spite of the dialectical intentions, structures often appear in analyses as something abstract and outside the situated interplay between persons in a context – as a kind of untouchable 'frames' or conditions of determination (compare, for e.g., Dreier, 2007, 2008).[2] An abstract conceptualization of structure splits up the societal structures that people live and develop through – and their *acting* and *situated interplay* in which human beings structure the possibilities of each other.

This leads to conceptual problems in relation to understanding the child as a living and acting subject as well as in relation to understanding the social context for the development. 'Context' easily becomes a more or less empty concept that we all agree about and use as a guarantee for remembering the social world. But still we are in need of concepts to analyse the social life as something that persons *create together*. I think we need to analyse inter-subjectivity – to analyse the dynamics when subjects act together structuring the possibilities of each other.

In continuation of this I want to concretize the concept of structure as related to human participation in concrete social practice. In this way you might say that I use the concept of 'structure' as a twofold possibility – pointing to the active 'structuring' that persons create together when they act – *and* pointing to the social structures that make up conditions for their acting. To put it in other words structures are seen (1) as a focus on the historical arrangements of societal contexts and their tasks, means and objects – for example the societal connections between the school, the family and the social arrangement of special help. And (2) as well as the structuring process when participants are taking part and acting together in different and local social practices – a focus on the collective interplay in a context.

The point is to keep this as a dialectical unity. Even though means and objects of a context are historically developed they are indeed not unambiguous but in continuous negotiations and changes. Through their collective interplay subjects change the historical arrangements, and the connections between the places are in a continuous historical restructuring – as you may see illustrated in this book: Psychologists in the field of children are moving towards more consultative methods of working with teachers and others in schools and settings – expanding their role in the direction of working with organizations, teachers, classrooms and inclusion (Leadbetter, this volume; Vassing, this volume). This way of working *changes the relations between places* as schools, families and institutions – and especially it changes the relations between the helping system and the general system for children's life (for parallels especially in relation to collaboration between the systems see Daniels, this volume).

This attempt to follow up on the challenge about the concept of social practice raised by Hedegaard et al. is meant to strengthen our possibilities to analyse (and influence) the situations where children are in difficulties in their daily life. For instance the classroom may be analysed as a local practice that forms part of a societal structure (as for instance the position of the school in a structure consisting of family, kindergarten and other educational institutions). The school is not an accidental practice and the social life here should not be understood as abstract, isolated and detached 'relations' but as collective ways of relating to the agenda of the school. The participants relate to what is going on here and how this is meaningful to them. In school there is for instance learning, achievement, evaluation, competition, differentiation, inclusion as well as exclusion at stake. In school children are learning to take part in a very special practice and they are engaged *in relating to* the possibilities as well as contradictions here – they are engaging in the meanings this has to them in a concrete way.

In this understanding we must investigate social structures through the personal ways subjects relate and ascribe meanings to these – as expressed in their participation and experiences. For example in the field of children we build up structures for helping children in need, and when we explore the perspectives of the children we realize how children in a life across arrangement of help and general institutions get complicated conditions of participation in relation to these structures (Morin, 2008).

Sometimes it is stated by professionals in this field that the children enter *the same* classroom (and when they perform differently it must have to do with other things than what is going on here), but with the concept of social practice we might analyse how the classroom does not have the same meanings and does not set the same conditions for different children (Højholt, 2001; Stanek, in prep).We have to analyse the situated interplay closely, the different conditions for taking part here, the different *positions* in the classroom, the *reasons* children may have to act as they do, the social dynamics when some children are excluded and others, highly appreciated etc. (for the analytical concepts see Dreier, 2003). If we do not observe and analyse these dynamics in a situated way it seems that we turn our back to this part of the life of children and seek the background for their difficulties in other contexts as for instance their families, culture or isolated individual functions – without connecting to the *meanings in concrete life*. In this way it becomes complicated to work for changes in conditions – and for inclusion.

Participation as a key concept

The concept of participation may be seen as an attempt to develop dialectical concepts, which may help us to focus on *what* the children participate in, and on *how* the children participate in their personal ways. Development becomes related to personal ways of taking part in different social communities.

Such theoretical considerations build on the current critique of mainstream developmental psychology (as formulated by Burman, 1994; Hedegaard, 2002; Rogoff, 2003), and try to meet the challenge of developing conceptualizations by anchoring the personal process of learning and developing in the personal participation in social practice. 'Participation' has become a central concept in several variations of the cultural historical traditions, and I will emphasize that I attach weight to the dialectical unity of subjective activity as a personal way of dealing with situated social conditions in a practice. This attention is a little different than for instance Rogoff et al. (2007), who relate to a concept of 'cultural repertoires' (from earlier experiences) whereas I emphasize the situated, actual interplay between participants in a common practice. This turns my attention – and research activities – to the concrete interplay between participants, for example, in a classroom or in the interdisciplinary work related to supporting children in difficulties (Højholt, 2006).

In relation to improving the support for children's possibilities of participation in the social contexts of their daily life – and in relation to improving their processes of learning – it could be relevant with an elaboration of the concept of participation. I have discussed this concept as specified by Leontiev in relation to understanding the actions of a human being as *part of* a division of labour – and understanding the behaviour of a child as given grounds in relation to what the child is participating in (Højholt, 2006 p. 87f.; Leontiev, 1978). But here I would like to expand this with the formulations of Anna Stetsenko who, in her interpretation of Vygotsky, argues for more 'emphasis not on participation in practices but on contribution to them' (Stetsenko, 2008, p. 478).

Stetsenko argues that this focus points to 'a more active, self conscious, and directional process' (ibid.) and that all human activities (including psychological processes) are instantiations of contributions to collaborative transformative practices (p. 471). She relates this to what she promotes as an activist standpoint and to overcoming the opposition between knowledge and transformation, and this is indeed relevant to the practical support for children (I have tried to discuss this in Højholt, 2005; 2006). It is relevant in relation to developing the support in the direction of *creating social changes in the practices where children participate* and not just work isolated with each individual apart and in another context.

Here I would like to emphasize the relationship between these social changes and the possibilities of the single child to participate in a way that makes it possible to *contribute* to social activities and thereby to the personal learning process of its own. Learning becomes connected to 'finding a way to contribute to the continuous flow of socio-cultural practices' (Stetsenko, 2008, p. 487).

So, my intention with this discussion is to suggest *directions* for the work with social changes. When we connect the personal process of learning so closely to contributions to social practice we have a guideline for the practical help for children in difficulties: we may search for creating *possibilities for contributions* in concrete communities of relevance. And with the previous section in mind I could add: contributions not just in relation to choosing a colour for the drawing but in relation to how we are together here – to the structuring of the social life that we are part of. Our traditions about working with the training of individual children in isolated contexts must be transgressed by possibilities for organizing interventions in the social possibilities for participation – for contributing and finding personal meanings by engaging in social practice.

Methodological considerations

I have tried to illustrate, above, how theoretical clarifications may be important to the development of support for children, and I have slightly touched on the relationship between such theoretical discussions and more methodological questions about how to create knowledge relevant to the ongoing development of societal efforts in relation to improving children's life conditions.

In this section, I will sum up that the consequences of the above discussions point to developing participatory observations aimed at overcoming the tendency in psychology to focus on one single individual separately. In psychology, we have developed methods for describing and evaluating the behaviour and competences of individuals, and even though we have worked for several years with the individual in its surroundings I think we are still in need of traditions for studying *the general practice* that persons are creating together in their common interplay in relation to specific historical locations.

In the presented research[3] we try to observe the social dynamics in the interplay between children as well as grown-ups, to watch how the participants structure conditions to each other, to follow the varying positioning in a social practice, how the premises are set to become involved in activities, to speak up, to influence what is going on. This could be in the classroom or at an interdisciplinary meeting in order to decide the support for children (here we find parallels to the study of Hugh Mehan about the very different possibilities for influencing the descriptions of problems at such meetings, 1993). We are curious about how the ways in which the grown-ups organize their work (and thereby organize the conditions for the children) have influence on the interplay of the children. And we are curious about how the cooperation between the grown-ups has influence on their way of approaching the problems. In short we try to observe and to ask for conditions, meanings, different perspectives in a social interplay where different parties take part from each of their positions.

To gain knowledge about how concrete children live their lives and what seems important to them – as well as knowledge about the structural arrangements of social practice where children participate – we need knowledge from the perspectives of the children (Hedegaard et al., in prep). The concept of the perspectives of the children is meant as an analytical concept in relation to anchoring personal perspectives in locations in social practice. In order to contextualize the research about children, we have to investigate how children live their lives, what children *do*, what different social contexts *mean* to them, what concrete children are engaged in and what this looks like from their perspectives.

And to understand the personal engagements of a child, we have to look not only at the child itself but also 'in front' of the child – what is the child looking at, occupied with, taking part in? Children are like other persons aiming at something, and we must explore their personal *reasons* related to their engagement in concrete social situations with different things at stake.

The children's perspectives on dilemmas in their lives may teach us about the structure of contexts we have arranged for children and what kind of challenges and possibilities children deal with here. In relation to this we want to explore the arrangements we make for the children – our teaching, our special help, our pedagogical effort – in the light of how it works in the daily life of the children (considerations about the perspectives of the children are unfolded more in Højholt, in prep).

'Where do I belong?'

In Denmark we refer about 14 per cent of all children to some kind of special help and in short it can be said that this is very expensive, that we do not know if it works and that the system of special help has been criticized quite a lot – among other things for marginalizing the children, or with Hugh Mehan's words: 'Handicapping the handicapped' (1986).

For the moment 'inclusion' is a key word in relation to these problems; and in the mentioned research we are studying different kinds of support for children related to the inclusion of children in difficulties in ordinary schools. These interventions vary – in some cases the children are placed in 'special-education arrangements' at the school and in other cases at special institutions. In both cases a smaller group of children work with special teachers in relation to their difficulties. Different parties such as teachers, pedagogues, special teachers, consultants and psychologists are involved. Typically psychologists are involved in the process of referring the children to support and often they are also involved in different kinds of counselling for children as well as parents and professionals.

One of the initiatives we have observed is the so-called family classes and this construction is for the moment a very popular intervention, among other things, because it offers *an alternative to removing* a child to a permanent special-education arrangement: The children join the family class part of the week and for some months and then they are supposed to stay full time in their basic class again. Also this construction represents a possibility for *cooperating with parents in a new way* since a parent of the child joins the family class. In praxis the family classes in Denmark vary in methods but in some sense they use to build on the ideas of systemic family therapy. In the family classes where the research group makes observations the practice is organized around procedures of setting up goals together (children and parents join these procedures – a goal could be to raise your finger when you want to speak up), working with school tasks (children and parents cooperate), systems of scoring the behaviour of the child in relation to the goals (everybody is involved).

In this situation of observation we are sitting in a class room where about five children are working with their parents. Christina is a girl from seventh grade and she and her mother participate in the family class:

> Christina and her mother have done their school work successfully. Christina has received good 'scores' and her mother is now helping another pupil (part of the method).
>
> The mother seems to accomplish the expectations of a mother here, and she even converses with the researchers. Christina walks around and looks like a reserved teenager.
>
> When the lesson ends, her mother says: 'Now you are going to your basic class.' Christina answers in quite a bitter way: 'I don't want that "shit class"'

Christina's comment is in contrast to the success in the family class and her good scores here. But it can be seen in continuation of many observations of children pointing to their occupation – and preoccupation – with their possibilities of participation among other children.

In our project here, we have noticed that the children in the interventions tell about their classmate from the class they come from, talk about where they belong and about how they get playmates in the new (helping) context. Some of the younger children (about third grade) formulate the dilemmas like: *'Who are my friends', 'where do I 'belong', are my friends here or in the normal class, and how do I get friends here as well?'*

Observations with Jacob (in another family class) illustrate how some boys from third grade are occupied with getting in touch with each other – watching the other boys in the family class, turning their attention to the activities of the others, addressing the others with questions about what they are doing, invitations for doing something together – or teasing each other turning into lots of conflicts (for more details see Røn Larsen, in prep). The children are dealing differently with their learning situations across the arrangements for special support in the family class and the general learning in their home class system but they all relate to the other children and where they want or do not want to engage.

Christina seems to choose another way than Jacob, who engages very actively (but in a way that seems to disturb his process of relating to the school tasks), by choosing a more reserved approach. There is nobody of her age in the family class – and in her seventh grade there may be many sorts of difficult interplay to participate in, for example, related to the new relations the girls are developing to each other at this age, the new relation to the boys and to the teachers with whom Christina may have conflicts. It is my experience that these kinds of dilemmas are interwoven (Højholt, 1999, 2001, 2006).

But in the family class we do not have *access* to these interplays – neither Christina's *personal criteria of relevance* nor her *subjective reasons* for participating the way she does. The point is that we do not know – and the professionals do not know – we are in the wrong context in relation to gaining knowledge about these questions.

In this way Christina's comment illustrates a fundamental dilemma for the work of inclusion: The family class is, as the rest of the interventions we are presented for in relation to inclusion, *organized apart* from the home class. Children live a compound life together with other children and more than anything they seem directed towards peers. Children do not just live together – they *learn together* as well (Hedegaard, 2002; Højholt, 2008; Morin, 2008). Children's personal problems take place in an everyday and common life – but when we want to help them, we go somewhere else.

In this way I find that Christina's statement tells us several important things about the way we organize our support, and about how children and their grown-ups may have different perspectives about *what is important* and what is troublesome. It also tells us about how the life of children is connected and that we cannot understand the perspectives of the children just from looking at one place. In relation to research as well as practical support the example can be seen as an argument for investigating meanings across life contexts.

The organizational gap between 'special help' and the school

In order to explore the conditions of the children as well as the possibilities for support, we have interviewed the different teachers involved. The teachers in the family class are disappointed that their colleagues in the basic classes do not seem to see a task in relation to this intervention. The teachers in the family class want the regular teachers to follow up on the goals and scores when the child is in their class, and they want them to work with possibilities for the child to change here. On the other hand, the teachers from the basic classes seem a little mystified about what is going on in the intervention and feel they are not being involved. They do not know what kind of task they are expected to carry out, and it seems that the tasks are not explicitly connected to their daily work but only to the special methods of the intervention (for parallels from another study: Knudsen, 2007).

I want to understand this paradox (that I meet every time I interview different parties related to the same children) – in respect to the *division of tasks* between the grown-ups (Højholt, 2006). As mentioned in the introduction to this book the individualization of children's difficulties must be seen in the light of division of labour in the school and the isolation of responsibility in relation to this. In this way the processes of exclusion must be seen in connection to common contradictions and dilemmas that the participants in the school handle in each their conflictual cooperation (Axel, in prep).

The professionals take part in a quite divided structure, and they each have the responsibility for more or less isolated contributions. They are receiving tasks based on *individual descriptions* of children without insight into the interplay of the children, and the tasks are formulated in relation to specialized methods and techniques. Furthermore they have to *document individual progress* in relation to special functions. For the moment political demands of more and more measurement and documentation of efforts in relation to standardizations of individual performance are raised in Denmark.[4] This political movement reflects a specific (individualistic and decontextualized) approach to the learning of children and to what is 'professional' in relation to support for children (expertise becomes related to universal and abstract knowledge, see for example Parsons, 1954). In relation to the discussion here I want to point to the consequences for the cooperation between the grown-ups: How this demand enlarges the split between them and between the different life context of children as well as between *conditions* for learning and *support* for learning and developmental processes.

So the tasks of the professionals are not formulated in connection to each other – nor in connection to the compound life of the children. The tasks are formulated in relation to specialized methods and techniques for preparing the children *individually* to meet the challenges in the class room and not in relation to conditions of participation here. In this way the professionals cannot relate their tasks to each other – the tasks address isolated children, isolated problems and 'special functions'.

In this way it seems as if the arrangements for help 'lock themselves in' and 'shut the life of the children out'. What happens between the children is in this way placed outside reflections as well as outside help from the grown-ups.

Cooperation between the grown-ups

So far the analysis has turned our attention to the practical and theoretical structuring of our possibilities for organizing the support for children in difficulties. Because the first empirical example pointed to the split between the special intervention and the general education I will now present an example where this connection is handled in a different way. This may also serve as an argument for the possibilities in relation to a dialectical concept of structure with which I want to point to *practical possibilities* for changing structures.

A teacher – Karen – from a special institution where they work with family classes as well, tells about a process where a boy is now back in his basic class full time – together with Karen. Karen underlines: '*When I am there I am not just there for Jacob. I am there for the entire class*'.

Karen makes observations of the children in the school yard, she has common meetings with all the parents and she talks to the children about general dilemmas among them, as for instance the interplay between boys and girls and among these groups. The conclusion is that the entire class has had an 'added bonus' because of Jacob and the special teacher.

But what was the problem in relation to Jacob? We interview his teacher and his pedagogue, we make observations in his basis class as well as in his family class and at the interdisciplinary meetings about him (Røn Larsen, in prep). We get a picture of a quite engaged boy who involves himself actively in the social life around him. In the ordinary class he seems to have a hard job combining participation in the tasks from the teachers and participating in the group of boys. There is no *unambiguous* process of exclusion (as we often see when we observe children in a situated way), but it is difficult for Jacob to become accepted and his efforts seem to become increasingly desperate. I ask the pedagogue why he could not stay in the class and she explains that maybe there is something with his brain, but anyhow that is not the reason why he could not be in the class. And then she tells me about a quite troublesome and noisy group of boys with a tough language and tone among themselves. This is not easy to handle for the grown-ups and especially in the group of parents there are many conflicts.

When I follow different cases of children referred to psychologist and special support, I become aware of the meanings of the entire group of parents. Very often it seems that when other parents complain to the leader of the school it plays a significant role in the process of exclusion. The conflicts between parents may be seen as an illustration of the connection to political questions about how and for whom we want to organize the school. In the mentioned example it is interesting that when the pedagogue estimates the role of the teacher from the special institution she emphasizes the meetings with the entire group of parents: 'this group of parents need to be a community' and 'she gave them common tasks in relation to the children.' And when the process turns in a positive direction Jacob's father evaluates it like this (at an interdisciplinary meeting): 'Well there is nobody who complains now!' At the same meeting Jacob's mother tells that a parent of a girl in the class called her to tell that Jacob had played with her daughter – and this mother thought that Jacob's mother should not just hear bad things about her boy but also that she has a very nice boy.

In this way the meanings of other parents may play a part in processes of exclusion as well as in processes of support and inclusion. And it is interesting that the picture of Jacob changes during these processes.

Still, of course, Jacob plays a part in his way of relating to all these connections in his life. I believe that children's perspectives are constantly changing and that they are quite sensitive to changes in their life (Schwartz, in prep) but in the time period in which we follow the processes, Jacob seems to find it difficult to combine his participation in different places, and the observations of his desire to participate and make himself part of the group of boys point to a preoccupation in relation to this. We analyse this, in our research, in connection to his possibilities of participating and *contributing* to the communities in his life. It is as if there is no peace in his participation, his participation is not a matter of course – it is *at stake*. This may connect to a general dynamic in the interplay in the class (the pedagogues made small interviews with all the children in the class and the children talked about different *general problems* and conflicts among them) and it may connect to the situation were he is pointed out as a case, receiving special help and not being in the class all the time. He is not an obvious part of the community. Exactly in these conditions there are movements and openings, and I find these dynamics in the communities of children very important to our chances for supporting children in difficulties.

For a period of time we observe a productive development in the cooperation between the grown-ups as well as in the participation of Jacob – and he leaves the family class to stay in his basis class. The teacher reports that he (at least for a period) turns his attention to follow the rules of the school and to be cooperative (and in relation to this the teacher realizes how much the other boys make trouble and encourage Jacob to do the same). I do not think all problems are solved in this way, but the example illustrates what other kinds of 'successes' point to as well: Such processes are characterized by *cooperation between the grown-ups* – in this case cooperation between a school and the special school and between these professionals and the entire group of parents.

It is cooperation about *general dynamics* in the communities of children and their conditions for being together. It is important for me to emphasize since 'cooperation' has become a concept of fashion in the professional work, but in the research we often see quite a lot of parties cooperating about an individualization of problems without creating changes in the possibilities for participation of the children in difficulties. The *accesses* to work with structuring processes in the general possibilities of the children seem to be at stake in relation to supporting children across their life contexts.

The cooperation between the grown-ups seems to be a key for changing structures between the places, but the content in the cooperation is also highly important: Are we cooperating about scoring Jacob individually at different places or are we cooperating about how he can become a contributing participant in communities at different places? And are we involving parents as clients to change or as parties with perspectives on the problems and contributions to understanding as well as overcoming them?

So this is an example of potentials for another way of organizing and thinking about the relation between interventions and school, another way than the first mentioned 'gap'. In this way we see concrete processes exceeding the limitations of individualistic understandings in our material as well. Not once and for all but as examples of *interplay pointing to possibilities.*

Conclusions

In the article I have tried to connect the practice of support to theoretical discussions about relating learning to participation and contribution and to concrete social practice structuring the individual conditions of taking part. My main point is to argue that the support must become directed to understanding and changing such social dynamics and the relations between concrete children in difficulties and the social practice where they take part.

To work with children's participation in communities requires reflections on how the children set up conditions for each other and on how the professionals arrange situations for the interplay among the children. But first of all it implies cooperation between the grown-ups: Cooperation across different sectors – across the system of special help and the system of general education. Using the theoretical concepts I deal with in the chapter this involves:

- working with the structures of interconnected contexts (the relation between 'special help' and the general institutions)
- *and* working with the structuring process in a context – for example how children make up the conditions of each other.

In this way I hope to make the conceptualization of the 'structure' more concrete – and to point to possibilities of working directly with the participation of children in the contexts of their everyday lives. The psychologists play a very important role in such processes.

The psychologist can *go across* in the life of the children, starting up observations of social interplay between children and of the personal engagements, dilemmas and difficulties in relation to this. This may inspire other groups of professionals to observe the children in other ways and to *discover* new aspects and possibilities. But often the professionals are quite deadlocked in conflicts with each other and it can be difficult to exchange about the problems. Especially in relation to these conflicts the psychologist has an important task about *drawing the general connections* between the different experiences. The connections between the different tasks and interests among the grown-ups are not obvious but can be made explicit if the psychologist illustrates how the children are connected in a common life across contexts and how the personal and the social dilemma is connected. As I have tried to illustrate, the difficulties may be seen as an occasion for strengthening the whole community – and processes of exclusions mean insecurity to everybody. Especially in relation to the entire group of parents, the teachers may need help from the psychologist to make this kind of generalization.

There is no universal model for such processes but a perspective about working with conditions for participation in communities: To work with the general (excluding) practices and not just with the excluded individuals – preparing them to fit into the general as if this was not full of contradictions.

Notes

1. The book is the first in a series from the Fourth Congress of International Society Activity Theory and Cultural Research, held in Aarhus, Denmark, 1998 – with the theme 'Activity Theory and Cultural-historical Approaches to Social practice'.
2. Even though this picture may seem obviously one-sided most child research is concerned about how to find the links between classes of isolated societal 'factors' or variables – and the behaviour of children (e. g. Jørensen et al. 1993) and much research is then concerned about how social factors such as economic weakness lead to psychological needs – for an overview see Petersen, 2009.
3. The research is carried out together with researchers from Roskilde University and Aarhus University and in two different municipalities in Denmark – see http://www.ruc.dk/paes/forskning/fais/
4. In Denmark this follows a specific history of bad performance in relation to international standards (the PISA tests). The political answers to this are for instance national tests and demands of new standardized evaluations and documentation in relation to all efforts and interventions.

References

Axel, E. (in press). Conflictual Cooperation, submitted, *Nordic Psychology*. Dansk Psykologisk Forlag, Copenhagen.

Burman, E., (1994). *Deconstructing Developmental Psychology*. London and New York: Routledge.

Dreier, O. (2003). 'Personal Locations And Perspectives – Psychological Aspects of Social Practice', in O. Dreier, *Subjectivity and Social Practice* (2nd edn). Aarhus: Centre for Health, Humanity, and Culture, University of Aarhus.

—(2007). 'Generality and Particularity of Knowledge', in Vasi van Deventer; Martin Terre Blanche; Eduard Fourie; Puleng Segalo (eds), *Citizen City. Between Constructing Agent and Constructed Agent.* Concord, Canada: Captus University Publications, pp. 188–196.

—(2008). *Psychotherapy in Everyday Life.* Cambridge: Cambridge University Press.

Hedegaard, M. (2002). *Learning and Child Development: A Cultural Historical Study.* Arhus: Aarhus University Press.

—(2008). 'Children's Learning through Participation in Institutional Practice: A Model from the Perspective of Cultural-Historical Psychology', in Bert van Oers; Elbers; Rene van der Veer; Willem Wardekker (eds), *The Transformation of Learning: Perspectives from Activity Theory.* Cambridge: Cambridge University Press, pp. 294–318.

Hedegaard, M., Chaiklin, S. and Jensen, U. J. (1999). 'Activity Theory and Social Practice: An introduction', in M. Hedegaard, S. Chaiklin and U. J. Jensen (eds) *Activity Theory and Social Practice.* Aarhus: Aarhus University Press, pp. 12–30.

Hedegaard, M.; Højholt. C. and Ulvik O. S. (eds) (in prep). *Children's Perspectives and Everyday Practices.*

Højholt, C. (1999). 'Child Development in Trajectories of Social Practice', in W. Maiers, B. Bayer, B. Duarte Esgalhado.(eds) *Challenges to Theoretical Psychology*, Captus Press, North York, pp. 278–285.

—(2001). *Samarbejde om børns udvikling* [Collaboration on the development of children]. Dissertation, University of Copenhagen. Copenhagen: Gyldendal.

—(2005). 'El desarrollo infantil a través de sus contextos sociales', *Revista de Psicología y Ciencia Social,* editada por la Facultad de Estudios Superiores Iztacala, de la Universidad Nacional Autónoma de México, 7(1–2), 22–40.

—(2006). 'Knowledge and Professionalism – from the Perspectives of Children?' *Journal of Critical Psychology*, Cardiff University, Wales, pp. 81–106.

—(2008). 'Participation in Communities – Living and Learning across different Contexts', in *ARECE – Australian Research in Early Childhood Education*, Faculty of Education, Monash University, Australia, l5(1), 1–12.

—(in prep). 'Children's Perspectives and Common Learning Processes', in M. Hedegaard, C. Højholt. and O. S. Ulvik (eds), *Children's Perspectives and Everyday Practices.*

Jørgensen, P. S.; et al., (1993). *Risikobørn, hvem er de – hvad gør vi?* [Children at risk, who are they – what do we do?]. Socialministeriet, Det tværministerielle Børneudvalg. København.

Knudsen, H. (2007). 'Familieklassen – nye grænser mellem skole og hjem'. [The family class – new borders between school and home], in L Moos (ed.), *Nye sociale teknologier i folkeskolen.* [New Social Technologies in the School]. København: Dafolo, pp. 105–122.

Lave, J. and Wenger, E., (1991). *Situated Learning: Legitimate Peripheral Participation.* New York: Cambridge University Press.

Leontiev, A. N. (1978). *Activity, Consciousness and Personality.* Englewood Cliffs, New Jersey: Prentice-Hall.

Mehan, H. (1993). 'Beneath the Skin and Between the Ears: A Case Study in the Politics of Representation', in S. Chaiklin and J. Lave (eds) *Understanding Practice.* New York: Cambridge University Press, pp. 241–267.

Mehan, H., Hertweck, A., and Meihls, J. L. (1986). *Handicapping the Handicapped*. Stanford: Stanford University Press.

Morin, A. (2008). 'Learning Together – A Child Perspective on Educational Arrangements of Special Education', in *ARECE – Australian Research in Early Childhood Education*, Faculty of Education, Monash University, Australia, pp. 27–38.

Parsons, T. (1954). *Essays in Sociological Theory*. New York: The Free Press of Clencoe.

Rogoff, B. (2003). *The Cultural Nature of Human Development*. New York: Oxford University Press.

Rogoff, B., Moore, L., Najafi, B., Dexter, A., and Correa, M. (2007). 'Children's Development of Cultural Repertoires through Participation in Everyday Routines and Practices', in J. E. Grusec and P. D. Hastings (eds). *Handbook of Socialization: Theory and Research*. New York: The Guilford Press, pp. 490–515.

Røn Larsen, M. (in prep.). *'Professionelles samarbejde og strid om børn i vanskeligheder'* [Profesionals Conflictual Cooperation about Children in Difficulties]. Ph.D. dissertation, Roskilde University.

Schwartz, I. (in prep). 'Understanding and supporting children in troublesome life situations', in M. Hedegaard, C. Højholt. and O. S. Ulvik (eds), *Children's Perspectives and Everyday Practices*.

Stanek, A. (in prep). *Børnefællesskaber i overgangen fra at være store børnehavebørn til at blive små skolebørn*, [Communities of Children in their Transition from being Big Kinder Children into being Small School Children]. Ph.D. dissertation, Roskilde University.

Stetsenko, A. (2008). 'From relational ontology to transformative activist stance on development and learning: expanding Vygotsky's (CHAT) project', *Cultural Studies of Science Education*, vol. 3, 471–491, Springer Science+Business Media B.V.

Supporting Children and Schools: A Development and Practice-Centred Approach for Professional Practice and Research

Mariane Hedegaard and Seth Chaiklin

Chapter Outline

The pedagogical psychological support for children and schools with problems is being reconstructed in many social service centres because of societal/political demands (e.g. for inclusive schools; for inter-agency cooperation; for cost-saving) and because of changing professional standards for looking at the child in institutional practice rather than diagnosing the child (Højholt, this volume; Vassing, this volume; Edwards, Daniels, Gallagher, Leadbetter and Warmington, 2009). The main aim of this chapter is to present an approach to pedagogical psychological support for children and schools that is relevant to these new demands. The *development and practice-centred approach* draws inspiration from consultation approaches where a professional cooperates with other professionals and clients to develop and realize intervention plans; but also extends and refines existing consultation traditions by using cultural-historical theory to conceptualize both children's development and school practice, and organizing the intervention based on that analysis. The development and practice-centred approach can be applied in a variety of practical situations that arise for schools and/or children, including support for families and schools, and for individual children with disabilities, learning problems, social problems and so forth. It can also be used to conceptualize interventions for group, classroom, or school-level problems (e.g. bullying, students who resist learning).

The development and practice-centred approach involves four main phases. First, a development and practice analysis provides a way to characterize relevant dimensions in a problematic situation. This analysis uses a theory of children's development to focus on what is meaningful from children's perspective in relation to their life course through the institutions in which they live their everyday lives. In the second phase, success goals for intervention are formulated, where these goals are grounded in the development and practice analysis, and aligned with theoretical conceptions about intervention, practical possibilities for action, and specific methods for intervention. In the third phase a plan of intervention is formulated in cooperation between professionals and clients that aims to realize the success goals. The fourth phase involves the clients starting to carrying out the plan, with consultant support, including ongoing evaluation and possible revision or adjustment of the development and practice analysis, success goals, and intervention plan (i.e. the results of the first three phases), in light of the experiences with the intervention.

The chapter's presentation has four interdependent parts. The first part explains how the development and practice-centred approach is not only influenced by, but also extends consultation approaches to support children and schools. The extension is grounded in Hedegaard's (2009) cultural-historical theory of child development. The second part elaborates the four phases in the development and practice-centred approach, with special focus on the child's social situation and practice in the classroom, giving a specific model for how professionals in social service could approach problems in school. The third part gives an example of how the development and practice-centred approach was used in 'The Project School' – an intervention project for refugee children who were not succeeding in the existing school system. The fourth part highlights implications and possibilities for research, discussing two different kinds of research orientations in which the development and practice-centred approach can be used.

The consultation tradition and an argument for its extension through inclusion of a cultural-historical theory of development

The formulation of the development and practice-centred approach to support children and schools[1] with problems is inspired by the particular consultation approach that focuses on communication between professionals to support children and school (*Dansk Pædagogisk Psykologisk Rådgivning* [special issue], 2007; Carlberg, Guvå and Teunell, 1984; Hansson, 1995; Johannessen, Kokkersvold and Vedeler, 2001; Lambert and Hylander, 2004). This communication-oriented consultation approach focuses on the concrete practices in which the child participates (see also Vassing, this volume), transcending the functional approach to support, which diagnoses what is wrong with a child who has problems in school.

The communication-oriented consultation approach is grounded in part in ideas of systemic theory, which have their origin in Bateson's (1972) reflections in 'Steps to an Ecology of Mind' (Johannessen, 1990; Johannessen, Kokkersvold and Vedeler, 2001). Another important inspiration was Caplan's theory (Carlberg, Guvå and Tuernell, 1984; Hansson, 1995). Caplan was a pioneer in developing psychological support for children from war. He developed his consultation method in Israel in the late 1940s, when there were not enough resources to support children with problems. He saw the school as an arena for supporting children to learn new strategies and motives oriented to a future.

Consultation methods have been developed further in Israel (Ayolon, 1983), as well as other countries such as USA (e.g. Erchul and Sheridan, 2008), the Nordic countries (e.g. Lambert and Hylander, 2004), and the United Kingdom (e.g. Wagner, 2000). Consultation approaches are becoming more common within psychological educational practice (Doughterty, 2009), being used in several school counselling centres in Denmark, or in the United Kingdom (e.g. Larney, 2003) or in intervention research that focuses on how different professionals within social services for children can be supported to cooperate (Daniels et al., 2007; Edwards et al., 2009).

While consultation approaches overcome, to some extent, the individualizing tendencies of functional approaches that classify and label children into age-specific expectations, they do not go far enough. Current approaches to consultation for pedagogical psychological support are too narrow in their conceptualization of both the child's social situation and the classroom as context. One needs a broader perspective that encompasses (a) the fact that children's life and school activity take place in relation to several institutional practices, (b) that conceptualizes and attends to the child's motives and (c) that considers the child's life course in relation to these practices. This broader perspective is motivated by an assumption that children are more likely to engage successfully with interventions that are sensitive to the demands and orientations in their lives, and reflects a key idea that interventions should be formed in relation to a theoretical understanding about child development.

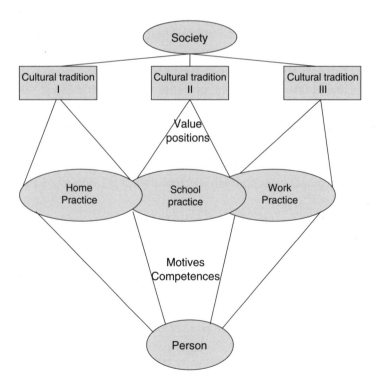

Figure 5.1 A model of different institutional practices in a child's life

The broader perspective in the development and practice-centred approach draws on Hedegaard's (2009) cultural-historical conception of development, which builds on Vygotsky's (1998) theory of development (see also Chapter 1, this volume). Key assumptions in Hedegaard's theory are:

- A child's social situation of development is created through the activities in everyday practice in which a child takes part.
- A child participates in several different societal institutions and practices; the child's social situation of development is constituted through the network of relations (e.g. in the form of demands and expectations) that arise in these practices.
- The central relations in a child's social situation of development are created by coordination of activities around the child.
- Each society, with its different cultural traditions and connected value positions, gives diverse possibilities for life-trajectories (Hundeide, 2003, 2005).

These assumptions are reflected or summarized in the model of institutional practices, depicted in Figure 5.1. The middle layer of the model indicates some of the main institutional practices in which children normally participate in their daily life. Institutional practices are enacted through participants' activities (e.g. in school teachers' and children's interactions around teaching and learning). At the same time, a practice transcends a specific person's activities through the values and demands of cultural tradition for how activities should take place within an institutional practice. These values and demands are indicated with the top layer, which represents both that a society creates and gives conditions for its institutions, and that these conditions are modulated by the dominant cultural tradition in society, as well as other cultural traditions. The child (bottom layer of the model) develops motives and competences through participation in the different institutional practices.

In relation to the model, the core ideas in Hedegaard's conception of child development are:

- Institutional practice and children's development are connected to conceptions of a good life, where these conceptions can vary both between institutions and among participants within a single institutional practice.
- A child's development is viewed as qualitative changes in the child's motives and competences. These changes arise because of new demands and objectives that arise as a consequence of changes in the child's social situation in an existing institutional practice or when a child enters a new institutional practice.

One can use the model as a general organizing framework for analysing the practices within which a child develops. For example, a child's social situation can be conflictual because the child is positioned in institutions that have specific values conflicts, either between two institutions (e.g. between home and school) or within the same institution (e.g. between parents or between different teachers). These conflicts have consequences for understanding the child's social situation and the possibilities for development. Sources of conflict include different cultural traditions for practice or different values and objectives in the institutional practice (Hedegaard, 1999, 2005). Value conflicts are often particularly visible among families that have immigrated to a new society, where these families have participated previously in institutions with other practice traditions, and where the parents bring values about family practices and other institutional practices from the society from which they emigrated. Under these circumstances, children from immigrant families can often end up in dilemmas between value positions they meet at home and value positions that dominate in school.

A development and practice-centred approach to support children and schools with problems

The previous section introduced the idea that interventions for supporting children and schools should be organized in relation to an analysis of children's development in institutional practices. The present section introduces a particular way to conceptualize and carry out such interventions. The general approach is similar to other communication-oriented consultation approaches, in which the consultant's role is to cooperate and communicate with other professionals to formulate intervention plans to support a child (or children) with problems to continue to participate (or be included) in a better way in the everyday practice in which s/he already participates (or should participate), and where the professional caregivers have primary responsibility for carrying out the plan. The special characteristic in the development and practice-centred approach is that the plan for intervention draws explicitly on an analysis of the children's social situation and the practices in which the child participates, where the cultural-historical theory of child development (see previous section) provides important conceptual resources for this analysis.

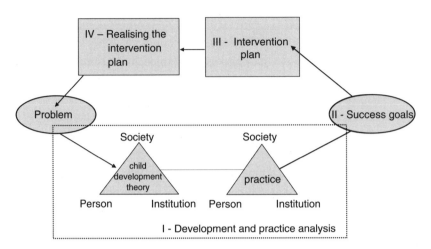

Figure 5.2 A model for practitioners and researchers to conceptualize an approach to shared agency for supporting schools and children

As mentioned in the introduction, the development and practice-centred approach involves a four-phase process. These phases, depicted in Figure 5.2, are used both to conceptualize the formation and conduct of interventions, and to structure the interaction between consultant and consultee. As a conceptualization, the four phases reflect an analytic perspective about important characteristics that should be included in a good intervention plan. As shown in Figure 5.2, the first three phases are to analyse the development and practice (I), formulate success goals (II), and outline an intervention plan (III). Each phase provides preconditions, constraints and requirements for the succeeding phases giving the consultee(s) a theoretical foundation for carrying out the intervention plan (IV), with advice, support, feedback, and evaluation from the consultant.

The four phases also provide a structure around which the consultant organizes a cooperative interaction with the consultee(s), where the aim is to develop the development and practice analysis, success goals and an intervention plan. It is important for the consultees to participate in forming these analyses with the consultant, both as part of coming to understand the intentions in the plans and to provide important local information for the analyses. These first three phases can be considered as the preliminary steps in the simultaneous beginning of the fourth phase (where the consultee has the primary responsibility for carrying out the intervention).

By structuring the interactions with the consultees in relation to the four phases of the theoretical conception, the consultant has a better chance of addressing the theoretically-motivated requirements of the development and practice-centred approach. In first three phases, the consultant usually takes a more leading role – both in terms of leading or organizing the analyses and in terms of bringing theoretical conceptions into the analytic and synthetic work. The consultees take the leading role in carrying out the plan (the fourth phase), supported by the consultant. As such, the development and practice-centred approach is not a specific technique or method; rather it requires the professional to concretize and adapt the general four-phase structure both in relation to the specific situation in which one is working and in cooperation with consultees. We characterize the professional's role as a three-quarter relation. Before discussing each of the four phases in more detail, it is necessary to elaborate the idea of the three-quarter relation, because it provides an important perspective for how the consultant conceptualizes the interaction with the consultees in the development and practice-centred approach.

Three-quarter relation

The *three-quarter relation* is a neologism created in the context of practice-developing research (Chaiklin, 2006). It expresses a particular kind of interactive relationship between a professional and other practitioners in the professional work situation, where the interest is to get a particular theoretical or conceptual model established in that work.

In a three-quarter interaction, a professional (often a consultant) has a vision of specific theoretical aspects that need to be realized or addressed in an ongoing practical situation, but is unwilling to form a completely worked out comprehensive vision of the exact form by which this will be achieved (e.g. a concrete intervention plan). In effect, the concrete formulation of the professional's vision is three-quarters[2] complete. This unwillingness reflects both a recognition that one lacks essential or critical knowledge about the specific conditions, and an insight that changes in professional work must be realized by the involved practitioners. Therefore practitioners must be involved both for their knowledge and for getting their engagement to carry out the intervention plans.

In the three-quarter relation, the consultant has no intention or interest in being neutral, or to come to the interaction passively, ready to act only on that which is formulated independently and self-sufficiently by the other

interpreted by focusing on her or his intentions in interactions and the possibilities s/he has for activities in the practices s/he participates in (Hedegaard, 2008).

To highlight the importance of considering the child's motives in analysing the situation, the following interview extract with Alber shows how his motives changed because of the demands and threats he met in school.

Alber:	In year seven, I was told that if I did not get through year seven without fighting with the older guys I would be thrown out of school.
Interviewer:	*Was it a teacher who told you?*
Alber:	Yes but it was not like a threat, she just told me that I should take care. And then I promised myself not to fight. I have not done this the last couple of years.
I:	*You did not fight with anybody after year seven?*
Alber:	No for the most, no (laugh a little). Perhaps I did in between, but it was not like when I was smaller, then I did it completely wildly. I hit and kicked and all this. In year eight and nine it became more discussion, I could start to say something and answer back if I had to.
I:	*Was there something that made you sad in school?*
Alber:	In year eight, yes, I remember I was sitting in the lesson, just after the school kitchen lessons. I was sitting crying because I could not get myself to hit and kick. Really I sat in a corner in the lesson and cried by myself, I did not want to write anything or do anything. I thought I would leave school and other things, but . . .
I:	*But you did not?*
Alber:	I did not because I hoped it would go over.
I:	*In this period, when you decided not to fight, you were teased a lot. Did you get any support from the teachers?*
Alber:	No I do not think so, they were not otherwise than they used to be.

In year seven, Alber's motive was to defend himself to keep his self-respect in school; his strategy for achieving this is to fight when he is attacked or teased. This motive, with its associated strategy of fighting, conflicted with his growing motive for education, which required that he stay in school. As Alber became more conscious of the value of education, influenced in part by a teacher's comment in year seven to think about a future, he sought to change his strategy for solving his problems with the other children so he could stay in school. In year eight his motive for education came to dominate his motive for self-respect, which became subordinated to this new motive. This change in his motive hierarchy led to a change in his strategy for self defence.

In Alber's perspective, the school did not seem to care about the children's social relations and the social climate in the class. Therefore when Alber accepted the school's objective as his motive, he had to change his strategies of self defence. In this case, Alber could solve his own problem, but not all children from immigrant families can do this. Analysis of children's motives can help clarify underlying reasons and directions for children's actions in institutional practices.

Second phase: forming success goals

Success goals are an attempt by the consultant and the consultees to formulate specific objectives towards which to work. Ideally these goals should be grounded in the development and practice analysis, with special attention to the three perspectives: societal, institutional (i.e. school and family) and child/children, where one seeks to form goals that can address these needs, objectives and motives.

Third phase: forming an intervention plan

After forming success goals, the consultant and consultees must form an intervention plan for realizing these success goals. The specific plan must reflect the professional's understanding of what conditions enable realization of the success goals, what resources and capabilities are available, and what strategies can be employed to work toward these goals. In forming the plan, the consultant should draw on the development and practice analysis from the first phase, and work in dialogue with the consultees to form a plan that reflects that understanding. In other words, the three-quarter relation still applies here, even if there is a collaborative effort to form an intervention that addresses the success goals.

Most intervention plans require cooperation and communication between the partners, both within the consultees (e.g. teachers, parent, or child) and the consultants (which could be several professionals in a social service centre for children). Often several professionals share agency in realizing plans (Edwards, 2005; Leadbetter et al., 2007). This cooperation can be difficult to achieve, as shown by research on the missing cooperation and coordination between professionals (e.g. Højholt, 1992) and in research on cooperation and shared agency in social services (Edwards et al., 2009).

Fourth phase: realizing intervention plans and evaluation

The consultees have the main responsibility for realizing the intervention, but the consultant should provide support, including formative evaluation, feedback and possible adjustment in the plan. Therefore the relation and interaction between the consultant and other professionals involved in the plan must allow for the possibility for the consultant to get in contact with the school or child (see also Kennedy, Cameron and Monsen, 2010).

Using the development and practice-centred approach for supporting refugee children in difficult positions in school

To illustrate the four phases in the development and practice-centred approach for pedagogical psychological support we draw on an intervention project from the late 1990s. First the background to the problem is described followed by a discussion of how the first three phases were accomplished, along with the specific content of these phases. Next some issues that arose in the fourth phase are discussed. The illustration ends with a comment about establishing an intervention in practice.

Background to problem

The initial problem was raised by school authorities in a large municipality in Denmark (Hedegaard, Frost and Larsen, 2004). A group of teenage boys from refugee families of Palestinian origin had all been expelled from one or more local schools. Most of them had been involved in minor criminal activity and no other schools in the area would accept them. The municipality had a legal responsibility to ensure that these boys were educated, plus they wanted to prevent the criminal activity. To address these problems, the municipality arranged a one-day conference with professional experts from the city: researchers, psychologists, school leaders and other persons who had knowledge about children within migration contexts. The conference led to a joint decision by three administrations in the municipality (School, Social and

Cultural) to construct a *Project school* as a developmental research project with pedagogical staff who had competence and experience in working with children with immigrant background, and Hedegaard as a researcher and consultant (for the first two years of the project).

To start, a week-long workshop was held with the pedagogical staff and the steering group (representatives from the three administrations, and the head of the school). The workshop started with the consultant presenting theories about child development, and about teaching and learning, with a special focus on immigrant children's life conditions. Thereafter the workshop participants worked on tasks created by the consultant, using the three-quarter relation to bring her knowledge into the discussion, and to bring out practical experience of the other professionals. The aim of the workshop was to analyse the situation in terms of development and practice, form success goals, and discuss ideas for school practice (i.e. an intervention plan in relation to the success goals).

Development and practice analysis

The problem presented by the municipality is clear. They have a need to keep the youth off the street and engaged in some school activity (see Table 5.1). From the school's perspective, the interest was to establish the boys' engagement in the school (see Table 5.1). To understand the challenge for the school one has to understand the situation for children from refugee families coming from war areas. War destroys social relations between the family and a community and within a family because of loss (e.g. family members, place to live, support for daily living) (Blackwell, 1993). Most refugee families, when

Table 5.1 Interests and motives for main actors in the situation.

Society (municipality)	• to abide by the Danish law that all children must engage in some school activity until they are 16 years old • to keep the children off the street and out of criminal activity
School	• establish cooperation between the parents, their children and educators to re-establish the trajectory of education • develop new methods for pedagogical and social work with the youth
Parents	• to have their son in the normal Danish school • to have their son educated in relation to future employment
Boys	• to be with friends • to be acknowledged as other youth in Denmark

coming to a new country, have difficult family relations, and few or no social relations with the new community. Refugee children in an exile country have worse conditions for establishing social relationships than children in war (Hedegaard, Frost and Larsen, 2004), and they have developed strategies to survive in a country at war. These strategies are often misplaced in the host society and a future perspective is difficult to establish.

In a school context, there is often a tendency for teachers and school psychologists to see refugee children's problems as coming from another context (e.g. home and local community) (Rousseau, Drapeau and Corin, 1996). More generally, when any child is referred to a psychologist then the psychological description of the child often dominates over descriptions given by teachers and parents that draw on social and historical accounts (Mehan, 1993). It would be easy, in this situation, to focus on the difficult behaviour of the boys, or have them tested and identified as having learning difficulties. But these approaches do not consider the possibilities for action within the context of these institutional practices.

In particular, the parents were motivated for the boys to be in a Danish school. This could be a source of institutional support in the situation, even from parents who did not always have many resources to offer. And finally, the boys were oriented to have a 'normal' life as youth in Denmark.

Success goals

The success goals should take account of the main involved motives and interests in the situation, and aim at creating conditions for the development of the children, while being within the capabilities and possibilities of the institutional practices. The main goals were formulated as trying to develop the boys' motives and competences for subject matter and supporting their social relations so that they could re-establish a trajectory in relation to school education. These goals were seen as important for helping the boys develop as qualified participants in different activities, thereby helping them to develop a positive orientation to their future. At the same time, realization of these goals would address the institutional objectives and societal needs, that the boys acquire strategies in relation to school life and the surrounding society.

Formulation of intervention plan

The intervention plan did not focus on specific children or specific problems. Rather the idea was to create an educational offering that would allow the boys

Table 5.2 Educational principles for the activity in the Project School: Radical-local on the left, traditional opposites on the right

Subject matter content relating theoretical principles with concrete examples	Empirical knowledge
Students cultural background guided the choice of teaching content	Personal experience and traditional teaching material guided the content
Using teaching forms that favoured students' exploration, formulation of conceptual relation and modelling of insights	Master desk teaching
Cooperation and group work	Individualized teaching

to pursue their motives, while developing their motive for education, which would then provide better conditions for addressing or realizing the other success goals.

The plans for classroom teaching took the success goals into consideration by building on principles from an earlier research project with immigrant children in New York City (Hedegaard and Chaiklin, 2005). The principles from that project – radical-local teaching and learning – are listed on the left side of Table 5.2. In practice, school teaching must draw from both sides of Table 5.2, but the educational methods on the left side were predominant during the first two years of the Project School.

The use of radical-local teaching and learning was motivated by the belief that drawing on content from the boys' cultural background would motivate them to make positive contributions to the teaching from the beginning, and make it more likely that they will attend school. This would re-establish their educational trajectory and keep the boys of the streets during school hours, which would satisfy both the municipality's needs and interests and the parents' motives.

Realization and evaluation of plans

Weekly meetings took place between the consultant and the teacher group to discuss the teaching and to plan future teaching. In these sessions the consultant brought observation protocols from her classroom participation as the foundation for the discussions that evaluated how the intervention was working, and considered possible adjustment in the plans for classroom activities.

The Project School worked with new educational methods. When the school started it was seen as something new and promising for the professionals and as a last chance for the families to help their boys get a school education. But it was a challenge to get the school to function well. The pressure and challenge in the first weeks to get any activities established was so difficult that two of the professionals (a teacher and a pedagogue) left and were replaced in the team.

To initiate and establish interest in the teaching, teachers drew on material that focused on the boys' cultural background, but it was still a challenge to get the boys to meet every morning. This was solved by considering a school subject in which the boys had some competence. Each morning started with mathematics teaching. This made it more attractive for them to attend. The school teaching came to function within the first half year. The boys came to school, and were seldom sick or truant. In interviews after nine months, they expressed a desire for more teaching, supporting the success goal that was formulated with a focus on developing the boys' capabilities to engage with school. The school hours were subsequently increased an hour, from four to five hours of lessons.

Another challenge was to convince the parents that this was a good school; they wanted their boys to be in the normal Danish school, not a special arrangement. To address this concern, the plan was to get the parents involved in the school, which in turn was expected to make the boys more likely to participate in both school and after-school arrangements. The social worker succeeded in establishing a fathers group that met at the school once a week after the children had left, which functioned as an important signal to both the parents and the boys. From a radical-local teaching and learning perspective, we would have liked that the parents contributed to the content of the class activities (as in the research of Moll and his co-researchers, e.g. Moll and Greenberg, 1990; Moll, Amanti, Neff and Gonzalez, 2005), but language and the families' conditions stemming from the war made this difficult.

Establishing interventions in practice

The Project school was a developmental practice research project aimed at developing the school practice for refugee children. The support for the boys and the Project school was a balance of repeated analysis of the situation, revising success goals and cooperation among the involved professionals together with the parents and the boys, adapting the intervention to the concrete situation.

The transition from initial project to sustained innovation was not easy, and in this case did not succeed. When Hedegaard (2006) visited the school as an observer six years later, it had changed greatly from the first two years.

The school had a new leader, who had other pedagogical ideas, such that the educational principles listed on the right side of Table 5.2 came to dominate. Consequence discipline was introduced. The students were isolated in booths, and the learning principle was organized around master desk teaching with a focus on empirical knowledge exemplified with experiences, rather than cooperation between students. The students started to be truant from school; ten years after its start, the school was closed down. This unfortunate development provided a natural experiment for comparing the validity of the conceptual principles used to organize the original intervention plan (which had more attention to the motives of the pupils) with the intervention plan of the new leader, underlining the importance of institutional practices for sustaining interventions.

Using the development and practice-centred approach in research activities

To this point, the development and practice-centred approach has been presented as a conceptual perspective for interventions to support children and schools. However, the approach has implications and possibilities for research. This final part highlights this point by discussing two different kinds of research orientations in which the approach can be used.

Generating new knowledge

A researcher can use the conceptual framework of the development and practice-centred approach as a way to identify important conceptual and theoretical issues that would improve the knowledge used by the consultant in the four phases. For example, some aspects in the development and practice-centred approach, especially the development and practice analysis and the formulation of theoretically-motivated intervention plans, depend on research knowledge (e.g. about children's motives) or theoretical analysis (e.g. about processes of development through participation in practice). Even if a researcher is not actually conducting an intervention, it is still meaningful to orient the investigation to topics that would be used in the approach, including such aspects as the motives of the different actors in the situation, the conflicts and contradictions in institutional practices involving children, the efficacy of specific analytic principles used in designing or motivating an intervention (e.g. the effects of instructional modifications in relation to children's motives). In other words, research topics can be chosen with an aim to strengthening the conceptual and analytic resources used in development and practice-centred approach, where the value and relevance of the chosen topics can be understood in relation to the professional work. The example of the Project School described in the previous section can be understood as having a research dimension in that it explored, among other things, how to adapt analytic principles of instructional design to educate children who have previously had problems with school.

Developing professional practice

The second kind of research orientation shifts the focus to issues in the development of professional practice. In this instance, the professional practice can be understood as referring to a range of social service professionals (e.g. psychologists, social workers, special education teachers) who are involved with giving support to children and schools with problems. Two main questions that arise in this research orientation include (a) what does it mean to develop this professional practice?, and (b) how can one make interventions into a specific professional service such that it moves toward adopting and/or extending the ideas of a good professional practice?.

These two questions are central in the practice-developing research perspective (Chaiklin, 2006). This research perspective provides a way to use the development and practice-centred approach in research that aims to develop professional work and practice in relation to support for children and schools.

Special requirements of practice-developing research include: (a) a theoretical analysis of the practice with which one is working, along with a formulation of what is considered to be a development in that practice, (b) a theoretical analysis of the conditions that are necessary (or will make it more likely) to realize that development, and (c) principles for how these conditions can be realized through concrete actions in the professional work.

In relation to the first requirement, if one does not have a theoretical conception of the practice being developed, then it is difficult to identify what it would mean to develop the practice. The concept of *practice*, as used here, refers to the ideal that one is trying to realize. In the present case, the ideal of providing professional support for children and school is reflected in what one is trying to produce through the professional work and what basic relations must be addressed to realize that product. The development and practice-centred approach can be seen as trying to support children's development (i.e. to produce conditions that contribute to a good life for children), where the basic relations that must be addressed are the ways in which professional caregivers are working with children. The underlying assumptions of the approach (e.g. about focusing on children's development, about making interventions that are directed to the ongoing activities and related to children's motives) can be understood as reflecting a general conception about professional practice that aims to support children and schools, and not just a specific technique for organizing professional intervention. The general conception is needed to address the aspect of the first requirement about 'what counts as a development', where the idea would be to support changes in professional work that better realizes the ideal in the development and practice-centred approach. At the same time, this aspect provides a challenge to the development and practice-centred approach, because of the need to evaluate whether the specific details of this approach will, in fact, be adequate to realize the ideal towards which it is oriented.

The second requirement asks for an explicit analysis about how this development is going to be realized in concrete situations. The research strategy of practice-developing research is to form a theoretically-motivated practice development project that aims to develop better methods for realizing a practice together with institutional capabilities to maintain that new development. That is, the goals of the developmental project are formed in relation to a theoretical conception of the practice, and the interventions and interactions in the project are motivated by theoretical principles. If these conditions are fulfilled, then the way in which the project proceeds (i.e. both how it is implemented, and what happens in the intervention) becomes the object of research. The research dimension comes from an explicit theoretical focus on the specific conceptual and practical problems in professional development; and not simply from an attempt to use the development and practice-centred approach in a practical situation.

The third requirement introduces another dimension of interest. Given a commitment to a particular conception of practice (such as the development and practice-centred approach), then what strategies should one use to get that approach established in concrete professional work. A key idea in practice-developing research is that it is important to integrate new ways of acting in relation to tasks which practitioners are already trying to solve in their daily work. Conceptual models are better embedded in action by engaging professionals in tasks that embody the conceptual model, giving possibilities to develop an understanding through action. The challenge (for the person who wants to introduce new ideas) is not simply to explain them intellectually, but to give practitioners an opportunity to develop an understanding of these ideas as part of their work.

Conclusion

This chapter has introduced and illustrated the development and practice-centred approach to support children and schools. It has emphasized a need for a broader perspective that draws on theory of child development and analysis of practice in analysing situations that are presented as problems. It has introduced a four-phase structure for conceptualizing the formation and planning of interventions, drawing on the broader perspective, and sketched some considerations about how to work with these ideas in practice. An example was presented to give an impression of how to work with the four-phase structure of the development and practice-centred approach and to highlight that such an approach is not always an easy task. Finally, it was pointed out that the approach can also be used for research purposes, both to develop better conceptual foundations for the approach, and to engage in the development of professional practice.

The development and practice-centred approach places greater demands on professionals to take responsibility for using their conceptual and analytic skills to interpret concrete situations and to organize a collaborative process to form success goals and intervention plans. Similarly, it places greater demand on being willing to enter into an interactive, collaborative process with others. The critical question is whether qualified and adequate support for children and schools can be achieved without meeting these demands.

Notes

1. The arguments in this article are meant to apply for giving support to children in day-care institutions and community programmes, as well as school. For the sake of readability we write *support for children and school*, where this broader scope is intended.
2. The exact amount is not essential. The term *three-quarters* is meant to indicate that one comes with a fairly full vision (whether in 70%, 85% etc.) rather than an open and equal interaction.

References

Ayolon, O. (1983). 'Coping with terrorism', in D. Meichenbaum and M. E. Jaremko (eds), *Stress Reduction and Prevention*. London: Plenum, pp. 293–339.

Bateson, G. (1972). *Steps to an Ecology of Mind*. San Francisco: Chandler.

Blackwell, R. D. (1993). 'Disruption and Reconstitution of Family. Network, and Community Systems following Torture, Organized Violence, and Exile', in J. P. Wilson and B. Raphael (eds), *International Handbook of Traumatic Stress Syndromes*. New York: Plenum Press, pp. 733–741.

Caplan, G. (1974). *Support Systems and Community Mental Health*. New York: Behavioral Publications.

Carlberg, M., Guvå, G. and Teurnell, L. (1984). *Konsulentarbejde i daginstitutioner: Psykologer beskriver teori og praksis*. Copenhagen: Dansk Psykologisk Forlag.

Chaiklin, S. (2006). Practice-Developing Research: Introduction to a Future Science. Unpublished manuscript, Danish University of Education.

Daniels, H., Leadbetter, J., Warmington, P., with Edwards, A., Martin, D., Popova, A., Apostolov, P., Middleton, D. and Brown, S. (2007). Learning in Multi-Agency Working. *Oxford Review of Education*, 33, 521–538.

Dougherty, A. M. (2009). *Psychological Consultation and Collaboration in School and Community Settings* (5th ed.). Belmont, CA: Brooks/Cole.

Edwards, A. (2005). Relational Agency: Learning to be a Resourceful Practitioner. *International Journal of Educational Research*, 43, 168–182.

—(2009). Relational Agency for the Wellbeing of Children and Young People. *Journal of Children's Service*, 4, 33–43.

Edwards, A., Daniels, H., Gallagher, T., Leadbetter, J. and Warmington, P. (2009). *Improving Inter-Professional Collaborations*. Oxon, England: Routledge.

Elder, G. H. (1998). The Life Course as Developmental Theory. *Child Development*, 69, 1–12.

Erchul, W. P. and Sheridan, S. M. (eds). (2008). *Handbook of Research in School Consultation*. New York: Erlbaum.

Hedegaard, M. (1999). 'Institutional Practices, Cultural Positions, and Personal Motives: Immigrant Turkish Parents' Conceptions about their Children's School Life', in S. Chaiklin, M. Hedegaard and U. Juul Jensen (eds), *Activity Theory and Social Practice*. Aarhus: Aarhus University Press, pp. 276–301.

—(2005). Strategies for Dealing with Conflicts in Value Positions between Home and School: Influences on Ethnic Minority Students' Development of Motives and Identity. *Culture and Psychology*, 11, 187–205.

—(2006). 'Undervisning i klasser med mange indvandrerbørn' [Teaching in schools with many immigrant children], in B. Elle, K. Nielsen and M. Nissen (eds), *Pædagogisk psykologi - Positioner og perspektiver*. Roskilde University Press, pp. 123–146.

—(2009). A Cultural Historical Approach to Development. *Mind Culture and Activity*, 16, 64–81.

Hedegaard, M. and Chaiklin, S. (2005). *Radical-local Teaching and Learning*. Aarhus: Aarhus University Press.

Hedegaard, M. and Fleer, M. (2008). *Studying Children. A Cultural-Historical Approach.* London: Open University Press.

Hedegaard, M., Frost, S. and Larsen, I. (2004). *Krigsramte børn i exil.* Aarhus: Klim.

Højholt, C. (1993). *Brugerperspektiver. Forældrers læreres og psykologers erfarenhder med psykosocialt arbejde.* Copenhagen: Dansk Psykologisk Forlag.

Hundeide, K. (2003). *Barns livsverden. Sociokulturelle rammer for barns utvikling* [Children's life world. Sociocultural frames for children's development]. Oslo: Cappelens.

—(2005). Socio-Cultural Tracks of Development, Opportunity Situations and Access Skills. *Culture and Psychology,* 11, 241–261.

Johannessen, E. (1990). *Gruppekonsultatsjon med barnehagepersonale. Doktorgradsavhandling.* Oslo: Barneversakademiet/Statens Speciallærerhøgskole.

Johannessen, E., Kokkersvold, E. and Vedeler, L. (2001). *Rådgivning. Traditioner, teoretiske perspektiver og praksis* (2. utg.). Oslo: Universitetsforlaget.

Kennedy, E. M., Cameron, R. J. and Monsen, J. (2010). Effective Consultation in Educational and Child Psychology Practice: Professional Training for Both Competence and Capability. *School Psychology International,* 30, 603–625.

Lambert, N. M, Hylander, I. and Sandoval, J. H. (eds). (2004). *Consultee-Centered Consultation: Improving Professional Services in Schools and Community Organizations.* Mahwah, NJ: Erlbaum.

Larney, R. (2003). School-based Consultation in the United Kingdom: Principles, Practice and Effectiveness. *School Psychology International,* 24, 5–19.

Leadbetter, J., Daniels, H., Edwards, A., Martin, D., Middleton, D., Popova, A., Warmington, P., Apostolov, A. and Brown, S. (2007). Professional Learning within Multi-Agency Children's Services: Researching into Practice. *Educational Research,* 33, 521–538.

Mehan, H. (1993). 'Beneath the Skin and between the Ears: A Case Study in the Politics of Representation', in S. Chaiklin and J. Lave. (eds), *Understanding Practice: Perspectives on Activity and Context.* Cambridge: Cambridge University Press, pp. 241–268.

Moll, L. C. and Greenberg, J. B. (1990). 'Creating Zones of Possibilities: Combining Social Contexts for Instruction', in L. C. Moll (ed), *Vygotsky and Education: Instructional Implications and Applications of Sociohistorical Psychology.* Cambridge: Cambridge University Press, pp. 319–348.

Moll, L. C., Amanti, C., Neff, D. and Gonzalez, N. (2005). 'Funds of Knowledge for Teaching: Using a Qualitative Approach to Connect Homes and Classrooms', in N. Gonzalez, L. C. Moll and C. Amanti (eds), *Funds of Knowledge: Theorizing Practice in Households, Communities, and Classrooms.* Mahwah, NJ: Erlbaum, pp. 71–88.

Rousseau, C., Drapeau, A. and Corin, E. (1996). School Performance and Emotional Problems in Refugee Children. *American Journal of Orthopsychiatry,* 66, 239–251.

Vygotsky, L. S. (1998). *The Collected Works of L.S. Vygotsky. Volume 5: Child Psychology* (M. Hall, Trans.). New York: Plenum.

Wagner, P. (2000). Consultation: Developing a Comprehensive Approach to Service Delivery. *Educational Psychology in Practice,* 16, 9–18.

Developing Educational Psychological Consultative Practice in Schools Framed within Cultural-Historical Theory of Child Development

6

Christine Vassing

Chapter Outline

The transformation of educational psychological practice in school is widely debated primarily with a focus on the negative consequences of an individualized focus on children with problems (assessment) to a focus on a how a systemic approach (consultation) extend the possibilities for understanding and acting in relation to problems experienced within school. This paradigmatic shift is also described by Leadbetter (this book). While praising this development of the practice of educational consultative psychology, professionals using this approach are still holding on to the tradition of assessment in some cases (Shwery, 2004). The assessment tradition is related to the origin of educational psychology within schools where the task of the psychologist has been to diagnose children through testing and thereby legitimize processes of segregation (Leadbetter, this book; Chaiklin, 2005). Assessment, as a practice of educational psychologists working in schools, relates to a functionalistic and individualized child developmental approach. With this approach, child development is separated into functions such as emotional, social, behavioural and cognitive (for instance, found in the theory of Piaget, 2000). Underlying the tradition of assessment is an assumption that a certain level in a child's development should be achieved by the child before the he or she is able to learn from teaching activities in school. This level is measurable through the testing of the child's functions on norm-based scales. Instead of viewing teaching and learning activities as mediating children's development, the level of development of children is seen as a precondition for their access to participate in the teaching. With this approach it becomes hard to see the child as a whole person, to understand the child's intentions across functions and to acknowledge that teaching and learning occurs in social relations as well as to recognize that children contribute to the practice of learning and development in school too (Hedegaard and Fleer, 2008; Hedegaard, 2009).

Efforts at redefining the practice of educational psychologists working in schools from assessment practice to consultative practice has been documented internationally in several studies (Mägi and Kikas, 2009; Tanggaard and Elmholdt, 2006;2007, Hylander and Guvå, 2004; Guvå, 2004; Leadbetter, 2004; 2006; Klassen et al., 2005; Engelbrecht, 2004; Larney, 2003; and Wagner, 2000).

Educational psychological consultation includes diverse primarily systemic approaches to working with schools/teachers and other professionals often about children with problems. The consultation process typically takes place as a conversation between a psychologist and teachers including other school staff such as school principals and specialized teachers (Leadbetter, 2004; Wagner, 2000). The psychologist works with the teacher to achieve the main objective of creating changes in the teacher's relationship to a child for example by supporting the teacher in re-conceptualizing the problems she experiences (Hylander, 2004). Others have focused on the potential of creating organizational changes in school (Leadbetter, this book, Tanggaard and Elmholdt, 2006). In systemic consultation the psychologist does not interact with the child directly (Shwery, 2004).

Consultation has been used as an educational service to schools in the United States since the 1960s (Caplan, 2004; Lambert 2004) and in Sweden since the 1970s (Hylander and Gvuå, 2004), but the concept has gained new interest in relation to the political movement of inclusive education (Salamanca declaration, 1994; Tanggård and Elmholdt, 2006). For instance in the study by Anderson et al., teachers rely very little upon support from the psychologist when trying to create inclusive classrooms and with regard to this, Anderson et al. argue for a transformation of the role of the school psychologist away from 'assessment, identification and placement' toward the needs of teachers when creating inclusive classrooms (2007, p. 144).

School legislation across a variety of countries states that the purpose of schooling is the child's learning and development (See for instance Folkeskolens formålsparagraf, 2006; Danish Ministry of Education, British education act, 2002). Studies and theories[1] on renewing educational psychological practice in schools discuss consultation when seen from the perspectives of different professionals, including teachers, school principals and educational psychologists and in some of these, the relation between different professional perspectives (See for instance Mägi and Kikas, 2009; Davies et al., 2008; Tanggaard and Elmholdt, 2007; Farell et al., 2005; Leadbetter, 2004; Stobie et al., 2002; Wagner, 2000). The studies do not integrate theory of child development or relate professional (teachers) perspectives to children's perspectives. The consequences of educational psychological consultative practice on the lives and developments of school children subsequently reside in the dark. With regard to the ultimate goal of schooling referred to above this is an important matter even if the objective of some consultation approaches is changes at the organizational level of school.

While maintaining the fundamental idea derived from systemic consultation of supporting and creating processes of communication between the psychologist and the teacher(s) where the direct intervention in relation to the children is carried out by the teacher(s), the model of consultation that will be presented in this chapter also transcends systemic approaches of consultation: In conducting participatory observations to capture the child's perspective in the teaching practice, to be used within the consultation process, the psychologists interact directly with the child/children (Hedegaard, 1994; Hedegaard and Fleer, 2008). By framing consultation within a cultural-historical approach it is possible to conceptualize children's participation as intentional and dynamically related to institutional practices, for instance school, yet again dynamically related to societal goals for children's development (Hedegaard, 2009). The main objective to be achieved through using the suggested consultation model is children's development. This is done through supporting interventions in the concrete interplays within teaching settings in schools.

The conditions under which these interplays between teachers and children occur are also addressed by the model. In this way the model aims at overcoming an individualized and failure-oriented approach to child development, as well as the absence of ideas regarding child development in systemic consultation, discussed above.

The argument for developing a model of consultation (the child developmental consultation model) is in this chapter supported by a teaching experiment with a group of psychologists working as consultants in schools organized and carried out by the researcher. This teaching was inspired by ideas of the double move in teaching (Hedegaard, 2002; Hedegaard and Fleer, 2008) and practice developing research (Chaiklin unpublished; Hedegaard and Chaiklin, this book).

Cultural-historical theory of child development that includes the perspective of the child

Cultural-historical theory of child development conceptualizes children's development as social and relational. Development initiates through the child's intentional activity within and across practices in cultural-historical institutions (Elkonin, 1999; Hedegaard 2009). Four concepts derived from this overall tradition were used in the study: the concept of participation in practices in different institutionalized settings (Elkonin, 1999; Hedegaard 2009; Hedegaard and Fleer, 2008), the zone of proximal development (Vygotsky, 1982; Hedegaard 2009), the concept of crisis (Vygotsky, 1998; Hedegaard, 2009) and the perspective of the child (Hedegaard, 1994; Hedegaard and Fleer, 2008; Hedegaard, 2009).

The social interplays in which the child participates are always institutionalized within different practice traditions and are therefore also influenced by the values within these traditions (Hedegaard and Fleer, 2008; Hedegaard, 2009). By participating in and across institutionalized social practices, the child is both influenced by and contributes to these practices, which transform the child's relation to the world (Hedegaard, 2009). Studying the child's intentional activities within and across different institutionalized practices can allow one to identify such changes in relation to both the changing child and the changing practice. Development is a dialectical, mutually contributing relationship between the child, other children and, for instance, teachers within a school, which acts as one type of practice tradition guided by societal values of what constitutes a good life for children. Central to children's participation in school and other institutions aiming at supporting children's development is the dialectical process of appropriating motives and competences (Elkonin, 1999).

In Hedegaard's theory of child development, she uses two central concepts, the zone of proximal development and crisis derived from Vygotsky (2009). The zone of proximal development (ZPD) can be used to describe the difference between what a child can do independently and what this child can do in cooperation with others, sometimes illustrated by the use of some cultural artefacts such as a calculator (Vygotsky, 1982). In the ZPD, Vygotsky emphasized how support from a more competent person could enhance the achievements of a child in situations of assessment and initiate the mental development of the child through participating in teaching activities. In contrast to the functional tradition Vygotsky (1982) and Hedegaard (2009) conceptualize teaching and learning as mediating and creating child development.

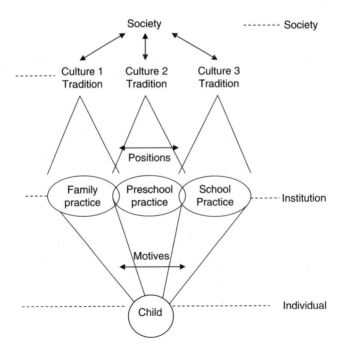

Figure 6.1 This model by Hedegaard depicts the structural relationships of a child's development according to the ideas presented above (2009)

Vygotsky conceptualized developmental crises as normal, necessary and constructive processes dialectically related to more stable periods in a child's development and not as a pathological state or a deviance (1998). He conceptualized crises as 'turning points' characterized by 'abrupt and major shifts, displacements, changes and discontinuities', as 'stormy', 'impetuous', 'catastrophic' and 'revolutionary' where 'the child changes completely in the basic traits of his personality' (1998, p. 191). In this way, crises signify that a child is developing. Hedegaard defines the concept of crises to changes that occur in

'the child's social situation via biological changes, changes in everyday life activities and relations to other persons, or changes in material conditions'. (2009, p. 72)

Conceptualizing developmental crises as central for dialectical appropriation of motives and competences taking place through children's participation across different practices, crises have to be seen as recurrent events in children's development. And the task of the educational psychologists is subsequently to foster conditions that support children to develop motives and competences through their crises.

Taking the perspective of the child as a method to capture children's development in and across different practices

When conceptualizing problems related to children's learning and development as related to the concrete interplay between children and teachers situated within and across different practice institutions, it is also important to view these interactions from the child's perspective. That is to capture the child's intentions, motivations, engagements, projects and motives in his or her activities as meaningfully related to other perspectives in the activity setting that are the teacher's, the other children's etc.(Hedegaard, 1994; Hedegaard and Fleer, 2008; 2009). The perspective of the child includes the leading activity of children of a certain age (Elkonin, 1999), but it is also a perspective of the specific child (Hedegaard, 1994; Hedegaard and Fleer, 2008). To take and use the child's perspective means to 'focus on the intentions that guides the child's actions, and from the pattern of actions and communication, interpret the projects and motives that engage the child' (Hedegaard and Fleer, 2009 p. 19) and then use this information to develop the activity settings within a practice, for instance the teaching activities within school practice.

By using participatory observations able at capturing the dialectics between the teachers' perspective (which in turn, reflects the institutional perspective of school) and the children's/child's perspectives in the teaching and learning activities, it is possible to both describe and intervene in the teaching with a developmental aim. This approach can counteract processes of individualizing, de-contextualizing and displacing problems too (Højholt, 1993).

Consultation framed within cultural-historical theory of child development

Consultation framed within cultural-historical theory of child development as presented and discussed above becomes a practice where the psychologist uses and shares with the teachers the following concepts: the perspective of the child, the zone of proximal development and the concept of crises with the aim of conceptualizing and supporting the development of the children in the teaching activities.

The development of *the perspective of the specific child* in relation to the teacher's perspective is created through discussions in consultation practice where the psychologist shares with the teachers transcripts of her participatory observations of focus children in the classroom. The psychologist can support the teacher in supporting the child in a number of ways. The psychologist can ask questions, give advice, listen etc.; however, this process of communication must always be focused on facilitating the child's development through teaching by including societal goals of child development framed within *the ZPD of a specific child*.

The concept of *developmental crises* can be used to support re-definitions and explanations of the problems and how they may be solved.

By using the psychologist's participatory observations of children in the classroom in consultation the perspective of the child is included in developing the teaching practice; what the child does can be related to what the teachers do at a micro-analytical level. The mediation of the observation transcripts can support the teachers in seeing their activities and perspectives as related to the children's and support them in making both small and large changes in his or her teaching approach. This is to the benefit of not only the individual child but also the other children, with the ultimate aim of aiding the development of the whole group of children in the classroom. This is possible because the concepts suggested for use in the consultation are derived from cultural-historical theory of child development and as such are social and relational like the ZPD. Thus, this model not only differs in transcending consultation as an indirect service (in the sense that the psychologist interacts with the children directly in the course of observing them through her observations) (Hedegaard, 1994; Hedegaard and Fleer, 2008), but it is also explicitly aimed at facilitating child development through teaching as a social practice constituted by different perspectives.

Existing models of consultation have been described as being 'non-prescriptive', 'non-hierarchical' and 'egalitarian' (Hylander and Guvå, 2004; Lambert, 2004; Wagner, 2000), and in general, they are concerned with the well-being of the teachers who have implicitly been expected to solve the problems in relation to the children. The child developmental consultation model directly and explicitly addresses and conceptualizes children's development through teaching as the goal of consultation practice (Figure 6.2).

Figure 6.2 represents the activity relations in the reformulation of educational psychological consultative intervention in schools – the child developmental model. The different types of activities are participatory observations,

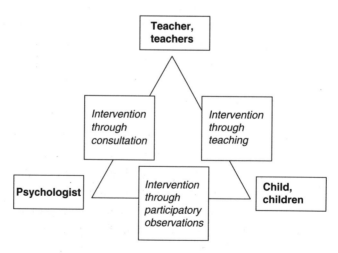

Figure 6.2 The child development consultation model. The figure shows the leading activity in the relationships between the psychologist, teacher (s) and the child/children

consultation and teaching. All of the relationships are supposed to be dynamic and reciprocal. The children both contribute to and are influenced by the observation activity and the teaching activity. The teachers and the psychologist are actively engaged in conceptualizing the problems encountered by the teachers together. By utilizing transcripts from the psychologist's participatory observations of the particular child of interest in class they influence each other's understandings and formulations of the problems and interventions. The focus is on developing the activity settings at school; however, it is important to note that children develop through participation across different practice traditions. The intervention implemented through consultation in the school should support the child's participation in settings elsewhere.

A teaching experiment with educational psychologists working as consultants in schools

Background for teaching and the participants' pre-conceptions

With the aim of gaining knowledge about how the group of educational psychologists, subjected to the research project, conceptualized their own practice, saw as problems and conflicts in their practice and how they tried to handle these problems and conflicts, the researcher participated in a seminar organized by the management of the psychologists' (September 2008).

The content of this seminar reflected the daily practice of the psychologists in relation to the local politics within their organization (their activity plan) and the legislation regarding children and young people within the local community. In addition, copies of the Salamanca declaration, among other documents, were handed out to the participants. One of the aims of the seminar was to support the 'work unit in moving away from an individualizing, diagnostic culture toward an inclusive and resource-oriented culture'. Despite commitment to progress and future practice as highlighted through activity plans, more traditional methods were not excluded. Assessment was listed as one out of several methods/services that could be applied by the psychologists. Many discussions at the seminar were derived from and centred on the difficulties of transcending an individualized failure-oriented perspective and applying a relational, resource-oriented and inclusive approach. The discussions revealed problems within and across the approaches. Two themes were of particular interest to the researcher: how they conceptualized or re-conceptualized their role/professionalism and in relation to this how they conceptualized the perspective of the child when working as consultants.

In an effort to move past the individualizing and diagnostic culture, the participants (psychologists, speech pedagogues/teachers, a physiotherapist and different consultants working in or in relation to school and day care) were very cautious not to act as experts or to use categories from the assessment paradigm when working as consultants. Instead, they suggested that they could be the 'expert in relationships' or that they could act as 'catalysts of processes'. At the seminar, such re-definitions of their expertise were not related to ideas of child development or to ideas of children's perspectives and conceptualizing their role as 'experts in relationships' and 'catalysts of processes' seemed not to able at solving their dilemmas in relation to working with children's development through consultation: A relatively undisputed statement about the advantages in stating that the problems belong to the child ('it is sometimes helpful to state that a child has got problems') at the first teaching session rather demonstrated a regression to than a transcending of an individualizing and diagnostic culture.

At the seminar, enabling teachers to see the perspective of the child was considered to be a task of the educational psychologist. The 'child's perspective' was conceptualized much like the 'child's voice'. Accounting for this perspective was thought to protect the rights of the child and his or her parents by including their opinions in the referral process once the child was referred for educational-psychological intervention. The focus of attention was how the referred child's explicit and conscious understanding of the problems could be included or of how children could get in touch with the educational psychologists by themselves, for instance by phone.

Understanding and using the child's perspective as a critical concept in supporting children's development in school through consultation, as suggested in this chapter, was not present in the psychologists' discussions at the seminar.

The above reflections all influenced the structuring of the teaching sessions as can be seen in the teaching design that will be presented shortly.

The aim of the teaching experiment

The aim of the teaching experiment conducted by the researcher was to facilitate a re-modelling or a re-conceptualization of consultation practice in relation to the problems the psychologists encountered when working as consultants in relation to the theoretical framework (not fully formulated) put forward by the researcher (Chaiklin, unpublished; Hedegaard and Chaiklin, this book). The re-modelling or re-conceptualization of their consultation practice was structured by the objective of overcoming an individualized failure-oriented approach to the learning and development of school children, as well as a consultation approach absent of ideas about child development. This objective related itself to the aim of the specific educational psychological practice of moving away from 'an individualizing, diagnostic culture toward an inclusive and resource-oriented culture' but by advocating the use of cultural-historical theory of child development including the child's perspective within consultation, the aim of the specific educational psychological practice was also transcended.

The teaching experiment was related to other interventions within the overall research project pursuing the goal of displaying the ideas in the child developmental model (Figure 6.2) related to the goal of the specific practice of educational psychology in schools (see above). By studying and documenting the developmental changes, the research project including the teaching experiment exceeded the purpose of 'just' supporting the educational psychologist in transforming their practice: The researcher also participated in the experiment with the aim of creating knowledge of how to achieve development of educational psychological practice in general through a teaching experiment (Chaiklin, unpublished; Hedegaard and Chaiklin, this book).

Design of the teaching experiment

The teaching experiment took place at the work unit of the educational psychologists and consisted of six sessions, each about two hours. All of the teaching sessions were documented through participatory observations[2] and displayed different sub-goals all related to the overall aim of transcending an individualized failure-oriented approach to the learning and development of school children, as well as a consultation approach absent of ideas about child development:

- The goal of the *first teaching session* (November 2008), displaying the fundamental idea in the model (represented in Figure 6.2), was to make the psychologists reflect on their consultative relation to teachers as mediating changes in the relations between teachers and child/children.

- The goal of the *second teaching session* (March 2009) was to support the psychologists in re-formulating and re-contextualizing the concept of inclusion from a primary concern of how to include parents and children's opinions in the referral process to a concern of how they could support attempts in schools to create inclusive practices.
- The goal of the *third teaching session* (May 2009) was to qualify the psychologists' attempts to supporting inclusive practices within schools through the use of different concepts from cultural-historical theory of child development.
- The goal of the *fourth teaching session* (June 2009) was to provide the psychologist with a whole framework of cultural-historical theory of child development including the child's perspective that could support a transformation of their practice in relation to the problems they experienced.
- The goal of the *fifth teaching session* (September 2009) was to support a re-conceptualization of consultation in relation to the ideas presented by researcher including the use of participatory observations in consultation related to the ideas displayed by the psychologists.
- The goal of the *sixth teaching session* (October 2009) was to reflect on the conceptualization of educational psychological consultation constructed in cooperation between the psychologists and the researcher in relation to future practice.

Various methods were chosen to support the goals of teaching across sessions. *Role playing* and *fish bowl discussions* were used as key methods in the teaching and reflected quite different purposes. Role plays, inspired by forum theatre,[3] were used to reflect a typical real-life consultation setting in the psychologists' daily practice. Inspired by forum theatre, the role play could be interrupted to discuss the content of the play and to re-direct the play.

Fish bowl discussions[4] were used to create dynamic and goal-directed meta-reflections of the psychologists' daily practice by dividing the group of psychologists into subgroups of listeners (sitting outside of a virtual fishbowl) and discussants (sitting outside the virtual fishbowl). The subgroups switched seats along the successions of reflections. In addition to these methods, the psychologists were asked to make participatory observations (Hedegaard, 1994; Hedegaard and Fleer, 2008) of their consultation practice and of the children they had discussed with teachers in consultation in their classroom. This exercise should provide the psychologists with an opportunity to discuss the use of participatory observations in consultation (as a transgression of traditional consultation practice). Also various documents underlying their practice were included in the teaching, one among them is the *referral formula* of the work unit. The inclusion of the referral formula[5] in the teaching was considered to be of great importance since a prior study had documented how this document placed the psychologist in a fixed position (Højholt, 1993). Also extracts from the observations of the teaching sessions and the work seminar were used as *mirror data* (Edwards et. al., 2009).

Evaluation of the teaching experiment

Teaching the educational psychologists who are working as consultants in schools about developing their practice accomplished two goals. First, the teaching supported the psychologists' re-conceptualization of consultation framed within cultural-historical theory of child development, including the child's perspective. Second, the teaching supported initiatives to change the referral formula of the psychologists' work unit.

A development was observed in how the psychologists explicitly reflected about themselves, their own role in the schools and the goal of consultation. At the beginning the psychologists aspired at acting according to a relative and systemic worldview, in relation to teachers, other professionals and the parents as a goal in itself. The style of communication seemed to possess greater importance than the content of the communication and how that content would influence the children involved in their practice. Examples from the discussion at the first teaching session illustrate this point:

> When trying to act as good conditions for others – it is most successful when a symmetrical relation is created between me and the teacher, where I don't decide what is at stake.
> Maybe things change when one uses appreciation – acknowledge the knowledge they have both as teachers and as parents – that they are appreciated by the psychologist who they view as an expert.

At the fifth teaching session, where the psychologists were asked to discuss how they could use participatory observations to capture the child's perspective in consultation, the psychologists initiated a change in their focus from primarily reflecting on how to nourish their own relationship with teachers to include a focus on how consultation should mediate changes in the act of teaching in relation to the children. Having the psychologists reflect on the use of such observations in consultation facilitated their ability to conceptualize their relationship to teachers as mediating changes in another relationship (i.e. between the teacher/teachers and child/children). Furthermore, initiating a concrete formulation of the child's perspective related to activities within the teaching experiment can be seen in the conceptualization below, which was formulated in cooperation between the psychologists and the researcher/teacher:

> The purpose of consultative practice is the same as for school practice, that is, the learning and development of the child. The aim of consultative practice is to support 'a changed perspective' on the specific child in question. Not as a common or shared perspective in the sense that everyone holds the same perspective of the child or the problem but as a development of the interplay of the existing perspectives in relation to the interplay between the teacher/teachers and the child/children. This can be done through observations of the interplay of what the specific child does and says and what the teacher does and says. Also, teachers can themselves make observations of the teaching in relation to the specific child/children. Observation can be used in consultative practice as a space of reflection that should lead to enhanced possibilities of actions directed to support the children's learning and development.

The conceptualization shows a great change in the psychologists' view on consultation from being 'neutral' or 'relative' or at least implicit in relation to the outcome on the children (see the above examples) to being goal directed in relation to the children (explicitly concerned about the children's learning and development).

In discussing the aims and purposes of consultation that led to the conceptualization above, the psychologists suggested numerous other ways in which they could work as consultants in relation to teachers. In general, not all ideas from the tradition of assessment or from a consultative approach without incorporation of child development presented in the psychologists' practice were transcended. The conceptualization reflected a future aspiration of the psychologists, but the conceptualization will probably not be exclusive to other ideas or ways of working within this specific practice.

Two main obstacles hindered the psychologists from acting as consultants according to the conceptualization presented above, their referral formula and the school. First, the existence of *the referral formula* though not necessarily utilized in consultation seemed to position the psychologists within the tradition of functional assessment all though they had wishes to work outside of the assessment paradigm. As a consequence of the evaluation and discussion about the conceptualization above, management decided to change the referral formula of the work unit so that it would reflect their future aspirations of moving away from an individualized deficit-oriented approach.

The second, but possibly the greatest, obstacle for the psychologists in working as consultants is *the school*. The psychologists found it hard to make fundamental changes because of their interdependent relationship with the school, which still maintains traditions counteracting inclusive and developmental teaching practices. As school psychologists, they imagined that they would be able to make a difference, but they have found that a fundamental transformation depends on changes at other levels in relation to the school and school politics.

Consultation as mediating changes in the teaching practice through the use of participatory observations to capture the child's perspective and the teaching experiment as practice developing research

As described above, the development in the psychologists' explicit conceptualization of consultation as mediating changes in the teaching practice in relation to focus children occurred rather late in the course. It was provoked by the discussion regarding the use of participatory in consultation (at the fifth teaching session).[6] In contrast, when the psychologists acted in the role playing, they (critically) addressed the teaching in relation to the targeted child from the beginning. Addressing the teaching in the role playing was mostly done by raising different questions; some questions included the use of the concept of hindrance/barrier and the child's intentions, whereas others were posed to make the teacher reflect on what already worked. These questions and the discussions that followed in the role playing would probably not support fundamental changes in real world teaching because the players did not act from the knowledge that the use of participatory observations would have provided them. Prior to the fifth teaching session, the psychologists had been asked to make such observations of their real life consultative work or of the children whom they had discussed in consultation with teachers, but they had prioritized not to do this, excusing themselves by referring to limited time resources. Exploring the use of such observations should have given them an insight into how their own work (their comments, questions and advices in the consultation) was transformed by the teachers in relation to the focus child and the children as a group in the classroom, as well as given them an indication of how these children's development were supported by their intervention.

Engaging the psychologists in making participatory observations as part of their daily consultation practice does not happen just by the researcher's initiatives. The psychologists need to be able to envision how the appropriation and use of such observations can support them in handling recurrent problems within their consultation practice. This was attempted by the researcher through the use of the double move in the teaching experiment taking departure in the problems the psychologists experienced (displayed by the psychologists at the work seminar in the role plays as well as in the fish bowl discussions) and providing them with theory, relevant to realizing and developing the goals of this practice of moving toward a relational, resource-oriented and inclusive culture, and by which they could discuss and develop their practice with the aim of overcoming recurrent problems.

The conditions for the psychologists' work need to provide them with opportunities to act differently according to the goals of practice development too (for example in legalizing and supporting the allocation of time resources from, for instance, assessing children to working with participatory observations in consultation). At this moment the leadership of the work unit can support psychologist in this by leaving some of their work methods behind, such as assessment, so that the methods and the practice reflect their aspired goals. Leaving the assessment approach behind is possible within current legislation; the use of participatory observations to capture the perspective of the child within the teaching activities can serve as valid approach when aiming at describing, supporting, and developing school children through consultation: children involved in educational psychological practice will have greater chances of being included as intentional participants in school practice among other institutional practices instead of being individualized, isolated or segregated as within the assessment paradigm. Future focus should be on how descriptions of children based on participatory observations can be used to create better conditions for children's learning and development in school through consultation.

As is likely true for any educational psychology service in schools, the work unit of the psychologist subjected to researcher's investigation, was under great pressure from long waiting lists. Adding to this the work unit also exhibited an eagerness to satisfy the needs and meet the expectations defined by school, parents and others, which did not necessarily possess any inner coherence or correspond to what the work unit want their practice to be about. These external pressures did not seem to support a transformation of practice. To handle such pressure and dilemmas the psychologists and their leadership need to be further supported in working on a model of how to develop their practice and sustain that development with the aim of creating/improving conditions that can realize their goals (Chaiklin, unpublished)

Another dimension might also need to be added: declaring a political goal of moving away from an individualistic and diagnostic perspective towards a relational and inclusive perspective does not mean that politicians, researchers, psychologists, their leadership, schools or teachers are convinced by or committed to working in this direction. The above might provide an outline of how such a political goal can be worked on and maybe also transcended.

Notes

1. Theories and studies that I have been able to uncover.
2. Different persons all with a degree in psychology and an interest in the field including theory and methods carried out the observations. Researcher carried out the interpretation of all of the observations.
3. www.peopleandparticipation.net
4. At Center for Systemudvikling, Aarhus University (2001) the approach was used as reflecting different perspectives for instance in a work organization.
5. The referral formula, more or less identical across services of educational psychology to schools in Denmark, consists of three to four pages where the teachers/school should answer questions and provide descriptions of the problem related to the child of concern. There is space for parents' comments and feedback as well, but the formula primarily centres on the teachers' understanding of the individual child's problems (including family background and history of the child with special attention to previous referrals to medical specialists). In the formula, the reason for the referral should be categorized according to the child's malfunctions, such as in the area of attention/concentration or of behaviour.
6. Although, as I later state the psychologist had not made the observations we discussed, what they would have seen if they had been observing.

References

Anderson, C. J. K., Klassen, R. M. and Georgiou, G. K. (2007). Inclusion in Australia: What Teachers Say they Need and What School Psychologists Can Offer. *School Psychology International*, 28, 131–147.

The British Education Act (2002). www.opsi.gov.uk

Caplan, G. (2004). 'Recent Advances in Mental Health Consultation and Collaboration', in N. M. Lambert, I. Hylander and J. H. Sandoval (ed.). *Consultee-Centred Consultation – Improving the Quality of Professional Services in Schools and Community Organizations*. New Jersey: Lawrence Erlbaum Associates. pp. 21–35.

Chaiklin, S. (2005). 'Danish Pedagogical Psychology in Historical Perspective', in Ringsmose, C. and Baltzer K. *Specialpædagogik ad nye veje*. Copenhagen: Danmarks Pædagogiske Universitet.

—(unpublished manuscript). *Introduction to a Future Science*. Copenhagen: Danish University of Education.

The Danish Ministry of Education (2004). Folkeskolens Formålsparagraf. www.uvm.dk

Davies, S. B. B., Howes, A. J. and Farell, P. (2008). Tensions and Dilemmas as Drivers for Change in an Analysis of Joint Working between Teachers and Educational Psychologists. *School Psychology International*, 29, 400–417.

Edwards, A., Daniels, H., Gallagher, T., Leadbetter, J. and Warmington P. (2009). *Improving Inter-Professional Collaborations – Multi-Agency Working for Children's Wellbeing*. Oxon, UK: Routledge.

Elkonin, D. B. (1999). Toward the Problem of Stages in the Mental Development of the Child. *Journal of Russian and East European psychology*, 37, 11–29.

Engelbrecht, P. (2004). Changing Roles for Educational Psychologists within Inclusive Education in South Africa. *School Psychology International*, 25, 20–29.

Farell, P., Jimerson, S. R., Kalambouka, A. and Benoit, J. (2005). Teachers' Perceptions of School Psychologists in Different Countries. *School Psychology International*, 26, 525–544.

Guvå, G.(2004). 'Meeting a Teacher Who Asks for Help but Not for Consultation', in N. M. Lambert, I. Hylander and J. H. Sandoval (ed.). *Consultee-Centred Consultation – Improving the Quality of Professional Services in Schools and Community Organizations*. New Jersey: Lawrence Erlbaum Associates. pp. 257–264.

Hedegaard, M. (1995): *Beskrivelse af småbørn*. Aarhus: Aarhus University Press.

—(2002).*Learning and Child Development: A Cultural Historical Study*. Aarhus: Aarhus University Press.

—(2009). Children's Development from a Cultural Historical Approach: Children's Activity in Everyday Local Settings as Foundation for their Development. *Mind, Culture and Activity*, 16, 64–81.

Hedegaard, M. and Fleer, M. (2008). *Studying Children – A Cultural Historical Approach*. New York: Open University Press.

Højholt, C. (1993). *Brugerperspektiver – Forældre, læreres og psykologers erfaring med psykosocialt arbejde*. Copenhagen: Dansk Psykologisk Forlag.

Hylander, I. (2004). 'Analysis of Conceptual Change in Consultee-Centered Consultation', in N. M. Lambert, I. Hylander and J. H. Sandoval (ed.). *Consultee-centred Consultation – Improving the quality of professional Services in Schools and Community Organizations*. New Jersey: Lawrence Erlbaum Associates. pp. 45–61.

Hylander, I. and Guvå, G. (2004). 'Development of Consultee-Centered Consultation in Sweden', in N. M. Lambert, I. Hylander and J. H. Sandoval (ed.). *Consultee-Centred Consultation – Improving the Quality of Professional Services in Schools and Community Organizations*. New Jersey: Lawrence Erlbaum Associates. pp. 65–77.

Lambert, N. M. (2004). 'Consultee-Centered Consultation: An International Perspective on Goals, Process, and Theory',. in N. M. Lambert, I. Hylander and J. H. Sandoval (ed.). *Consultee-Centred Consultation – Improving the Quality of Professional Services in Schools and Community Organizations*. New Jersey: Lawrence Erlbaum Associates. pp. 3–19.

Larney, R. (2003). School-Based Consultation in the United Kingdom: Principles, Practice and Effectiveness. *School Psychology International*, 24, 5–19.

Leadbetter, J. (2004). The Role of Mediating Artefacts in the Work of Educational Psychologists during Consultative Conversations in Schools. *Educational Review,* 56, 134–145.

Mägi, K. and Kikas, E. (2009). School Psychologists' Role in School: Expectations of School Principals on the Work of School Psychologists. *School Psychology International* 30, 331–346.

Piaget, J. (2000). *Barnets psykiske udvikling.* Copenhagen: Hans Reitzel.

The Salamanca Declaration (1994). www.unesco.org.

Shwery, C. (2004). Teacher Resistance to School Based Consultation with School Psychologists: A Survey of Teacher Perception. *Journal of Emotional and Behavioural Disorders,* 12, 30–37.

Stobie, I., Gemmell, M., Moran, E. and Randall, L. (2002). Challenges for Educational Psychologists and their Services: A Qualitative Analysis. *School Psychology International,* 23, 243–265.

Tanggaard, L. and Elmholdt, C. (2006). Bevægelsen mod Konsultative praksisformer i PPR. *Pædagogisk Psykologisk Tidsskrift,* 43, 373–498.

—(2007). Learning Trajectories among Educational Psychologists. *Studies in Continuing Education,* 29, 295–314.

Vygotsky, L. S. (1982). *Barnets psykiske udvikling.* Copenhagen: Nyt nordisk forlag, pp. 106–148.

—(1998). *The Collected Works of L.S. Vygotsky.* Child Psychology, Vol. 5, New York: Plenum Press, pp. 187–205.

Wagner, P. (2000). Consultation: Developing a Comprehensive Approach to Service Delivery. *Educational Psychology in Practice,* 16, 9–18.

Change and Development in the Professional Practice of Educational Psychologists in the UK

Jane Leadbetter

Chapter Outline

Introduction

This chapter analyses the transformation of the professional practice of educational psychologists in the UK, from a cultural-historical perspective. Through applying activity theory, as an approach to depicting and examining specific shifts in practice at significant chronological points in the history of the profession, the chapter seeks to explore why changes have occurred, what external forces have acted to influence change and how the profession has responded to these. In the latter part of the twentieth century there were consistent moves to change the focus of professional educational psychology from a mainly individual child focus to a wider, more systemic approach. This transformation is considered, particularly in relation to the use of consultation as a way of engaging with the wide variety of people with whom educational psychologists work.

Finally, activity theory is used to articulate some of the more recent changes taking place in the work of educational psychologists, particularly in multi-agency settings, with specialist teams and with parents. New concepts are introduced in order to describe and explain how professionals can relate to children in schools and schools as organizations. The chapter seeks to clarify which knowledge has dominated through progressive periods of time and which knowledge has developed and been incorporated over time.

A century of professional educational psychology in the United Kingdom

The current employment and legislative context for most educational psychologists (EPs) working in the United Kingdom is very different from that which pertained when the first educational psychologist was appointed in London in 1913. Most newly trained EPs work for Local Authorities and the vast majority spend their entire professional careers working within Local Authorities. The employment context has some similar features across the UK and the legislative framework that applies to a high proportion of the work of EPs is, in the main, consistent across the UK. However, there is variety in terms of the range of work and the way services are delivered across the UK. More interestingly, the way the work has changed since the first EP was appointed reflects factors that have influenced the development of the profession. This progression can be examined and analysed in a number of ways but within this paper, activity theory is used to describe context and activities at important times. Transformations in role can be observed in relation to many factors and these can be analysed using a cultural-historical approach.

In 1913, Cyril Burt (later Sir Cyril Burt) was appointed by London City Council as a part-time school psychologist. He was appointed to use the newly constructed intelligence tests to select children who would benefit from the new forms of specialist schooling that were being set up. He was also expected to undertake research as part of his role. Now, nearly a 100 years on, the roles educational psychologists take up have some elements in common with the first assigned role Burt took up but there are also fundamental differences and there have been some interesting turns along the way. The following sections trace the transformation throughout the century but first it is important to outline the theoretical basis upon which this analysis is based.

Activity theory

The study of activity has been a focus for Soviet researchers and theorists since the birth of the study of psychology. Although definitions of activity and beliefs about its roots, function and relationships to other concepts have varied over time and are still strongly debated today, Daniels (1996), suggests;

> Since the time of its inception in the 1920s, this category has undergone a metamorphosis and has been the subject of so many disputes that it cannot be adequately comprehended out of the context of its history. (1996, p. 99)

Activity theory itself is grounded in the assumption that the study of 'activity' in itself is meaningful and can be used as a significant unit of analysis, (Engestrom, 2001; Leadbetter, 2004, Bakhurst, 2009). Thus at a meta-level, activity systems can be constructed to show change and development over time due to external social, cultural, legal and historical factors. However, alongside this wide-ranging analysis, activity can be studied at a micro-level; paying attention to the actions undertaken by EPs, the tools used and the range of others involved in the work, in order to understand the changes in working practices and also the relationships between the actions taken and the changing contexts. Therefore;

> Activity theory posits psychological development and thus psychological analysis as grounded in practical cultural activities. (Daniels, 2001, p. 76)

Activity theory is therefore a useful framework or tool to study transformations in professional practice.

Activity theory is not without its critics. Ratner, (1997) while accepting that activity theory has helped cultural psychologists because the research and conceptualizations are usually based in real activities and 'socio-technical systems' suggests that this is not always the case. He cites examples where activity theorists have not always considered the concrete social organization of activity and have therefore not always taken account of wider socio-cultural factors,

(1997, p. 101). This is perhaps a fair criticism and it is important, when adopting such an approach, to ensure that wider historical and cultural influences are not ignored.

More recently, Bakhurst, (2009) has suggested that activity theorists have been over-ambitious in their attempts to provide a single theory of 'activity'. This, he says, is a difficult, if not impossible task as in aiming to create an overarching theory it becomes increasingly abstract and therefore the validity and usefulness becomes diminished.

Activity theory has been developed in a range of directions and within diverse contexts. However, the analysis described here has drawn upon the development and theorizing of activity theory undertaken by Engestrom and his team in Helsinki, in a wealth of published literature. (see Engestrom et al., 1999). Engestrom·has suggested that there are five principles that are central to activity theory in its current form and these are taken by Daniels (2001, p. 93–94) to represent a manifesto. In brief, they are as follows:

A collective, artefact-mediated and object-oriented activity system, seen in its network relations to other activity systems, is taken as the prime unit of analysis.

. . . The multi-voicedness of activity systems. An activity system is always a community of multiple points of view, traditions and interest.

The third principle is historicity. Activity systems take shape and get transformed over long periods of time.

The fourth principle is the central role of contradictions as sources of change and development.

The fifth principle proclaims the possibility of expansive transformations in activity systems. (Engestrom, 1999, p. 4–5)

Engestrom conceptualizes an expanded activity system to include a 'macro-level' analysis that emphasizes collective and communal factors. He introduces the notions of 'Rules', 'Community' and 'Division of Labour'. A diagram showing an activity theory model is contained in Figure 7.1.

Engestrom emphasizes the importance of the interaction between the various elements within this expanded activity system and also the importance of the constant changing of the subjects and objects. Mediation is also a fundamental concept within Vygotskian theorizing, in contrast to other post-Vygotskians such as Leont'ev whose theory of activity focused upon activity and action, (Wertsch, 1995 p. 20). In discussing mediation Wertsch posits that

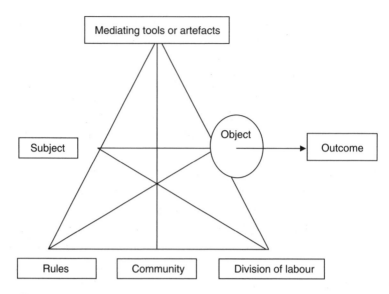

Figure 7.1 Activity theory model

as well as being empowering, in that it can open up opportunities for new action, mediation can also be constraining. He suggests that,

> When analysing or planning for new forms of mediation, the focus is typically on how these new mediational means will overcome some perceived problem or restriction inherent in existing forms of mediated action. However, one of the points that follows inescapably from the view of mediated action . . . is that even if a new cultural tool frees us from some earlier limitation of perspective, it introduces new ones of its own. (1995, p. 24–25)

This is an interesting and often neglected attribute of mediation, which is normally seen as a positive force or intervention and thus it will be examined within the analysis described here.

Developing an understanding of mediation is clearly important and Kozulin (1990), in interpreting Vygotsky's work suggests that he envisaged a theoretical programme in which there existed three types of mediator: signs and symbols; individual activities; and interpersonal relations. (see Daniels, 1996). However, there are important points of difference in terms of the role of mediated action within activity theoretical work. Engestrom et al. (1999)

argue that socio-cultural approaches tend to privilege mediated action as the proper unit of analysis, (Wertsch et al., 1995). They do not emphasize ideas of historicity or object-orientedness: elements that have a strong emphasis within the works of Engestrom and his followers. Clearly, mediation is another complex and keenly debated concept within socio-cultural and activity theory discourses, but for the purposes of this chapter one emphasis is upon the nature of the mediating artefacts that are used during the work of EPs and teachers and upon the tools and instruments used in EP practice over its 100-year history.

In describing the analytical concepts used in this chapter it is also important to highlight an important distinction in the study of artefacts, relating to the functions of psychological and material tools. Cole makes a clear distinction between tools and artefacts, (1996). He views tools as a subcategory of a wider overarching concept of artefacts. As part of this premise he cites the fact that people, as well as objects may be used as mediating artefacts. Certainly artefacts can be viewed, analysed, categorized and defined in a variety of ways. Clearly the different methods of analysis will each be grounded in slightly different theoretical positions and will serve specific lines of research or enquiry. This richness of approach is not necessarily a bad thing as Engestrom and Miettinan (1999), point out,

Activity theory needs to develop tools for analysing and transforming networks of culturally heterogeneous activities through dialogue and debate. (1999, p. 7)

A chronological, activity theoretical analysis of the work of educational psychologists

This chapter is concerned with transformations in the practices of educational psychologists over time. Through examining cultural and historical conditions and influences, the contradictions and reasons for change can be uncovered. Therefore activity theory is used as a framework for analysis. For each time phase, the subjects are taken as the body of educational psychologists working in the UK and for each phase, the objects, outcomes, tools, rules, community and division of labour are described.

Early developments: 1913–1940

Earlier in this chapter, mention is made of the appointment of the first educational psychologist in the UK, Cyril Burt. During this period of time, the objects were mainly the children who were referred to EPs testing and thus the main tools or instruments that were used or 'mediated' the work of EPs were psychometrics. However, the techniques associated with developing research methods were also valuable tools as Burt tried to understand and describe populations according to emerging norms.

Outcomes, at this time tended to be mainly the results or diagnosis, resulting from the psychometrics that may have led to differential placement or the allocation of educational resources. Speculating about key influences over 80 years ago is somewhat difficult but it is likely that the rules that governed practice were, as now, the relevant legislation. Thus, Education Acts, which entitled pupils to educational opportunities, formed the backcloth to the lone EP attempting to classify children. The wider community in activity theory terms can be thought of as the local context and the national government, directing the operation of the newly created Education Boards.

Division of labour and, subsumed within this, the politics of power, was a key influence as the client group was initially identified from a medical basis with doctors playing a key role. Hence the role of EP as tester stemmed both from the technologies available but also the position that education found itself in with respect to the more established medical fraternity. The extent to which this role development was dependent upon the key interests, skills and preferred style of the (then) lone EP is difficult to ascertain. Certainly, given the circumstances of Burt's appointment and his opportunity to draw up his own terms of reference, it is safe to assume he was happy in his work. Such degrees of freedom are not necessarily apparent in the wider development of EP role as this analysis of the development of the profession demonstrates.

Educational psychologist's work from 1940–1968

Through examining the socio-cultural and historical contexts, transformations in practices can be observed and this is certainly the case for educational psychologists. The Second World War provided ample opportunity for psychologists to develop their therapeutic and supportive skills as many children were evacuated from their families, resulting in disturbances to family life. Additionally, with fathers away from the home, uncertainty surrounding individual and collective futures existed. In many families, mothers were going out to work for the first time and there were severe pressures on families and children resulting in greater numbers referred for child guidance. By about 1944, there were about 70 child guidance clinics in the UK (Dessent, 1978).

The publication of an Education Act in 1944 introduced, among many changes, the concept of educational sub-normality and also established maladjustment as a handicapping condition in the same way that blindness or deafness existed. In terms of the industry of categorization, labelling, discriminating and selecting, this created ever-new vistas for psychologists. At this time, many psychologists were spending some of their time working as part of a child guidance team and part of the time within a school psychological service. This latter development was essentially post-war and marked the beginnings of educational psychologists working directly in schools. It would be gratifying to report that EPs worked *with* schools but in fact they tended to replicate the practices undertaken in clinical settings, namely testing, within various corners of school buildings. However, the 1944 Education Act, by including more children within the legitimate remit of education, at least provided a forum for questions to be asked about provision for these new groups of children. Numbers of educational psychologists increased, so that a report by UNESCO in 1948, indicates that there were about 70–100 educational psychologists in England and Wales, but many of those were part-time.

The 1950's saw the development of School Psychological Services alongside Child Guidance Clinics with a typical arrangement being that educational psychologists spent part of their time each week in each of the two settings. An impetus for change came from the frustrations of psychologists feeling that the role within child guidance was essentially restricted and medically based and that there was more scope for the development of the role within more educational settings. This pattern continued throughout the 1960's and culminated in the commissioning and publication of a government report on 'Psychologists in Education Services', more commonly known as the Summerfield Report (1968).

While acknowledging the danger of oversimplifying complex situations by using a basic analytical model, it is still possible to conceptualize the developing role of EPs during the period of time described above. Using activity theory terms the relationships and influences can be summarized as follows: The object remains the same in that children are still referred for assessment but the outcomes broadened somewhat including not only diagnosis and placement but also some therapeutic work. The tools were still predominantly psychometrics but also some therapeutic interventions including psychodynamic approaches and play therapy. There was little change in the rules, although the more specific legislation concerning the categorization of children required the development of more sophisticated tests (tools). Division of labour shifted slightly to give schools a more important role so that referrals could be made by medics and schools and schools became possible sites for interventions.

The reconstructing movement: educational psychologist's work from 1968–1981

It might be suggested that progress was slow but from the late 1960's in line with other major cultural movements progress quickened. The Summerfield Report (1968) provided data on the amount of time EPs spent in different activities – the first of many such surveys. The results reflect a continuation of earlier trends as the two key activities were 'psychological assessments' and 'treating children'. Within this breakdown, approximately 10% of the time was spent assessing children in child guidance settings and between 20% and 70% assessing children in schools and other settings.

> The work analysis thus showed a preponderance of individual clinical, diagnostic and therapeutic work with little indication of involvement in advisory, preventative or in-service training work. More over, the scientific research role of the educational psychologist, so strongly advocated and practised by Burt received little mention. (Dessent, 1978, p. 31)

This balance of work seems to have been rarely challenged even while the number of psychologists continued to increase on a greater scale than before. The increase in posts was in part due to the fact that more children were coming within the purview of education as the 1970 Education Act deemed that children previously labelled educationally sub-normal, ESN(S), should now become the responsibility of education departments. To an extent, this group of pupils paved the way for psychologists to begin to employ behavioural principles in their work, something that had not been prevalent up to this point. However, this new approach was necessary in order to design suitable curricula, teaching programmes and behaviour-management techniques.

The decade following the publication of the Summerfield report saw the development of a role that came to be known as a traditional role for educational psychologists. Writers such as Phillips (1971) stated that the core skills and responsibilities of EPs were identification, diagnosis and treatment, the main client groups being children with learning or adjustment problems. Most EP practice at this time seemed to conform to this definition. However, many practitioners were becoming openly dissatisfied by the circumstances they found themselves in and the prescribed role they were occupying.

Against the custom and practice formed over many decades, in different parts of UK, new techniques, roles and models of practice were being discussed and in some cases put into practice. Leyden (1978) portrays a picture of the climate and culture against which this happened.

> Faced with school populations of 20,000 to 30,000 and a system of open referrals with no initial screening, the enthusiasm for testing began to wane, initially on the simple grounds that it was inappropriate and impossible for the large number of children referred. (p. 163–164)

The seminal text 'Reconstructing Educational Psychology' (Gillham, 1978) brought together a collection of writers, all educational psychologists, who represented the frustrations and dissatisfactions, felt by many, surrounding the role of educational psychologists. The book also included descriptions of possible alternative models of working and modes of employment. Criticisms centred on chapters entitled; 'Medical and psychological concepts of problem behaviour', 'The failure of psychometrics' and 'The psychologists' professionalism and the right to psychology'.

Tizard, in 1976 suggests:

> To apply psychology was to assign individuals to points in a multi-dimensional matrix. This would enable them to be sorted into appropriate categories, for which there were appropriate educational niches or forms of remedial treatment. (p. 226)

Clearly, the medical model was still perceived to be dominant. An interesting point emerges here as some psychologists sought to shed themselves of roles they felt to be inappropriate. Throughout the history of the profession there is a theme that educational psychologists' roles have always been defined by others rather than by themselves. For most of the time up to the late 1970's, it seems that there was little incongruence between the two groups. Leyden, (1978) suggests that from the early beginnings of the profession, most EPs were faced with a definition of their area of competence made by other people.

At this point in the history of the profession, when role definition was particularly crucial, Topping suggested that, even though many EPs were beginning to question a medical model of professional practice, this premise

> . . . remains firmly part of the cognitive map of the teaching profession, and teacher's expectations of psychologists' in many areas are still couched in terms of the "assessment and treatment" of individual children, who, by virtue of needing such attention, must be "abnormal". (1978, p. 21)

Thus pressures relating to expectations from the medical profession shifted, or were perhaps augmented by pressures arising from the new colleagues with whom EPs worked, namely teachers.

One chapter in 'Reconstructing Educational Psychology' portrays the role of the EP as an agent of change working with school systems (Burden, 1978). A conceptualization of the role of the EP as being concerned with the wider environment, employing systemic and preventative approaches, was a welcome relief to many EPs dissatisfied with the narrowly defined role previously outlined. This conceptualization of role also represents the beginnings of 'the great debate', as it came to be known (Reid, 1976). Other writers since this time have typified the tensions, which exist between the push to undertake crisis-driven individualized work with children and the belief that preventative, systemic applications of psychology are more effective.

Continuing to position the EP as the subject, the objects can be viewed as referred, named children. A significant development, certainly for school age children, is that referrals tended to come from schools rather than from medics. In some cases and in some parts of the country, the objects could be seen to be whole class or whole school problems, demanding a more environmental, systemic approach. Outcomes also broadened to include some systemic, project-based work with schools alongside assessment and placement of individual pupils.

The tools available to EPs had begun to broaden to include skills in project work and evaluation mirroring the expansion in content of EP to include new areas of psychology including instructional psychology, behavioural approaches and systemic problem-solving. However, this new knowledge and these embryonic skills did not replace the core tools of the trade; assessment and testing methods and materials.

During this time the prevailing rules were perhaps set as much by tradition and other peoples' expectations as by heavy legislative strictures or guidance, as discussed earlier. The community (in a broad sense) had widened out to include teachers and schools as key players in the system and the division of labour had also moved a little but still consisted of teachers referring problems (usually children) and EPs mainly assessing and occasionally intervening. Again, it is important to acknowledge that this is a simplification and generalization of what went on over a significant period of time. The purpose of such an analysis and the benefits that ensue lie in highlighting the changes over time and in understanding the reasons for these changes.

The impact of legislation and statutory duties: 1981–1998

The next period of time saw a significant shift in role definition for EPs as the profession gained, for the first time, a statutory function within special needs legislation. This was heralded by many as an important shift, in that the status, position and specific skills and knowledge of EPs was recognized for the first time. However, with hindsight other commentators have reflected that it was the beginning of a different type of straightjacket for the profession. The 1981 Education Act introduced a statutory requirement for all children who may have special educational needs to undergo a full assessment by a range of professionals, including, in all cases, an educational psychologist, employed by a Local Education Authority. Gillham (1999), commenting on the effect of the 1981 Act on the profession of educational psychology suggests,

> The 1981 Education Act leading to the implementation of the statementing procedure and its corollaries can now be seen as nothing less than a tragedy for the profession. (p. 220)

The results of the implementation of the 1981 Education Act and its revisiting in many subsequent Education Acts and sets of guidance have been huge for all institutions, schools, Local Authority departments and professionals working in the field of special needs. At the time of the 1981 Act, although the role of the EP was only one part of the whole assessment process, in terms of the long-standing rivalry between medical staff and psychologists, EPs were given some supremacy. This occurred because their advice was often viewed by LEA officers as the most important advice submitted and in many LEAs the EP was required to draft or even write the final statement as well as submitting their psychological advice. However, this role definition, while providing job security for many, did little to further the cause of applied educational psychology in schools.

The moves to more inclusive education being offered to some children have also added complexity to the role of the EP. In order to be placed in a special school or to be allocated resources in a mainstream school, a statement was needed. This, in turn necessitated an assessment of need that in turn requires EP involvement and advice. This train of bureaucracy is costly in terms of time and money and has also changed the relationship between schools, LEAs and support services. In many areas of the country, EPs were placed in positions, either officially or unofficially, where they are required to make decisions about whether a child's level of need requires an assessment or provision. This invidious position is concerned with measuring against locally or nationally agreed criteria and does not involve the application of psychology. Selecting pupils to benefit from assessment has put EPs in direct conflict with parents and teachers in both mainstream and special schools. This developing role has felt uncomfortable for many EPs, partly because the system is complex and distracts time from more interventionist work but also because in many areas it has forced practice back in time in that briefer, but less rigorous assessments were being carried out upon greater numbers of children to meet bureaucratic requirements.

During this time there was a significant shift in object and division of labour as school staff and EPs came closer together through the necessities of legislation. Hence the object of EPs activities included more work with teachers and the division of labour involved teachers doing much more early work with children causing concern and involving EPs later in the process. Unfortunately, the outcome was a huge increase in the numbers of children being assessed, resulting in huge SEN budget increases. Tools for assessment widened to include more collaborative approaches such as the development and use of checklists used between EPs and teachers. The culture became more bureaucratic and litigious with criteria for resource allocation being invoked and tribunals where parents were able to contest Local Authority decision making becoming common place.

Using consultation: EPs work from 1998–2009

As statutory demands on educational psychologists have increased, there has been a continuing determination, on the part of EPs, to expand their activities beyond working with individual children. This has resulted in the use of a wide range of approaches, including sharing, or, some would say, giving away psychology, through training in schools and other settings. Some examples of this are described below.

There has been a growing interest in systemic approaches to school situations that has its basis in social psychology and family therapy. Coming from an interactionist perspective, many EPs have sought always to consider the child in a range of contexts and to look at the importance of school, classroom and teacher factors. Thus, the work of Dowling and Osborne (1994) and Stoker, (1987 and 1992) demonstrate the importance of EPs in crossing boundaries and making connections between systems at a number of levels. This work has more recently been extended to concentrate upon the environment as a primary focus and for interventions to be geared towards changing the environment to improve the situation for all pupils, not only named pupils experiencing difficulties, Daniels and Williams, (2000), Williams and Daniels, (2000).

EPs have also maintained an interest in therapeutic aspects of their role and in particular have developed approaches to support inclusive practice in schools, such as 'Circle of Friends' work, (Newton, Taylor and Wilson 1996; Shotton, 1998). They have also turned their attention to anti-bullying strategies and have been instrumental in developing approaches that are widely used in schools, (Sharp, 1996). All these approaches draw heavily upon a range of psychological models and theories but in particular are founded in social psychology and humanistic psychology. They provide examples of the innovative and valuable practice that can develop when some time or space is made within the EP role.

Practice is constantly changing in response to role demands and also to new knowledge and skill development within the profession (Leadbetter, 2000). More recently there has been a move towards a different model of engagement between schools and educational psychologists and this is characterized by the development of consultation in many EP services. Consultation, particularly with teachers, has grown in popularity as it is seen to offer opportunities for EPs to draw upon a broad range of psychological approaches, and work in a more equal partnership with teachers and others who wish to consult with EPs. Consultation has been defined in many different ways and is implemented in different EP Services in the UK with varying degrees of rigour. Some differences in the mode of implementation can be summarized as follows:

- Consultation as the model of service delivery within an EP Service;
- Consultation as a defined task with agreed characteristics;
- Consultation as a specific activity or skill. (Leadbetter, 2006)

Which ever of these approaches is used it shifts the tools upon which EPs draw to engage in their day-to-day work and it shifts the objects of their activity and the division of labour.

Wagner, (2000), has been at the forefront of the promotion and development of new ideas and methods in this domain. When aiming to answer the question; 'What is the problem to which consultation is a solution?' she suggests,

> Many Eps . . . report concerns about the continuing and grinding emphasis in their work on individual assessments and report writing. They lament a lack of creative and imaginative work with teachers, of preventative interventions in school and classrooms, and of effective joint school-family work. Above all, they sense that the educational psychology they are using is not making a difference in improving the development and learning of children and their schools. (2000, p. 9–10)

Within a consultation model the object of EP activity becomes the teacher or other who is directly involved with the child. Hence the EP works directly with the teacher and thus influences what happens to the child indirectly. Outcomes are defined jointly between EP (consultant) and teacher (consultee) and may involve joint problem solving, solution-finding and decision making. Tools include consultation enquiry forms, protocols for running sessions and use of different language and questioning. The division of labour shifts so that teachers and others bring concerns and EPs facilitate a process whereby actions are agreed jointly. This move to consultation does not impact upon all EPs or on all aspects of the work of EPs, but has been a noticeable shift. Recent changes in the organizational arrangements for EPs and others working in Children's Services in the UK is likely to mean further changes in the way EPs will be required to work and this is discussed later in the chapter.

Summarizing changes in practice in activity theoretical terms

Through this chronological analysis it is possible to consider how different elements of the activity systems described have transformed over time. Thus it can be seen that the objects of EPs actions have moved from; referred children > referred children and some systemic problems > helping teachers. Table 7.1

Table 7.1 Transformation in the work of EPs, over time using elements of activity systems.

Activity system elements	Early developments 1913–1940	Post-war developments 1940–1968	The reconstructing movement 1968–1981	Statutory duties 1981–1998	Using consultation 1998–2010
Subject	EP	EPs	EPs	EPs	EPs
Object	Referred children	Referred children	Referred children, some school-based problems	Work with teachers in schools and children being assessed	Teachers in schools
Outcomes	Diagnosis and placement of child	Diagnosis and placement and some treatment	Assessment and placement, some systemic work with schools	Assessment as part of statementing procedure, increase in budget for SEN	Joint decision making about actions to be taken by all parties
Tools	Newly devised psychometric tests, research surveys	Psychometrics and some therapeutic skills	Psychometrics, project work, behavioural approaches	Psychometrics, checklists, interviews, wider assessment approaches	Consultation forms, protocols, changes to language and questions used
Rules	Defined role as tester and researcher	Defined role as tester for newly defined categories	Assumptions of others, some legislative requirements	Legislation requiring EP involvement, criteria for resourcing. Contestation, tribunals	Legislation, accountability, more responsibility for delivery and funds in schools
Community	Government, medics, staff of newly formed special schools	Government, health service, education authorities and schools a little	Local authorities, schools, other related professions	Local authorities, schools, other related professions, parents	Local authorities, schools and other settings, other related professions
Division of labour	Medics identified children, EPs tested	Medics and schools identified children, EPs tested, some interventions	Schools referred children and sometimes wider problems, EPs assessed and sometimes intervened	Teachers do more early work, EPs involved later in process to ratify decisions often	Teachers bring concerns, EPs facilitate problem solving and solution finding

summarizes how the key elements of typical activity systems have been transformed over the time periods described earlier.

By recognizing and acknowledging how the past has been shaped by the historical context, cultural forces and in this case legislative changes, we can reflect on the way the profession has changed in the UK. There are clear connections to be made between the changes in role requirements and the tools that are chosen. In many cases it is possible that the tools are not those that EPs would prefer to use, but rules (e.g. time limits for submitting statutory reports) require quick solutions. In other cases it can be seen that the upsurge in a popular development in psychology has an impact upon the tools that are used; hence the approach of 'solution-focused' work has been assimilated in to much of the work done within consultation.

Current and future possibilities

Having undertaken a cultural-historical analysis, it is possible to change gaze and to speculate about 'where next?' drawing on observations of what has happened in the past. Thus, questions can be posed about where the object might move to next? It is certainly the case that parents are being accorded a more prominent role in some areas of work in Children's Services. In some EP Services, direct access to services for parents is being promoted, whereas in the past, EPs have sought to position themselves as working, as employees of Local Authorities, through schools, on behalf of children and families. Perhaps, within newly organized, child and family focused services parents and families will become more central objects.

Within the past few years, since the Every Child Matters (2003) agenda has been implemented, there has been a requirement for services engaged with children and families to work more closely together and develop new forms of multi-agency working (Edwards et al., 2009). Where this is happening, there are clear changes to the division of labour, whereby 'lead professionals' are appointed to work with families, sometimes taking on generic roles that might overlap with previous activities undertaken by a range of professionals. Hence, the division of labour shifts markedly, with 'teams around the child' being set up with specific roles assigned. EPs may find themselves undertaking more generic tasks in some cases (listening, supporting, advising) or in other cases may provide specific assessment information, or therapeutic interventions.

As these changes become embedded then it is likely that tools will change and new tools will be devised. A 'common assessment framework' has been donated and thresholds for actions agreed, across services (influenced strongly by a drive to improve child protection and safeguarding procedures). How EPs will respond to these changes, in terms of the tools they choose to draw upon is yet to be seen. Will there be a reversion to the traditional tools of the trade: psychometrics, as these are closed tests, limited to use by certain practitioners, or will there be a development of new tools with a psychological basis that will enable new forms of working?

Educational Psychologists are constantly adapting to the changing work contexts which characterize public sector practice. Activity theory can be used as a useful framework for understanding why changes have occurred in the past. However, in new contexts, where work boundaries are blurred, roles are merging, and practices are changing, different theoretical concepts may be needed to help make sense of what is happening. The Learning in and for Interagency Working (LIW) research project, (Edwards et al., 2009; Leadbetter, 2006, 2008) identifies several new concepts that can help to explain what happens in such new forms of working. Four such concepts are:

1. Boundaries and boundary crossing
2. Distributed expertise
3. Rule bending and rule breaking
4. Developing understanding of artefacts and the creation of new tools

Boundaries and boundary crossing can be viewed as:

- Places where professional identities can be called into question;
- Places and times where professionals were looking out from their home organizations toward other professionals and looking inward to the expectations of their primary workplace;
- Tensions that professionals experienced; holding onto the securities of established patterns of workplace practices while being pulled forward to new forms of collaboration by their beliefs that these would benefit children.

Distributed expertise can be viewed as:

- A collective attribute spread across systems that is drawn upon to accomplish tasks; expertise therefore lies in both the system and the individuals' ability to recognize and negotiate its use;
- Understanding some key areas which are identified as being important to practitioners
  o Knowing who is important in any activity
  o Knowing what their role entails and what they are able to do

o Having and showing clear sympathy or clear appreciation
o Knowing why they need to undertake specific activities.

Rule bending and rule breaking includes the following:

- Questioning rules or established social practices is one sign that a system is changing as a result of expanding understandings of the activity it is engaged in;
- Heroic actions and how to learn from them and embed them in practice;
- Rule-bending is a sign of both professional and organizational learning. It can also be a sign of values-driven professional practice. However it presents considerable challenges to organizations that are shaped by strong systems of accountability;
- As practitioners expand understandings of the problems of practice, they find not only can existing rules be unhelpful, but also that the resources and tools available restrict their responses and any fresh interpretations.

Developing understanding of artefacts and the creation of new tools includes:

- Acknowledging there is a need to create new tools;
- Embedding tools within systems;
- Evaluating the impact of a new tool on the expected outcomes and revising if necessary.

These concepts can be used to help EPs and their managers understand which areas of practice need to be developed to meet changing demands. In Table 7.2 there is an example of a matrix drawn up to help EP services decide which conceptual tool might apply in different situations. Thus the vertical axis describes different levels and formats of multi-agency working that might be in place within a local authority, within which EPs might work in different configurations. The horizontal axis contains the four conceptual tools described above and within a few cells of the matrix are examples of what the work might look like. This framework is currently being applied in some EP Services in the UK and may provide a new way of analysing working practices in order to inform appropriate changes.

Application of such ideas to team-working can help individuals to understand how they can make sense of what is, often being 'done to them' rather than them having power over their own destinies. Thus recognizing that some 'rule-bending' is necessary to improve practice can be transformational.

Understanding the contradictions that are presented, by new rules being invoked, such as joint referral mechanisms between teams, can lead to the

Table 7.2 Examples of types of multi-agency working and analytical tools

Examples of MAW	Boundary crossing	Distributed expertise	Rule-bending and risk-taking	Creating and developing new tools
Cluster based team (low level integration)			Changing traditional patterns of service delivery	
Joint referral and planning (medium level integration)	Co-working specific schools or families			New protocols, enquiry forms, ways of accessing service
Work in MAT e.g. CAMHS, LAC (high level integration)		Using others' expertise in training and consultancy		

creation of new tools; thus expanding learning and practice. Increasingly, within multi-agency working there is a need to acknowledge the multi-voicedness and the role that others play. Hence parents are, quite rightly, becoming more important players in the destinies of their children within the education system.

This chapter has demonstrated how activity theory can be applied to examine and understand transformations in the practices and in the work context of educational psychologists. The importance of historical and cultural factors is emphasized as is the relational nature of the elements of activity systems. Contradictions arising from external changes forced on professionals alongside internally driven developments have resulted in successive transformations, some positive, some negative. Very often earlier practices are not abandoned but new practices are incorporated into increasing complex work patterns. Finally, new concepts emerging from research into work-based practice are offered as tools for future use in further developing the professional practice of educational psychologists.

References

Bakhurst, D. (2009). Reflections on Activity Theory. *Educational Review*, 61(2), 197–210.

Burden, R. (1997). Research in the Real World: An Evaluation Model for Use by Applied Psychologists. *Educational Psychology in Practice*, 13(1), 13–20.

Cole, M. (1996). *Cultural Psychology: A Once and Future Discipline.* Cambridge, Mass: Harvard University Press.

Daniels, H. (ed.) (1996). *An Introduction to Vygotsky.* London and New York: Routledge.

—(2001). *Vygotsky and Pedagogy.* London: Routledge Falmer.

Daniels, A. and Williams, H. (2000). Reducing the Need for Exclusions and Statements for Behaviour. The Framework for Intervention Part 1. *Educational Psychology in Practice,* 15(4), 220–227.

Department for Education and Skills. (2003). *Every Child Matters.* London: The Stationery Office.

Department of Education and Science (1968). *Psychologists in Education Services. (The Summerfield Report).* London: HMSO.

—(1981). *Education Act 1981* London: HMSO.

Dessent, T. (1978). 'The Historical Development of School Psychological Services', in Gillham, B. (ed.) *Reconstructing Educational Psychology.* London: Croom Helm.

Dowling, E. and Osborne, E. (1994). *The Family and the School: A Joint Systems Approach to Problems with Children.* London: Routledge.

Edwards, A., Daniels, H., Gallagher, T., Leadbetter, J. and Warmington, P. (2009). *Improving Interprofessional Collaborations. Multi-Agency Working for Children's Wellbeing.* London: Routledge.

Engestrom, Y. (2001). Expansive Learning at Work. Toward an Activity Theoretical Reconceptualisation. *Journal of Education and Work,* 14(1) 133–156.

Engestrom, Y., Miettinen, R. and Punamaki, R. L. (eds.) (1999). *Perspectives on Activity Theory.* Cambridge: Cambridge University Press.

Gillham, B. (1978). *Reconstructing Educational Psychology.* London: Croom Helm.

— (1999). The Writing of Reconstructing Educational Psychology. *Educational Psychology in Practice,* 14(4), 220–221.

Kozulin, A. (1990). *Vygotsky's Psychology: A Biography of Ideas.* London: Harvester.

Leadbetter, J. (2000). Patterns of Service Delivery in Educational Psychology Services: Some Implications for Practice. *Educational Psychology in Practice,* 16 (4), 449–460.

—(2004). The Role of Mediating Artefacts in the Work of Educational Psychologists during Consultative Conversations in Schools. *Educational Review,* 56(2), 133–145.

—(2006). Investigating and Conceptualizing the Notion of Consultation to Facilitate Multiagency Working. *Educational Psychology in Practice,* 22(1), 19–31.

—(2008). Learning In and for Interagency Working: Making Links between Practice Development and Structured Reflection. *Learning and Social Care,* 7(4), 198–208.

Leyden. G. (1978). 'The Process of Reconstruction', in Gillham, B. (ed.) *Reconstructing Educational Psychology.* London: Croom Helm.

Newton, C., Taylor, G. and Wilson, D. (1996). Circle of Friends: An Inclusive Approach to Meeting Emotional and Behavioural Needs. *Educational Psychology in Practice,* 11(4), 41–48.

Ratner, C. (1997). *Cultural Psychology and Qualitative Methodology. Theoretical and Empirical Considerations.* New York: Plenum press.

Reid, R. S. (1976). Editorial *AEP Journal,* 4(1).

Sharp, S. (1996). The Role of Peers in Tackling Bullying in Schools. *Educational Psychology in Practice,* 11(4), 17–22.

Shotton, G. (1998). A Circle of Friends Approach with Socially Neglected Children. *Educational Psychology in Practice,* 14(1), 22–25.

Stoker, R. (1987). Systems Interventions in Schools – the Ripple Effect. *Educational Psychology in Practice,* 3(1), 44–50.

—(1992). Working at the Level of the Institution and the Organisation. *Educational Psychology in Practice,* 8(1), 15–24.

Tizard, J. (1976). Psychology and Social Policy. *Bulletin of the BPS* 29, 225–234.

Topping, K. J. (1978). The Role and Function of the Educational Psychologist. The Way Forward? *AEP Journal,* 4(5), 20–29.

Wagner, P. (2000). Consultation: Developing a Comprehensive Approach to Service Delivery. *Educational Psychology in Practice,* 16(1), 9–18.

Wertsch, J. V., Del Rio, P. and Alvarez, A. (eds) (1995). *Sociocultural Studies of Mind.* New York: Cambridge University Press.

Williams, H. and Daniels, A. (2000). Framework for Intervention, Part II. The Road to Total Quality Behaviour? *Educational Psychology in Practice,* 15(4), 228–236.

Part III
Support that Transcends Borders

Support for Children and Schools through Cultural Intervention

8

Harry Daniels

Chapter Outline

Introduction

This chapter will discuss the creation and maintenance of collaboration at two levels within a school: at the level of teaching staff relations and, although more briefly, at the level of the work of professional agencies. The focus will be on the formation of collaborative working cultures which support the development of responsive schooling and child welfare systems more generally. It will be argued that intervention in the cultural context of the institution which seeks to alter teachers' collaborative practices can make a difference to the instructional practices in classrooms. Collaboration between agencies can provide the 'seamless' or 'joined up' patterns of provision which are required to meet the complex and often fluctuating needs of children who are at risk of social exclusion. Collaborative problem solving between teachers can provide an engine for development in schools. The argument is that Cultural-Historical Psychology can provide a new perspective on possibilities for effecting change. The theoretical arguments which are drawn on in support of each intervention both between agencies and between teachers will be discussed both in theoretical terms and in relation to concrete practical examples.

Formative effects of school cultures

In what Minick (1987) refers to as the second phase of the development of Vygotsky's psychological theory, to be found in parts of 'Thinking and Speech', Vygotsky illustrates the movement from a social plane of functioning to an individual plane of functioning. Here Vygotsky argues that 'internalisation of socially rooted and historically developed activities is the distinguishing feature of human psychology' (Vygotsky, 1978. p. 57). Vygotsky provides a theoretical framework which rests on the concept of mediation by what have been referred to as psychological tools and cultural artefacts. This has found expression in the study of mediating role of specific cultural tools and their impact on development as well as the mediational function of the social interaction. From this point in the development of his work the challenges that confront us are at least twofold: first, have we developed an account of mediation that is both necessary and sufficient for a satisfactory account of the social, cultural, historical formation of mind and second have we developed a sufficiently robust understanding of the ways in which mediational means are produced? The first challenge will be discussed in relation to collaboration between agencies, the second challenge will be discussed in relation to collaboration between teachers.

In respect of the first challenge, Wertsch (2007) is developing an account of implicit mediation which echoes some of Bernstein's (2000) work on invisible mediation which can also be thought of as tacit mediation. It would seem that a similar challenge has also been noted by Abreu and Elbers (2005)

> . . . the impact of broader social and institutional structures on people's psychological understanding of cultural tools. We argue that in order to understand social mediation it is necessary to take into account ways in which the practices of a community, such as school and the family are structured by their institutional context. Cultural tools and the practices they are associated with, have their existence in communities, which in turn occupy positions in the broader social structure. These wider social structures impact on the interactions between the participants and the cultural tools. (p. 4)

In respect of the second challenge, a robust understanding of the ways in which mediational means are produced, Wertsch (1998) has advanced the case for the use of mediated action as a unit of analysis in social-cultural research because, in his view, it provides a kind of natural link between action, including mental action, and the cultural, institutional, and historical context in which such action occurs. This is so because the mediational means, or cultural tools, are inherently situated culturally, institutionally and historically. However as he had recognized earlier the relationship between cultural tools, power and authority is still under-theorized and in need of empirical study (Wertsch and Rupert, 1993). This recognition is an important step forward from the original Vygotskian thesis which as Ratner (1997) notes did not consider the ways in which concrete social systems bear on psychological functions. Vygotsky discussed the general importance of language and schooling for psychological functioning; however he failed to examine the real social systems in which these activities occur. The social analysis is thus reduced to a semiotic analysis which overlooks the real world of social praxis (Ratner, 1997). Nonetheless, some notable writers in the cultural-historical field have recognized the need for such a form of theoretical engagement (e.g. Hedegaard, 2001; Engestrom, 2007; Cole, 1996).

The ways in which schools are organized and constrained to organize themselves are seen to have an effect on the possibilities for peer collaboration and support at both teacher and pupil levels. However the theoretical tools of analysis of this kind of organizational effect are somewhat underdeveloped within the post-Vygotskian framework.

> As a rule, the socio-institutional context of action is treated as a (largely unanalysed) dichotomised independent variable – or left to sociologists. (Cole 1996, p. 340)

This chapter will provide a discussion of ways in which intervention in the socio-institutional context of schooling can offer support for pupils through their teachers and other professionals who work with them. It will start with a discussion of cultural intervention to support joined up working beyond the school and this will be followed by a discussion of intervention within the school.

Collaboration between agencies

This section of the chapter engages with questions concerning collaboration beyond the school. In doing so, it relates to the work described by Jane Leadbetter in Chapter 10 and Charlotte Højholt in Chapter 7. The UK government has given priority to tackling social exclusion which it has defined as: 'a shorthand term for what can happen when people or areas suffer from a combination of linked problems such as unemployment, poor skills, low incomes, poor housing, high crime, bad health and family breakdown' (Cabinet Office, 2001). The problems which give rise to social exclusion are regarded as linked and mutually reinforcing and it is recognized that they can combine to create a complex and fast-moving vicious cycle. A major policy concern is that many services are shaped by their histories and organized for the convenience of the provider, not the client (Cabinet Office, 2001). The present government has announced its concern with the development of 'joined up solutions to joined up problems'. Responsive inter-agency work in the emergent professional contexts created by the 'Joined up Working' agenda requires a new way of conceptualizing collaboration which recognizes the construction of constantly changing combinations of people and resources across services, and their distribution over space and time. However, it is clear that difficulties with cross- and inter-agency working persist and that formulation of policy alone may not be enough to effect the required changes in practice. An example of this obdurate problem is given in the Audit Commission (2002) report on processes within the statutory framework for identifying and meeting children's educational needs. Parents were reported as being very unhappy with the way that professionals failed to share information with each other. The report suggests that there is a general consensus that agencies need to work more closely together to meet the needs of young people with special educational needs (SEN), but different spending priorities, boundaries and cultures make this difficult to achieve it in practice (Audit Commission, 2002). They also note that while some Local Authorities have developed 'joined up' assessment arrangements in the early years sector, it appears that such working often declines once a child reaches school age (Audit Commission, 2002).

Collaboration between agencies working for social inclusion also now includes a capacity for collaboration with service users. Powell (1997), for example, in an overview of partnership in the welfare services, suggests that user involvement is more likely to flourish in inter-agency partnerships where the principles and ethics of collaboration have been explored and understood. Without doubt it constitutes a new form of work which will have to be learned. In some cases this may well be a painful form of learning as it will involve the development of new ways of professional being and the creation of what may well come to be known as new knowledge cultures (Knorr Cetina, 1997; 2001) in which understanding and professional expertise are distributed across what are at present highly boundaried agencies.

The Learning in and for Inter-agency Working project (LIW)[1] was concerned with the learning of professionals in the creation of new forms of practice which require joined-up solutions to meet complex and diverse client needs. We studied professional learning in children's services that aim to promote social inclusion through inter-agency working. Working with other professionals involves engaging with many configurations of diverse social practices, different figured worlds. It also requires the development of new forms of hybrid practice. They call for 'joined up' responses from professionals and stress the need for new, qualitatively different forms of multiagency practice, in which providers operate across traditional service and team boundaries. In this context the LIW Project is concerned with examining and supporting the learning of professionals who are engaged in the creation of new forms of multiagency practice most notably a form of work that has been termed co-configuration (Victor and Boynton, 1998). Co-configuration presents a twofold learning challenge to work organizations. First, co-configuration itself needs to be learned (learning for co-configuration). In divided multi-activity fields (e.g. health, education, social services, youth offending teams), learning takes shape as renegotiation and reorganization of collaborative relations and practices, and as creation and implementation of corresponding concepts, tools, rules and entire infrastructures as in the development of children's services. This occurs within and between agencies. Second, organizations and their members need to learn constantly from interactions with the user or client (learning in co-configuration).

Engestrom (1993) has shown that in examples of medical care in Finland, an increasing percentage of patients have multiple chronic illnesses for which standardized, single diagnosis care packages are inadequate. In Helsinki, 3.3% of the patients use 49.3% of all health care expenses, and 15.5% of patients use 78.2% of all resources. A significant portion of these patients are so expensive because they drift from one caregiver to another without anyone having an overview and overall responsibility for their care. Similarly, the Audit Commission (2002) has shown that 68% of SEN expenditure is focused on the 3% of pupils who have formal statements of SEN. While one would expect higher levels of need to attract a greater proportion of available resources, it is argued that the way in which funding is provided may fail to support inclusive practice and often does not result in 'joined up' working. Co-configuration work is a strategic priority because the different practitioners within services and agencies and the service users (students and parents) need to learn to produce well co-ordinated and highly adaptable long-term care and/or education trajectories.

The study demanded an analytic framework which would permit the examination of practitioners' understandings of their work and allow us to trace institutional history and current developments in their practice-oriented communication. Engeström's version of Cultural-Historical Activity Theory (CHAT) informed our initial examination of the institutional implications of collective learning occurring across multi-agency groupings. His elaboration of Vygotsky's notion of 'dual stimulation' was used in this project. A problem and a tool for solving that problem are presented to groups and approaches to problem solution are studied.

Vygotsky was concerned to study human functioning as it developed rather than considering functions that had developed. The essence of his 'dual stimulation' approach is that subjects are placed in a situation in which a problem is identified and they are also provided with tools with which to solve the problem or means by which they can construct tools to solve the problem. The crucial element in a Vygotskian dual stimulation event is the co-occurrence of both the problem and tools with which to engage with that problem.

When applied to the study of professional learning, it directs attention to the ways in which professionals solve problems with the aid of tools that may be provided by researchers. We studied professional learning in workshops which were broadly derived from the Developmental Work Research (DWR) 'Change Laboratory' intervention sessions, developed by Yrjö Engeström and his colleagues in Helsinki (Engeström, 2007) which incorporates a dual stimulation method. In laboratory sessions in the DWR projects the participants were helped to envision and draft proposals for concrete changes to be embarked upon. They discussed and designed interventions which were intended to bring about changes in day-to-day practices and, at times, in the social structures of the workplace. These actions were prompted by reflections on the tensions and dilemmas raised by data. Prior to the workshops, interview and observational data were used as a base from which to select data which mirror embodied tensions, dilemmas and structural contradictions in the practices of each site. In this way critical incidents and examples from the ethnographic material are brought into Change Laboratory sessions to stimulate analysis and negotiation between the participants.

Learning in and for inter-agency work project

Emergent multi-agency working, inter-professional practices and their learning challenges were elicited in a sample of 18 English Local Authorities (LA), in four regional workshops and in 18 individual telephone interviews. The three intervention sites were: a heavily boundaried extended school; a loosely coupled multi-professional grouping working with Children in Public Care; and a newly established area 'Multi-Professional Team' comprising education and social care professionals. One experienced Children's Services professional recruited from each LA joined the team as local researchers. Six DWR sessions at each site took place in 2006 and a seventh in response to an LA request. Prior to each DWR session, interview and observational data were collected from participants. These included everyday accounts of practices as they developed, which were analysed using CHAT concepts (e.g. rules that enabled or frustrated object-oriented collaboration). We collected narrative mini-case studies of challenges to practice that were presented in the sessions by the practitioners concerned. Full details are available in Edwards et al. (2009)

The analysis showed that practitioners were learning about children, other professionals and themselves while developing co-configured practices. Learning arose from contradictions in practices which were not the discrete province of any one profession; but required distributed systems of complementary expertise drawn from across professions. As was reported in Edwards et al. (2009) this lead, among other things, to an enhanced form of practice involving responsive decision-making and informed negotiations with other professionals and clients. It involved articulation of professional expertise when interpreting vulnerability with other professionals and making explicit responses to those interpretations. Professional knowledge was enhanced by working in relation to the priorities of other professions. It also led to the recognition of the rule-bending which occurs when professionals' clearly articulated knowledge confronts inflexible organizational regulations.

These findings and others reported in Edwards et al. (2009) point to the value of intervention which seeks to resolve contradictions that arise across professional boundaries. Whatever the methodology, and it is clear that the DWR approach is expensive, these findings suggest that support for children may need to be designed to impact on the broader figured worlds of professionals and take account of their emergent identities in practice if services for children are to be improved.

Intervention at the cultural level: teachers' collaborative problem solving

A good deal of the psychological intervention conducted in schools in the western world has focused exclusively on individual functioning rather than on the form of collective social activity in which the individual is located. There is clearly a need for such a theoretical orientation given that the training which teachers receive and the organizational structure of schools seem to discourage cultures of professional interaction and knowledge sharing. The reasons for this professional individualism, as Nias points out, 'are also profoundly cultural' (1993, p. 141). Hargreaves (2002) argues that when external accountability pressures mount on schools, as they most certainly have in the UK over the last 20 years, then the culture of the school mediates those pressures in very different ways. Hargreaves understands this move in terms of a shift in the emphasis on regulation by cultures of knowledge and experience to a system of regulation by contracts of performance. He suggests that when a school operates in the absence of a developed collective culture that external pressure can turn permissive individualism into corrosive individualism in which individuals compete and erode each other's status in a bid to comply with demands. He contrasts this move with that which may take place in schools with more highly developed collective cultures. In doing so, he contrasts those cultures which have been imposed, usually by a head teacher, and those which developed in a more 'bottom up' manner. In the imposed form he posits a move from contrived collegiality when there are few external demands and performance training sects which develop when external pressures rise. He contrasts this situation with that of a more democratic cultural development in which collaborative cultures become professional learning communities in response to increased external demands for accountability. The contrast between performance training sects and professional learning communities is discussed in the following terms:

> . . . Professional learning communities lead to strong and measurable improvements in students' learning. Instead of bringing about 'quick fixes' or superficial change, they create and support sustainable improvements that last over time because they build professional skill and the capacity to keep the school progressing. (Hargreaves, 2002, p. 3)

The literature suggests that schools which aim to develop support structures allowing for professional interaction and shared knowledge with fellow teachers are likely to have positive outcomes. This is partly a question of providing teachers with the opportunity to be reflective collaborative practitioners, (Fullan, 2005a and 2005b, 2006; Hargreaves, 2002), or teacher-researchers (Cochran-Smith and Lytle, 1993), but also of allowing the school to reallocate its time and resources as problems are solved in-house.

Teacher collaboration outside of the classroom is less well researched. This has been looked at in the work of Hanko (1989; 1990), Mead (1991), the Newcastle educational psychology service (Stringer et al., 1992) and in our own work (Norwich and Daniels, 1997; Creese, Daniels, Norwich, 1997b). These researchers, although differing in their focus, have developed and evaluated collaborative problem-solving schemes. Study of group peer support systems in the UK and USA show positive results. American research has indicated that Teacher Support Teams (TSTs) can contribute to a drop in the number of inappropriate referrals to outside services and other benefits (Chalfant and Pysh, 1989; Harris, 1995).

A TST is an organized system of peer support which consists of a small group of teachers who take referrals from individual teachers on a voluntary basis. The referring teacher brings concerns about classes, groups or individuals in order to discuss and problem solve with their peers. Follow-up meetings are held as necessary. The process is as confidential as the requesting teacher wants it to be.

TSTs are novel in that they are an example of a school-based development designed to give support and assistance to individual teachers. In this way, TSTs address a significant but neglected area of school development which has the potential to enhance the working conditions of teachers. They involve a sharing of expertise between colleagues, rather than some teachers acting as experts to others. They also provide an opportunity to support students indirectly by supporting teachers. As a form of group problem solving, they have the potential of extending staff's involvement in the development of special educational needs (SEN) policy and practice. They can help focus on the balance between addressing students' individual needs and bringing about change within school systems. TSTs aim to complement existing structures for supporting teachers at work. They do not intend to replace them.

Gerber and Semmel (1985) and Gerber (1988) have developed a theoretical position on the costs to class teachers of extending their range of tolerance, which takes account of the purpose of class teaching, structural constraints and teaching resources. They suggest that in the context of limited resources that tolerance conditions the relation between equity and excellence. There is a vicious circle in which children with SEN can come to threaten a teacher's professional self-evaluation and so receive inappropriate teaching. This process may be reconceptualized in terms of teachers coming to perceive some children as beyond their tolerance and capability. TSTs may act as a way of increasing teacher tolerance.

Creese, Daniels, Norwich (1997a) argued that schools' work with pupils can be understood in terms of the processes of *tolerance* and *active engagement* at institutional and teacher levels. Active engagement and tolerance can be seen as complementary and inter-related processes with active engagement referring to the ways in which teachers and schools include and provide for the diversity of pupils, and tolerance referring to the limits of the challenges within which schools and teachers can operate. Active engagement involves planned attempts to provide quality learning opportunities for children, to include them in the general planning and teaching of all children. It is expressed in both curriculum and behaviour management at a school level, the level and quality of internal and external support, and the differentiation of teaching and class management at teacher level. Tolerance, by contrast, involves enduring the challenges and unresponsiveness of pupils. At a school level, it is expressed through requests for external support, advice or exclusions, willingness to accept pupils with difficulties, satisfaction with special needs policy and practices and complaints to parents and Local Authorities. At a teacher level, it is expressed by attitudes to integration and inclusion, by views about the feasibility and desirability of making classroom and teaching adaptations and by personal teaching priorities. It is indicated by teachers' perceptions of: (1) how well they can cope with the range of teaching challenges; and (2) the teaching demands made by children in their class.

Active engagement and tolerance at a school level provide the context for understanding how a TST might influence the active engagement and tolerance of teachers who request support. Teacher tolerance in this framework is important, as this process has been overlooked in the moves to include more pupils with special needs in mainstream schools. In using the concept of teacher tolerance which was derived from Gerber and Semmel (1985), a number of theoretical assumptions are invoked. First, it is suggested that pupils come to be seen by teachers as varying in their difficulty to teach and manage and that teachers have a range of teaching tolerance for variations in attainment and social behaviour. Beyond the limits of tolerance pupils come to be seen as unresponsive to teaching and can come to lower the teacher's perception of her/his teaching competence and therefore her/his professional self evaluation. This can lead to feelings of insecurity and anxiety which in turn can result in less appropriate teaching and even further unresponsiveness from pupils. By this process teachers come to see certain pupils as beyond her/his teaching tolerance.

What is needed to increase teaching tolerance, given the social psychological, structural, functional and resource conditions, is an organizational strategy to extend and make good use of existing teaching resources. TSTs, by enabling teachers to support each other and share their teaching competence, provide such a strategy to increase the range of teaching tolerance and enhance active engagement in providing quality teaching for pupils with difficulties in making progress.

TSTs may be seen as a form of intervention which seeks to alter the socio-cultural context of schooling through the development of a culture of collaborative peer problem solving. It is thus an intervention which seeks to alter the context in order to enhance collective thinking. Teachers are, as Stringer (1998) suggests, 'seen as the target and agent of change'.

There is *a* theoretical position which has more than a passing resonance with the TST development process. Engeström defines the zone of proximal development as the 'distance between the everyday actions of individuals and the historically new form of the societal activity that can be collectively generated' (1997, p. 174). Under such societal interpretations of the concept of the zone of proximal development researchers tend to concentrate on processes of social transformation. This involves the study of learning beyond the context of pedagogical structuring, including the structure of the social world in the analysis, and 'taking into account in a central way the conflictual nature of social practice' (Lave and Wenger, 1991, p. 49).

TSTs seek to alter the communicative practices of teachers in schools. They engage with the tensions, dilemmas and even conflicts which teachers experience in the social worlds of the schools they inhabit. We know from our own work on TSTs that teachers come to value and enjoy collaboration with their peers in team settings. The overly cognitive interpretation of much of Vygotsky's work should not detract from affective and regulative considerations. Recent contributions have drawn attention to the need to develop a model of social formation of mind that extends beyond constraints of the cognitive domain.

> '. . . educationally significant human interactions do not involve abstract bearers of cognitive structures but real people who develop a variety of interpersonal relationships with one another in the course of their shared activity in a given institutional context. . . . modes of thinking evolve as integral systems of motives, goals, values, and beliefs that are closely tied to concrete forms of social practice. (Minick et al., 1993, p. 6)

Minick et al. argue that the concept of the ZPD should be redefined from a broader social and cultural perspective. Taken together, the positions established by del Rio and Alvarez (1995) along with that of Minick et al. point towards the need for more inclusive and coherent concept of development. Inclusive in that it should seek to take account of cognitive and affective domains. Coherent in that it should handle these domains as highly inter-related and/or embedded matters. The outcomes of our work on TSTs suggest that such theoretical development is necessary. The changes TSTs bring about lie in both cognitive and affective outcomes.

In order to try and discuss innovation and improvement of specific forms of multi-professional activity, Engestrom, Brown, Christopher and Gregory (1997) develop a three- level notion of the developmental forms of epistemological subject-object-subject relations within a Vygotskian framework. They call these three levels 'co-ordination, co-operation and communication'. Within the general structure of coordination actors follow their scripted roles pursuing different goals (see Figure 8.1).

Within the general structure of co-operation actors focus on a shared problem. Within the confines of a script the actors attempt to both conceptualize and solve problems in ways which are negotiated and agreed. (see Figure 8.1). The script itself is not questioned, that is the tacitly assumed traditions and/or the given official rules of engagement with the problem are not challenged.

Eraut (1994) drew an important distinction between reflection 'in action' and reflection 'on action'. While reflection in action may well occur in co-operative and co-ordinated systems, reflection on action is more difficult to attain. Engestrom et al. (1997, p. 373) discuss reflective communication 'in which the actors focus on reconceptualising their own organisation and interaction in relation to their shared objects and goals (see Figure 8.1). This is reflection on action. Both the object and the script are reconceptualised, as is the interaction between the participants.'

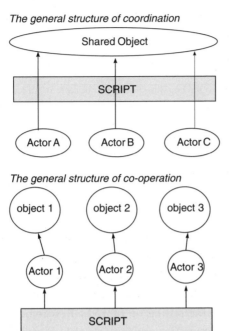

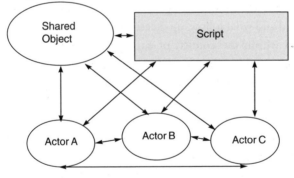

Figure 8.1 The general structures of coordination, co-operation and communication

Teacher support system projects

TSTs were originally conceived of as a system of support from a team of peers for class teachers experiencing teaching difficulties in relation to SEN. The model was that individual teachers request support on a voluntary basis from a team which usually includes the SEN coordinator, a senior teacher and another class teacher. The team along with the referring teacher collaborate in order to understand the problem(s) and design appropriate forms of intervention related to learning and behaviour difficulties.

> From a Vygotskian perspective, these mediating communicative patterns constitute tools for action and cognition. Though each participant in a discursive field need not think alike – indeed the discursive activities of disciplines largely rely on people not thinking precisely alike – each must draw on a common body of resources, cope with the same body of material and symbolic artifacts, master the same tools, and gain legitimacy for any new resources they want to bring into the field by addressing the same mechanisms of evaluation by which new concepts, tools, or phenomena gain standing in the discourse. (Bazerman 1997, p. 305)

Research about the outcomes of teacher peer support in the schools studied is encouraging. Two studies, a pilot project in three primary schools (Daniels and Norwich, 1992) and an Economic and Social Research Council project in a further eight primary schools (Norwich and Daniels, 1994) looked at the processes and outcomes of the setting up of TSTs. Researchers and schools collaborated to evaluate the operation and impacts of TSTs at the schools. This involved collecting information about the frequency of the meetings, the number of requests, the nature of the concerns expressed, what action was recommended and what follow-up meetings were organized. This information was analysed within the context of each particular schools with a view to understanding how a school's culture can contribute to supporting new schemes and how new schemes can contribute to a school's need to deal with and shape change.

In the primary school projects mentioned above (Daniels and Norwich, 1992; and Norwich and Daniels, 1994), the outcomes of the TST's work were positive. Both teachers who were members of the team and teachers who referred to the team for help reported that they felt their professional development was enhanced through the discussion and acquisition of strategies – either new, forgotten or not previously used – to deal with situations personal to them at that particular moment in time.

These included:

strategies for collaborating with other staff
this involved the direct involvement of the SEN coordinator or a TST member covering for a teacher

strategies for the teacher to use in-class

examples included the use of conduct charts, contracts and report books, the development of individual programmes and class management changes, such as use of group work and seating rearrangements.

strategies for lunchtime

for example, play materials were made available to some pupils to encourage more constructive play.

parental involvement

arranging specific meetings with parents and reaching agreement for parent to help-their children in specific ways at home (see also Chapter 4 by Charlotte Højholt for more on the involvement of parents).

communication with external support services

this involved writing to educational psychologists about statutory assessment or about bringing forward the date for the Statement review.

The TST members were themselves very positive about the value of their TST work for themselves as teachers. All were keen to continue as members. For the SEN coordinator in particular, TSTs were seen as positively affecting their work by promoting linking across the schools and preventing isolation.

Overall, it was found that there were fewer requests in relation to girls than boys, and to older than younger children. At the end of a two-term period, only a small proportion of the requests dealt with were judged as closed, in the sense that improvement was sufficient to merit the withdrawal of support. However, there was some improvement in about two-thirds of the requests overall, as judged by the TSTs. In all schools, the requesting teachers were mostly positive about the value for themselves of going to the team. The headteachers corroborated these views. Requesting teachers' perceptions of the nature of the support offered by the TSTs can be grouped under the following themes:

- enabled them to distance themselves from problems and re-examine their activities;
- enabled problems to be aired,
- enabled them to form their own strategies,
- enabled an opportunity to let off steam legitimately and that it was cathartic to talk to sympathetic colleagues with a non-judgemental attitude,
- enabled them to confirm approaches already being used,

- enabled an opportunity to discuss school policy which could then be raised at staff meetings.

In particular, the study showed how the TST supported teachers' perceptions of the difficulty of a situation. A validation of the teachers' perceptions led to an enhancement in the utility of their own intervention strategies, which were reaffirmed (Norwich et al., 1994).

Meadows (1998, p. 7) argued that "'collaboration with others . . . may make things achievable which were not and – indeed still are not – achievable by the individual acting alone". There can of course be many reasons for this social facilitation of development.' Our evaluation of TSTs reveals a range of outcomes associated with collaboration between teacher peers. As such it can be seen to provide support for some of the more recent developments in post-Vygotskian theory. Intervention in the cultural context of the institution which seeks to alter teachers communicative practices can make a difference to the instructional practices in classrooms. Collaborative problem solving between teachers can provide an engine for development in schools.

Conclusion

In this chapter interventions in the culture of education have been thought of as part of the way in which interventions can engage with the dissatisfaction and unhappiness experienced by pupils with additional needs. Such interventions have been discussed at the levels of staff relations and inter-agency working. These are interventions which involve changes in the division of labour within and between institutions. The focus has been on the development of collaborative working cultures. The argument has been that we need to extend the move that others have made to go beyond a focus on pathology or small-scale interaction in the identification of points for intervention in systems of schooling. From the standpoint of a view of culture as an ensemble of artefacts that is created and enacted or 'woven together' in the activities that constitute the practices of schooling it has been suggested that intervention that seeks to transform the division of labour within and between schools is of great potential value. More work needs to be done to understand the ways in which collaborative working provides tools for engaging with the demands of schooling. The suggestion is that as well-being and trust are built in collaborative working cultures then individuals feel more tolerant of the demands of work and more prepared to engage with problematic areas of work that lie outside narrowly defined targets. For many years it has been recognized that children who become marginal in welfare systems, such as those with Social, Emotional and Behavioural Difficulties (SEBD in England), need and deserve high-quality inter-agency service formulation and delivery. They are rarely in receipt of such services despite recurrent exhortations to 'join up'. Progress will be made if the position adopted is that these new ways of working need to be learned and that at present we do not know exactly what it is that must be learned. The culture of welfare work itself is in need of transformation. The weaving together of life experiences, attitudes, values and dispositions of pupils with the professional cultures and respective practices of teachers and others working in children's services will co-create very different possibilities and prognoses. In summary, it is suggested that different professional cultures will predispose the co-creation of different classroom cultures. One way to improve the possibilities and prognoses for pupils, who have the potential to become seen as having SEBD and other difficulties, is to intervene at the level of the cultures of professional collaboration and problem-solving within the school and beyond.

There are new support roles in this emergent world of child-welfare work. To fulfil these new roles professionals need new 'tools of their trade'. Arguably these new tools are to be found in the socio-cultural and cultural-historical traditions.

Note

1. TLRP-ESRC study ESRC RES-139-25-0100 'Learning in and for Interagency Working' was co-directed by Harry Daniels and Anne Edwards. The research team included Paul Warmington, Deirdre Martin,, Jane Leadbetter, David. Middleton, Steve Brown, Anna Popova, Apostol Apostolov, Penny Smith, Ioanna Kinti, Mariann Martsin, and Sarah Parsons.

References

Abreu, G. and Elbers, E. (2005). The Social Mediation of Learning in Multiethnic Schools: Introduction. *European Journal of Psychology of Education*, 20(1), 3–11.

Audit Commission (2002). *Statements and Assessments of SEN: In Need of a Review* (London, Audit Commission).

Bazerman, C. (1997). Discursively Structured Activities. *Mind Culture and Activity*. 4(4) 296–308.

Bernstein, B. (2000). *Pedagogy, Symbolic Control And Identity: Theory Research Critique* (Revised Edition), Oxford: Rowman and Littlefield.

Cabinet Office (2001). Preventing Social Exclusion. Available Online at: Http://Www Cabinet-Office. Gov.Uk/Seu/Publications/Reports/Html/Pse/Pse_Html/01.Htm. Last accessed March 2010.

Chalfant, J. C. and Pysh, M. (1989). Teacher Assistance Teams: Five Descriptive Studies on 96 Teams. *Remedial and Special Education,* 10(6), 49–58.

Cochran-Smith, M. and Lytle, S. L. (1993). *Inside Outside: Teacher Research and Knowledge.* New York: Teachers College, Columbia University.

Cole, M. (1996). *Cultural Psychology: A Once and Future Discipline.* Cambridge Mass: The Belknap Press of Harvard University.

Creese, A., Daniels H. and Norwich B. (1997a). *Teacher Support Team In Secondary Schools.* DfEE Report. London: DFEE.

—(1997b). *Teacher Support Teams in Primary and Secondary Schools.* London: Fulton.

Daniels, H. and Norwich, B. (1992). *Teacher Support Teams: An Interim Evaluation Report,* Institute Of Education, London University.

Del Rio, P. and Alvarez, A. (1995). Directivity: The Cultural and Educational Constructions of Morality and Agency. *Anthropology and Education Quarterly,* 26(4), 384–409.

Edwards, A., Daniels, H., Gallagher, T., Leadbetter, J. and Warmington (2009). *Improving Inter-professional Collaborations: Multi-Agency working for Children's Well Being.* Oxford: Routledge.

Engestrom, Y. (1993). 'Developmental Studies of Work as a Testbench of Activity Theory: The Case of Primary Care Medical Practice', in S. Chaiklin and J. Lave (eds) *Understanding Practice Perspectives on Activity and Practice.* Cambridge: Cambridge University Press, pp. 64–103.

—(2007). 'Putting Activity Theory to Work: The Change Laboratory as an Application of Double Stimulation', in H. Daniels, M. Cole and J. V. Wertsch (eds) *The Cambridge Companion to Vygotsky,* New York: Cambridge University Press, pp. 363–382.

Engestrom, Y., Brown, K., Christopher, L. C. and Gregory, J. (1997). 'Co-ordination, Co-Operation and Communication in the Courts: Expansive Transitions', in Legal Work in Cole, M. C., Engestom, Y., Vasquez, Olga (eds). *Mind, Culture and Activity: Seminal Papers from the Laboratory of Comparative Human Cognition.* Cambridge University Press: Cambridge, pp. 182–201.

Eraut, M. (1994). *Developing Professional Knowledge and Competence.* London: The Farmer Press.

Fullan, M. (2005a). Leadership and Sustainability: Systems Thinkers in Action. San Francisco: Corwin.

—(2005b). Professional Learning Communities Writ Large in R. DuFour, R. Eaker and R. DuFour (eds), On Common Ground: The Power of Professional Learning Communities. Bloomington, IN: National Educational Service, pp. 209–223.

—(2006). The Future of Educational Change: System Thinkers in Action. *Journal of Educational Change,* 7, 113–122.

Gerber M. M. (1988). Tolerance and Technology of Instruction: Implication for Special Education Reform. *Exceptional Children,* 54(4), 309–314.

Gerber M. M. and Semmel M. I. (1985). The Micro-Economics of Referral and Re-Integration: A Paradigm for Evaluation of Special Education. *Studies in Educational. Evaluation,* 11, 13–29.

Hanko, G. (1989). After Elton – How to Manage Disruption, *British. Journal of. Special Education.* 16(4), 140–143.

—(1990). *Special Needs in Ordinary Classrooms, Supporting Teachers* Hemel Hempstead: Simon & Schuster Education.

Hargreaves, A. (2002). 'Professional Learning Communities and Performance Training Cults: The Emerging Apartheid of School Improvement', in A. Harris, C. Day, M. Hadfield, D. Hopkins, A. Hargreaves and Chapman, C. (eds) *Effective Leadership for School Improvement.* London: Routledge, pp. 68–87.

Harris, K. (1995). School-Based Bilingual Special Education Teacher Assistance Teams. *Remedial and Special Education,* 16(6), 337–343.

Hedegaard, M. (2001). 'Learning through Acting within Societal Traditions: Learning in Classrooms', in M. Hedegaard (ed.) *Learning in Classrooms: A Cultural Historical Approach* Aarhus: Aarhus University Press, pp. 21–43.

Knorr Cetina, K. (1997). Sociality with Objects. Social Relations in Post-Social Knowledge Societies, *Theory, Culture & Society,* 14(4), 1–25.

—(2001). 'Objectual Practice', in T. R. Schatzki, K. Knorr Cetina and E. Von Savigny (eds) *The Practice Turn In Contemporary Theory.* London: Routledge. pp. 76–89.

Lave, J. And Wenger, E. (1991). Practice, Person And Social World, Chapter 2 in *Situated Learning: Legitimate Peripheral Participation,* Cambridge, Cambridge University Press.

Mead, C. (1991). *A City-Wide Evaluation Of Psg Training.* Birmingham: Birmingham Local Education Authority.

Meadows, S. (1998). Children Learning to Think: Learning from Others? Vygotskian Theory and Educational Psychology. *Educational and Child Psychology,* 15(2), 6–13.

Minick, N. (1987). 'The Development of Vygotsky's Thought: An Introduction', in R. W. Rieber and A. S. Carton (eds) *The Collected Works of L.S. Vygotsky, 1,* New York: Plenum Press, pp. 17–38.

Minick, N., Stone, C. A. and Forman, E. A. (1993). 'Introduction: Integration of Individual, Social and Institutional Processes in Accounts of Children's Learning and Development', in E. A. Forman, N. Minick and C. A. Stone (eds) *Contexts for Learning: Sociocultural Dynamics in Children's Development.* Oxford: *Oxford University* Press, pp. 1–22.

Nias, J. (1993). 'Changing Times, Changing Identities: Grieving for a Lost Self', in Burgess, R (ed) *Educational Research and Evaluation for Policy and Practice.* London: Falmer Press, pp. 24–45.

Norwich, B. and Daniels, H. (1994). *Evaluating Teacher Support Teams: A Strategy for Special Needs in Ordinary Schools.* Final Report to ESRC. Award Number R-000-23-3859 (Unpublished).

—(1997). Teacher Support Teams for Special Educational Needs in Primary Schools: Evaluating A Teacher-Focused Support Scheme, *Educational Studies,* 23, 5–24.

Powell, R. (1997). Understanding Partnership: Agency Collaboration and the Service User, in A. Pithouse and H. Williamson (eds) *Engaging the User in Welfare Services.* Birmingham: Venture Press.

Ratner, C. (1997). *Cultural Psychology and Qualitative Methodology. Theoretical and Empirical Considerations.* London: Plenum Press.

Stringer, P. (1998). One Night Vygotsky had a Dream: 'Children Learning To Think' and Implications for Educational Psychologists. *Educational and Child Psychology,* 15,(2), 14–20.

Stringer, P., Stow, L., Hibbert, K., Powell, J. and Louw, E. (1992). Establishing Staff Consultation Groups in Schools. *Educational Psychology in Practice,* 8(2), 87–96.

Victor, B. and Boynton, A. (1998). *Invented Here: Maximizing Your Organization's Internal Growth and Profitability*, Boston: Harvard Business School Press.

Vygotsky, L. S. (1978). *Mind in Society: The Development of Higher Psychological Processes.* Cambridge, MA: Harvard University Press.

Wertsch, J. V. (1998). *Mind as Action*, New York: Oxford University Press.

—(2007). 'Mediation' in H. Daniels, M. Cole and J. V. Wertsch (eds) *The Cambridge Companion To Vygotsky*, New York: Cambridge University Press.

Wertsch, J. V. and Rupert, L. J. (1993). The Authority of Cultural Tools in a Sociocultural Approach to Mediated Agency, Cognition and Instruction, 11(3–4), 227–239.

Relational Agency in Collaborations for the Well-Being of Children and Young People

9

Anne Edwards

Evolving concepts: social exclusion and prevention

In this chapter I work with the legacies of Vygotsky and Leont'ev and their development in particular by Engeström and by Wertsch to examine their implications for the professionals who support children. The ideas I offer have been refined in three research studies which have examined how practitioners, such as social workers, educational psychologists, teachers and voluntary sector workers, collaborate to support vulnerable children and young people. The three studies are the National Evaluation of the Children's Fund[1] (NECF) (Edwards, Barnes, Plewis and Morris et al., 2006) which was large scale,

40-month evaluation of the Children's Fund; Learning in and for Interagency Working[2] (LIW) (Edwards, Daniels, Gallagher, Leadbetter and Warmington, 2009), a four year study of professional learning in inter-professional work funded by the UK's Economic and Social Research Council (ESRC); and a 16-month examination of the impact of preventing social exclusion on schools[3] (PSE) (Edwards, Lunt and Stamou, 2010), also funded by the ESRC. All three studies have examined how practitioners from different backgrounds have learned to do something new: collaborate to reconfigure the life trajectories of children and young people who were at risk of not being able to take advantage of what society might offer them.

The ideas developed in this chapter include an account of local systems of support for children as systems of distributed specialist expertise that can be mobilized to strengthen children and young people. This account of expertise requires a focus on the relational aspects of professional practice, as workers need to be able to recognize the expertise of others, be able to work with it and in turn make their specialist knowledge available to others. I therefore use the idea of relational agency (Edwards 2005) to describe what arises when practitioners work purposefully together on a complex activity such as the reconfiguring of a child's trajectory, and explain the need for the opportunity to build some common understandings before the negotiations so necessary for relational agency can take place.

The ideas have all been developed in the context of studying the complex demands that have been made on practitioners who are involved in preventing social exclusion. The concept originated during the 1990s because of serious concerns about the fragility of society. As Room explained at the time:

> Social exclusion is the process of becoming detached from the organizations and communities of which the society is composed and from the rights and responsibilities that they embody. (Room, 1995, p. 243)

The shift, from seeing vulnerable children in terms of their being disadvantaged to being 'at risk' of being excluded from what society both offers and requires was future-oriented and allowed the State to think about how it might prevent the exclusion of children from what binds society together. The 'prevention of social exclusion' therefore emerged as a new core concept in welfare services in England in the late 1990s (Little, Axford and Morpeth, 2004).

The prevention of social exclusion demanded early intervention not only in the early years of life, but also at the initial signs of vulnerability. In England the influential report of Policy Action Team 12 argued that children and young people can become vulnerable at different stages of their lives through changes in their life circumstances and that early intervention needs to include acting at the early signs of vulnerability, regardless of age, to prevent ultimate social exclusion (Home Office, 2000).

Vulnerability of this kind therefore may not be evident unless one looks across all aspects of a child's life: parenting, schooling, housing and so on. There are two important ideas for professional practice here. First, social exclusion should be seen as a dynamic process and not a static condition (Walker, 1995). The dynamic is the outcome of interactions of effects across different domains of a child's life and therefore can be disrupted if the responses to it are also multi-dimensional. That means that practitioners, working together, can make a difference. Second, because vulnerability may not be evident until a picture of accumulated difficultly is picked up by looking across a child's life, all services which work with children need to be brought into the process of preventing it. These expectations have called for new forms of inter-professional work: new ways of looking at children with other professionals and new ways of responding to the picture of the child that emerges. I'm going to focus on prevention as that is where I've worked. However, the arguments I'll put forward I think also apply to high-end child-protection work where inter-professional collaboration is called for.

The implications of preventative work for practitioners

The need for practitioners to be able to understand the totality of a child's life circumstances has led to attempts at major reconfigurations of children's services in England through the Children Act (DfES, 2004). We have seen, for example, the merging of education and social care services under single directorates in English local authorities; the development of Children's Trusts to take forward service commissioning across agencies; and reorganization in central government to produce, in 2007, the Department for Children, Schools and Families (DCSF). These developments have the potential to produce the infrastructural conditions for inter-professional work, but they represent a massive shift. The development of Children's Trusts, for example, has been slow (Audit Commission, 2008).

A whole-system approach marks a considerable change for services which are used to working to their own professional standards on their own professional goals. In the LIW study we focused on the changes in practice identified by the practitioners as they began to work across organizational boundaries with other professionals.

LIW, like the other two studies, drew heavily on the Helsinki version of activity theory (Engeström, 1999; 2007), which allows an examination of relationships between changing practices and the systems in which practices are organized and sustained. Of particular relevance to the discussion in this paper is the idea of 'object of activity' as the problem space or task which is being worked on in these practices. In all three studies we attempted to identify what practitioners saw as the problem they were tackling in their work with children, what it was they were working on and trying to change. One might expect that in preventative work it would be a child's trajectory towards potential social exclusion which they were working on to disrupt and reconfigure. However, sometimes something else needed to be worked on first. It might, for example, be necessary to work on the barriers between practitioners to erode them, before they could tackle children's trajectories together. More details on the methodology can be found in Edwards et al. (2009).

As practitioners discussed what it was they were trying to do with children and families, they revealed the ideas they were using as they took forward collaborations. What practitioners needed to know and be able to do, in addition to their core expertise, fell into two sets of activity: changes in practices and changes in organizations.

Changes in practices

(a) *Focusing on the whole child in the wider context.* This was crucial to (i) recognizing vulnerability by building a picture of accumulated risk and (ii) orchestrating responses focused on children's well-being.

(b) *Clarifying the purpose of work and being open to alternatives.* Talking with other professionals about the purposes and implications, i.e. the 'why' and 'where to', of possible actions with children eroded inter-professional barriers by revealing common long-term values and purposes.

(c) *Understanding oneself and one's professional values.* Articulating their own expertise and values in order to negotiate practices with other professionals helped practitioners understand them better. Practices were enhanced by examining how practices which were driven by values such as children's well-being might be reconfigured in relation to other professionals and their purposes.

(d) *Knowing how to know who.* Knowing the people and resources distributed across local networks was an important capacity but was not enough. Knowing how to access and contribute to systems of locally distributed expertise by informing interpretations and aligning responses with others was crucial to successful inter-professional work.

(e) *Taking a pedagogic stance at work.* This involved: (i) making one's own professional expertise explicit and accessible by, for example, giving examples of what they do and why it matters and (ii) being professionally multi-lingual i.e. having a working knowledge of what mattered for other professions in order to 'press the right buttons' when working with them.

(f) *Being responsive to others: both professionals and clients.* Professionals demonstrated a growing awareness of the need to work relationally with each other and moved towards working more responsively with the strengths of their clients to build their resilience.

Changes in organizations arising from changing practices

(a) *Rule-bending and risk-taking.* Practitioners described taking risks involving rule-bending to pursue the well-being of children. Rule-bending, such as working directly with other agencies rather than keeping to line management systems, was a response to contradictions between emergent practices and the established systems of rules, protocols and lines of responsibility in their home organizations.

(b) *Creating and developing better tools for collaboration.* It was important for practitioners from all potentially collaborating services to be involved in developing new assessment tools so that the purposes of their services could be included and the assessments could be seen to be of value across services.

(c) *Developing processes for knowledge sharing and pathways for practice.* Another important tool for collaboration was the opportunity to discuss cases and, in those discussions, reveal and learn about the expertise available locally. These discussions helped practitioners develop an outward-looking stance and openness to collaboration as well as learning about other expertise available.

(d) *Learning from practice.* Lack of organizational adjustment, such as not adjusting line-management and supervision arrangements to reflect new demands arising from changing practices, was a major source of frustration for practitioners, leading some to identify the need to communicate with strategists in their organizations as a new skill to be learnt.

In summary, a strong message from the LIW study is that inter-professional practice is an enhanced form of practice which requires strong understanding of one's core expertise and also an additional layer of expertise which involves:

(i) responsive decision-making and informed negotiations with other professionals and clients;

(ii) articulation of professional expertise when interpreting vulnerability with other professionals and making explicit one's responses to those interpretations; and

(iii) enriched professional knowledge from working in relation to the priorities of other professions.

However, that list of professional attributes should not underplay some of the problems involved in inter-professional collaborations. Some are personally experienced. Jack has observed that professional identity for social workers is usually associated with the capacity to work with children in the greatest need (Jack, 2006), whereas preventative work removes them from that more high-status activity. There were several examples in the LIW study of people being reprimanded for 'going native' i.e. returning to their home organizations with new perspectives as a result of working preventatively with other agencies.

When we looked at systemic change, for example how social work services and schools dealt with the flexibility required for fluid inter-professional work, we found a major difficulty: the difference in time-scales between practice and strategy in services. This is a common problem when new practices are being developed (Schulz, 2003). In our study, practitioners, who were following children's trajectories and working out how to orchestrate their responses, were often sharply aware of the organizational implications of inter-professional work (hence the rule-bending); while the organizational conditions to support practices were frequently lagging behind the practices in their development in, for example, line management systems that did not reflect the need for responsive work with other practitioners. Mørch, Nygaard and Ludvigsen (2009) have described these disjunctures as differences between the time scales for adjustment and for generalization. The problems that arose for practitioners because organizational strategy was not keeping pace with constantly adjusting practice, suggested the need for systemic approaches to change to include time for systemic learning, what we called upstream learning. Time is needed for strategy to learn seriously from practice, and for the development of general strategies which are informed by the learning that is occurring in practice as practitioners develop new ways of working.

Expertise for child-centred practices

In LIW we conceptualized inter-professional preventative work as the fluid and responsive disrupting of children's developmental trajectories to, with children and their families, redirect their trajectories towards social inclusion. In activity theory terms, the child's wellbeing is the desired long-term value-laden goal, while the trajectory is the object of activity, which is worked on to change it so it may eventually achieve the more distant goal. That work involves practitioners in expanding their understanding of a child's trajectory by expanding their understandings of the child's life: their strengths, needs and so on. The idea of a trajectory was regarded as useful by practitioners because:

(i) It reflected an approach to preventative work which involved practitioners in following the trajectory of each child, often leading them to question the category systems of their home organizations.
(ii) It helped practitioners from different services to recognize that they shared the long-term goal of children's well-being which was based in sets of professional values which over-lapped.

Let us consider what is involved in negotiating collaborations around a child's trajectory. My own work (Edwards, 2005; 2010) suggests that expertise in the negotiated accomplishment of complex tasks calls for professionals to become adept at recognizing and working with:

(i) the professional resources that other practitioners bring to bear when interpreting a problem of practice; and
(ii) the resources that these practitioners use when responding to those interpretations.

These resources can, of course, be material artefacts, but they are also likely to be the specialist concepts and insights which are specific to different professional practices and cultures. However, almost invariably these concepts and insights are embedded within their practices and carried implicitly in how they construct the categories, or ways of thinking about clients, that shape their work. Makitälo and Säljö (2002), for example, demonstrated how work with clients in an employment exchange in Sweden was shaped by the institutional categories that were revealed in how practitioners talked about their work processes. The category system in use in the talk in that study served a number of functions, including shaping the provision of financial and other kinds of assistance to the unemployed and the use and production of the statistical information that informed the practices in the employment exchange.

In the LIW study we developed the concept of distributed expertise to capture how both particular ways of categorizing clients and material resources are spread across localities. Two elements are central to the idea of distributed expertise:

(i) cultural tools, whether they are material, for example an assessment system; or conceptual, such as specialist knowledge about autism, are loaded with intelligence, which can turbo-charge or strengthen the purposeful actions of practitioners; and

(ii) expertise may be distributed across a neighbourhood or local authority with practitioners contributing to it, drawing on it and engaging with it.

Decentering individual expertise in this way, as we shall see, requires additional personal expertise: the capacity to recognize and work with the resources that others can offer.

The LIW focus on expertise as distributed is in line with standard socio-cultural analyses of work systems, which see intelligence or knowledge as resources which are distributed across people and embedded in practices, and which are accessed by participants to enhance their actions. Bruner, for example, has talked about the 'extended intelligence' of research labs (Bruner, 1996); and Hakkarainen and his colleagues (Hakkarainen, Palonen, Paavola, and Lehtinen, 2004) have developed an extensive body of research on how knowledge is distributed across networks. What the LIW account adds, through working with welfare professionals, is an emphasis on longer-term value laden goals that give coherence to sets of distributed actions.

The idea of distributed expertise builds on Engeström and Middleton's description of expertise (Engeström and Middleton, 1996, p. 4) as the 'collaborative and discursive construction of tasks, solutions, visions, breakdowns and innovations' within and across systems rather than individual mastery of specific areas of relatively stable activity. Their line is particularly relevant to a study of new practices arising in response to new policies for work with children. It suggests that professional knowledge is not a stable body of knowledge simply to be acquired through participation in accepted practices. Rather, it can be reconstructed in an ongoing dynamic which takes into account historic values as well as new problems to be worked on. Expertise, in this definition, involves the capacity to learn and act on and transform the problems of practice with others.

Distributed expertise recognizes that expertise can involve a strong individually held knowledge-base and experience in interpreting and acting in specific situations. It augments that understanding by incorporating Engeström and Middleton's attention to the systemic conditions in which it is brought into play and by highlighting the need to attend to the processes of negotiating expertise in complex work situations which may be shaped by multiple motives. Consequently, access to the meaning-making and motives of other professional groups is crucial. Without access to the categorization, values and motives embedded in practices, negotiations to reconfigure a child's trajectory are likely to become formulaic rather than responsive and fluid.

Negotiating expertise

I am convinced that the expertise necessary for responsive work on complex tasks, like a child's trajectory, cannot be negotiated without some prior work. NECF alerted us to the importance of sustained inter-professional meetings which acted as spring-boards for later fluid and responsive working based on mutual trust. Our detailed analyses of inter-professional discussions in LIW revealed that inter-professional discussions of current and possible practices revealed the expertise that others had to offer and how they represented it: i.e. their professional categories. The later PSE study again showed us how practitioners found inter-professional meetings to be important. Time and again, echoing the NECF practitioners, PSE interviewees said that these meetings revealed to them new possibilities for collaboration which they knew would inform their practices: the attribute that began to develop in those meetings was, as in the LIW study, 'knowing how to know who' (Edwards et al., 2009).

Let us examine briefly what was happening in the inter-professional meetings that were part of the LIW study. In the analysis we focused on what Wertsch (2007) has described as the implicit mediation that occurs in everyday talk. The argument is that by revealing how we categorize the world we inhabit, we reveal how we think about it. By focusing on categorizations we were not attempting to get at tacit knowledge. The distinction between, on the one hand, the tacit knowledge that underpins professional action and, on the other hand, the implicit categorizations, values and motives that are mediated in inter-professional talk is important when thinking about developing inter-professional work. The latter usefully offer a window onto the former, but I suggest that inter-professional work does not require practitioners get to grips with the kinds of tacitly held understandings of other expert practitioners that have been discussed, for example, by Collins (2004) in his reflections on how one can get a close understanding of the work of others.

The practitioners we studied were not moving towards a form of hybrid practice that required them to do the carefully responsive work of other experts; rather they were developing the capacity to work with the expertise that others offered. Here our view is in line with Collins' notion of 'interactional expertise', where people are able to converse expertly about a practical skill without being able to practise it. To paraphrase Collins' argument it seems that interactional expertise captures what can occur when people talk together about practices which are cognate to and relevant to theirs, but are not practices they perform. The challenge for participants in LIW was to engage in a form of communication that revealed the complexity of the objects of activities in their practices and the motives they encapsulated.

Castletown, one of the case study sites in LIW, centred on a community school where school-based participants' contributions to inter-professional meetings focused on strengthening a tight boundary around the school that excluded the categorizations and meaning systems of other services and enabled the school to maintain established within-school social practices. At the same time, the other services that worked with children who attended the school were beginning to see themselves as elements in a system of distributed expertise which enabled them to look across the lives of vulnerable children; identify the complex components of risk of social exclusion; and work together to disrupt the children's high-risk life trajectories.

Practitioners' attempts at both defending the school boundary and disrupting it occurred through stories told in our activity theory-structured sessions which all attended. These stories carried in them the categorizations and values of the different professions. The official voice of the school offered frequent tales of horror and heroism (Orr, 1996) which offered a rationale for the boundary, as this extract from a senior member of the school staff (Carol) illustrates.

> Carol: Well the context is that if a child comes to school and they have come from a dreadful home situation where there is terrible violent crime and abuse and parenting is poor or non-existent because of addiction problems and so on and so forth and the kid hasn't had much . . . can't read or write to any standard that would allow him to access the curriculum . . . it can be awful out there, but you don't have to fail in school because we have got this for you, that person is there for you, if this happens you can do that. And I think it's a sanctuary.

Clive, an educational psychologist who was trying to take forward interprofessional work in the local authority, used the sessions as an opportunity to make visible the need for change by identifying the contradictions in the school and between the school and other services. At the same time, however, his language revealed the categorizations such as effects, targets and boundaries that made sense for him as an educational psychologist trained in systems theory. The following extract follows immediately after Carol's claim that the school was a sanctuary.

> Clive: It's interesting it makes me think of boundaries again. There is a sense in which although the child is the same child outside and inside we sort of feel we can almost draw a boundary around the school and say when you are in here you can leave it at the gates or we can minimize the effects yeah . . . I think we set ourselves a target which is almost unachievable, unattainable in the sense. Um and perhaps the way in which schools with others need to be bridging that boundary differently.

These conversations are important pre-requisites for a system of distributed expertise which enables fluid and responsive object-oriented work. Importantly they reveal professional motives and values and allow practitioners to see that they do actually share common values. The exchange between Carol and Clive developed to provide the opportunity for one of the teachers to echo the values and priorities of the educational psychologist, to begin to distance herself from the school's categories and to reposition herself as a potential collaborator (Edwards and Kinti, 2010). Recognizing the meaning systems and categorizations of other practitioners is, I suggest, a crucial pre-requisite to fluid and responsive work on children's trajectories.

All three research studies suggest that there is a three stage process of preparation prior to relational engagement in action.

(i) Recognizing similar long-term open goals, such as children's well-being, which give broad coherence to the specialist activities of practitioners

(ii) Revealing categories, values and motives in the natural language of talk about problems of practice.

(iii) Recognizing and engaging with the categories, values and motives of others in the processes of negotiating action on a complex object.

In Edwards' *Being an expert professional practitioner* (2010) I have discussed this process as building common knowledge at sites where different practices intersect. There I have argued that the common knowledge that is built in discussions that reveal what matters for each profession, mediates the interactions between practitioners when they need to act quickly to wrap support around a child or to orchestrate the refiguring of a life trajectory. These object-oriented intentional interactions in the field give rise to the core concept in this chapter: relational agency.

Relational agency

Relational agency (Edwards, 2005, 2009, 2010; Edwards and Mackenzie, 2005) can arise in purposeful responses to complex problems where more than one practitioner is involved and the resources of each are brought into play. The exercise of relational agency can be seen as a two stage process within a constant dynamic, which involves:

(i) working with others to expand the 'object of activity', or task being working on, by recognizing the motives and the resources that others bring to bear as they too interpret it; and

(ii) aligning one's own responses to the newly enhanced interpretations, with the responses being made by the other professionals to act on the expanded object.

I have suggested that because relational agency arises when working alongside others, it may strengthen the work of practitioners who can feel vulnerable when acting responsively without the protection of established procedures.

A key concept here is 'object-motive' which was developed by Leont'ev, a major contributor to activity theory.

> The main thing which distinguishes one activity from another, however, is the difference of their objects. It is exactly the object of an activity that gives it a determined direction. According to the terminology I have proposed, the object of the activity is its true motive. (Leont'ev, 1978, p. 62)

In summary, the object motive, how the object of activity is interpreted by participants in the activity, directs activities. A teacher looking at a child's developmental trajectory may interpret it in terms of academic performance reflecting the activity of schooling, while a social worker looking at the same trajectory may seek signs of vulnerability and risk of harm reflecting her professional activities and practices. The different interpretations of children's trajectories offered by practitioners therefore reflect the dominant activities of their professions and therefore also of the organizations they see as their professional homes. Recognizing the object motives of other practitioners may make for an enriched response which is likely to benefit the child but is not achieved without some effort.

Relational agency recognizes that practitioners need to have access to the object motives of their potential collaborators and that they often they need this access rapidly. Criticizing studies of collaboration because of their tendency to focus on *how* it is achieved rather than the motives that give shape to participation, Nardi has suggested that we should analytically focus specifically on object motives in order to examine the various motives for collaboration. (2005) She argues that more attention needs to be given to *why* people engage in collaboration and what are their 'passionately held motives' (p. 37).

Several implications arise from this move. First, if object of activity and object motive are not aligned in the same way for each collaborator, attention needs to be paid to aligning their different motives as they work with the same child in ways which enrich their understandings of the child. In other words, it is not enough to focus only on *how* a social worker and a teacher work with a child, exchange information and so on, we need also to examine *why* they are working with the child. This conclusion is echoed by a practitioner in NECF (Edwards, Barnes, Plewis and Morris et al., 2006).

> I think the very first step is understanding about what the sort of issues are . . . Professions have very, very different ideas about need, about discipline, about responsibility, about the impact of systems on families . . . So I think the first step is actually to get some shared understanding about effective practices and about understanding the reasons behind some of them. (Practitioner, NECF)

A focus on the why of collaboration also has implications for practitioners' professional and social identities in the kinds of object-oriented relationships that characterize relational agency. In summary, there are three points here.

(i) As practitioners work on objects of activity to transform them, the objects work back on them and impact on their subjectivity and how they, in turn approach the object in question. In this transactional relationship between subject and object, by transforming the object alongside other practitioners through contesting it and understanding it better, they also transform themselves i.e. they learn (Edwards, 2005).

(ii) Working relationally involves being aware of one's own expertise and professional values and revealing them to others. This awareness can enhance practitioners' sense of themselves as professionals rather than functionaries.

(iii) A capacity for working relationally with others can strengthen the actions of potentially vulnerable practitioners who are undertaking risky responsive work outside the safety of the social practices of their own organizations.

Working with service users

Strikingly, the professionals we worked with in all three projects found inviting parents or carers to participate as experts to be a step too far. The only exceptions in our studies were a few practitioners working in the voluntary and community sector who emphasized engaging the agency of parents and carers in the reconfiguring of their children's trajectories.

> . . . the main participation is in the individual packages we do with families, which are very much family-led really. It's around their description of the understanding

of their needs – the targets that we all agree to work towards, and their evaluations of the things at the end really. (Practitioner NECF)

This kind of approach was quite exceptional in our examination of inter-professional work. It appeared that the new policy emphasis on inter-professional collaborations was absorbing energy and, that by focusing on children's trajectories as objects of activity, practitioners were in danger of treating clients as objects of activity rather than thinking about how families' expertise might be brought into the collaborations.

The implications for the strategic development of children's services

One issue arising in all three studies is the capacity of systems to learn from practice. As I have already indicated, in the discussion of rule-bending, practitioners were frustrated by the inability of local authority strategists and senior managers to recognize how practices were changing and to support the changes. According to participants in the studies, the problem was that there were no channels of communication where strategists might learn from what was happening at ground level in ways that mirrored how different practition-ers learnt from each other. In our reports we have called consistently for atten-tion to 'upstream learning' across hierarchical boundaries in organizations to avoid the waste that occurs when it is absent.

As researchers we find ourselves doing the mediation between practice and strategy, but we can only do that on a temporary basis as we move on to other projects and lose sight of the most recent developments in practices. Also, in the UK, not every strategy group would see researchers as their first source of information (Edwards, Sebba and Rickinson, 2007). Nonetheless, there are some broad messages arising from our work on inter-professional practices for strategic planning. They centre on professional development and the con-ditions for it.

Inter-professional work involves the new skills outlined in this paper, together with core expertise; and the former is not a substitute for the latter (Edwards et al., 2010). I suggest, however, that although pre-service training can help beginning practitioners recognize and value the priorities of other services through lectures, reading and placements, the attributes necessary for relational practices need to be acquired and fine-tuned in practices. Here the conditions for them to arise and be supported are crucial.

While there is a place for stand and deliver training to update core professional knowledge, inter-professional collaboration calls for a different strategy. It needs an approach which enables people to look beyond their own professional boundaries to recognize both different expertise and priorities, but also common values. That recognition involves repositioning oneself as a practitioner and dealing with personally-felt contradictions. These processes will take time and are best experienced in the company of other professionals who are, at the same time, trying to understand what matters for you. Time is essential, as there may be conflict as well as curiosity before misunderstandings are ironed out. Our research suggests that inter-professional meetings should focus on problems of practice, so they are seen as worth attending, but the personal work of sharing categories and recognizing mutual interests that occurs there is the real agenda. Distributed expertise is necessarily locally situated and attention needs to be given to creating the conditions for its development.

Notes

1. The study was funded by the Department for Education and Skills between 2003 and 2006.
2. ESRC RES-139-25-0100 a TLRP study co-directed by Harry Daniels (Bath) and Anne Edwards (Oxford) with Jane Leadbetter, Deirdre Martin and Paul Warmington (Birmingham), David Middleton (Loughborough) and Steve Brown (Leicester) 2004–2007.
3. ESRC RES-00-22-2305 Expanding Understandings of Inclusion: implications of preventing social exclusion for practices in schools. Co-directed by Anne Edwards and Ingrid Lunt (Oxford) 2007–2008.

References

Audit Commission (2008). *Are We There Yet? Improving Governance and Resource Management in Children's Trusts.* London: Audit Commission.

Bruner, J. S. (1996). *The Culture of Education.* Cambridge: MA: Harvard University Press.

Collins, H. (2004). Interactional Expertise as a Third Kind of Knowledge. *Phenomenology and the Cognitive Sciences,* 3, 125–143.

DfES (2004). *The Children Act.* London: HMSO.

Edwards, A. (2005). Relational Agency: Learning to be a Resourceful Practitioner. *International Journal of Educational Research,* 43(3), 168–182.

—(2010). *Being an Expert Professional Practitioner: The Relational Turn in Expertise*, Dordecht: Springer.

Edwards, A. and Kinti, I. (2010). 'Working Relationally at Organisational Boundaries: Negotiating Expertise and Identity', in H. Daniels, A. Edwards, Y. Engeström, A. Gallagher and S. Ludvigsen (eds), *Activity Theory in Practice: Promoting Learning across Boundaries and Agencies*. London: Routledge, pp. 126–139.

Edwards, A. and Mackenzie, L. (2005). Steps towards Participation: The Social Support of Learning Trajectories. *International Journal of Lifelong Education*, 24(4), 287–302.

Edwards, A., Barnes, M., Plewis, I. et al. (2006). *Working to Prevent the Social Exclusion of Children and Young People: Final Lessons from the National Evaluation of the Children's Fund: RR 734*, London: DfES.

Edwards, A., Daniels, H., Gallagher, T., Leadbetter, J. and Warmington, P. (2009). *Improving Inter-Professional Collaborations: Multi-Agency Working for Children's Wellbeing*. London: Routledge.

Edwards, A., Lunt, I. and Stamou, E. (2010). Inter-Professional Work and Expertise: New Roles at the Boundaries of Schools. *British Educational Research Journal*.

Edwards, A., Sebba, J. and Rickinson, M. (2007). Working with Users: Some Implications for Educational Research. *British Educational Research Journal*, 33(5), 647–661.

Engeström, Y. (1999). 'Activity Theory and Individual and Social Transformation', in Y. Engeström, R. Miettinen and R. L. Punamäki (eds) *Perspectives on Activity Theory*. Cambridge: Cambridge University Press.

—(2007). 'Putting Activity Theory to Work: The Change Laboratory as an Application of Double Stimulation', in H. Daniels, M. Cole and J. V. Wertsch (eds) *The Cambridge Companion to Vygotsky*. Cambridge: Cambridge University Press.

Engeström, Y. and Middleton, D. (eds) (1996). *Cognition and Communication at Work*. Cambridge: Cambridge University Press.

Hakkarainen, K., Palonen, T., Paavola, S. and Lehtinen, E. (2004). *Communities of Networked Expertise: Professional and Educational Perspectives*. Amsterdam: Elsevier.

Home Office (2000). *Report of Policy Action Team 12: Young People*. London: Home Office.

Jack, G. (2006). The Area and Community Components of Children's Well-Being. *Children and Society*, 20(5), 334–347.

Leont'ev, A. N. (1978). *Activity, Consciousness and Personality*. Upper Saddle River N.J.: Prentice Hall.

Little, M., Axford, N. and Morpeth, L. (2004). Research Review: Risk and Protection in the Context of Services for Children in Need, *Children and Family Social Work*, 9(1) 105–117.

Makitälo, Å. and Säljö, R. (2002). Invisible People: Institutional Reasoning and Reflexivity in the Production of Services and 'Social Facts' in Public Employment Agencies. *Mind, Culture, and Activity*, 9(3), 160–178.

Mørch, A., Nygaard, K. and Ludvigsen, S. (in press). 'Adaptation and Generalization in Software Product Development', in H. Daniels, A. Edwards, Y. Engeström, A. Gallagher and S. Ludvigsen (eds), *Activity Theory in Practice: Promoting Learning across Boundaries and Agencies*. London: Routledge.

Nardi, B. (2005). Objects of Desire: Power and Passion in Collaborative Activity. *Mind Culture and Activity*, 12(1), 37–51.

OECD (1998). *Co-ordinating Services for Children and Youth at Risk: A World View*. Paris: OECD.

Orr, J. (1996). *Talking about Machines: An Ethnography of a Modern Job*. Ithaca: Cornell University Press.

Room, G. (1995). 'Poverty and Social Exclusion: The New European Agenda for Policy and Research', in G. Room (ed.) *Beyond the Threshold: The Measurement and Analysis of Social Exclusion*. Bristol: Policy Press.

Schulz, M. (2003). Pathways of Relevance: Inflows of Knowledge into Subunits of Multinational Corporations. *Organization Science*, 14(4), 440–459.

Walker, R. (1995). 'The Dynamics of Poverty and Social Exclusion', in G. Room (ed.) *Beyond the Threshold: The Measurement and Analysis of Social Exclusion*. Bristol: Policy Press.

Wertsch, J. (2007). 'Mediation', in H. Daniels, M. Cole, and J. V. Wertsch (eds) *The Cambridge Companion to Vygotsky*. New York: Cambridge University Press.

Diverse Needs, Different Provision: How Differences in Preschool Settings Support Children to Learn How to be Learners

10

Jan Georgeson

This chapter will use a study of four preschool settings to illustrate how different forms of provision can support children in different ways as they go through the transition from home to school. The study adopted the position that children's understanding about how to take part in teaching and learning activities begins with the earliest everyday exchanges between caregiver and child. Adults, both at home or in preschool settings, have their own understandings about how children learn and about what children will need to know to be part of the culture they have been born into and, more specifically, to take part in formal learning. Staff in preschool settings use this knowledge to organize provision and guide their interactions with children and this chapter argues that local practitioners in local settings are well placed to provide preschool experiences which are best matched to local children's needs. If staff in pre-school settings are familiar with children's home backgrounds, their current level of participation in learning activities and likely future needs, then they should be better able to support children to develop identities as learners that will help them settle into formal schooling. This can be particularly important for children who do not have access to this kind of preparation for schooling at home, or who find it difficult to move between the practices of different institutions.

The diversity of the UK preschool sector

Wide ranging social, cultural and political forces, which are beyond the scope of this chapter to describe, have given rise in the UK to different forms of early years provision with differing pedagogic traditions. What kind of a setting a child attends before starting statutory schooling depends on what their parents want, where they live, what they can afford and whether they need child care to enable them to work. Parents' needs for childcare and/or their interest in getting their child 'off to a good start' before they enter school have driven the expansion of private provision. At the same time, government initiatives such as Sure Start (community driven services for children and families in areas of deprivation) and now Children's Centres (universal local one-stop centres for a broad range of children's services) have increased the level of state funding for early years provision while also greatly extending its remit to push forward an agenda for social inclusion. All children are now eligible for a part-time government-funded nursery place from the age of three (or from two in some areas of high deprivation) in a setting chosen by parents. This can be anywhere that offers preschool provision which meets government require-ments, including private day nurseries, voluntary playgroups and independent pre-prep schools. All children then take up a statutory schooling place, in a school chosen by parents but where they meet the admissions criteria, from the term following their fifth birthday.

Preschool provision therefore spans the voluntary, private and state-maintained sectors but now works within common curricular guidelines set out in the Early Years Foundation Stage (DCSF, 2008). Settings, however, work within very different functional constraints (finance steams, session patterns, accommodation, staff qualifications). There is still considerable variation between settings on all the above parameters, in spite of 12 years of progressive standardization through government guidelines, inspection regime, qualification framework and workforce development. This includes the large and very 'diverse and disorganized' preschool sector (Vincent and Ball, 2001) outside government-maintained schools, as well as an increasing number of hybrid private, voluntary and state-funded services. There are still voluntary sector settings operating in shared community halls and relying on careful tracking of local and national government funding initiatives to stay financially viable. Elsewhere preschool departments in the independent school sector are thriving and, although managers of private day nurseries report a slight decrease in the demand for baby places, new private day nurseries are still opening, with existing nurseries still over subscribed and parents still struggling to find child care for their children while they work. While state-funded nursery schools are bracing themselves for changes in government funding formulae, recruitment to nursery classes in Foundation Stage units of state primaries remains buoyant.

Parents can choose which preschool their child will attend; preschool settings therefore seek to attract parents and provision is consequently shaped by settings' perceptions of what parents want. The opportunity to choose does not fall evenly across the social spectrum or geographical location and choices are often shaped by need (for example for childcare) and pragmatics (such as cost, or availability of transport). In some areas, competition for places in the most sought after primary schools, influenced by the publication of league tables of schools which perform best in national testing at 11, hastens children into school-based preschool provision to secure a statutory school place at the age of 5. This form of provision is not, however, available everywhere and does not suit all parents, particularly those who need full-time day care or those who object to the idea of sending their children into school at too tender an age. The forces of choice and competition lead to differentiation of provision; settings have grown up to respond to parents' needs and preferences and, although they have to meet certain requirements to be eligible for government funding, there is still room for considerable variation in ethos and approach.

There are two lines of argument – not necessarily mutually exclusive – which can be drawn up to consider the effects of this diversity of provision; one, that diversity perpetuates inequality; parents who are knowledgeable about the UK educational system, and have the financial means to use this knowledge, can place their children in settings which might give them an advantage over those who can't pay. And it is difficult to disagree with this.

There is, however, a second line of argument: diversity also promotes equality, because many preschool settings have evolved outside the maintained sector as a result of local need and so reflect local culture more closely than the more tightly regulated statutory-phase schooling. Preschools which have grown up in a community in response to local needs are, it could be argued, in a better position to act as a bridge between home and school culture and so are better able to support children with the transition between home and school.

This is not a new argument; Sally Lubeck was drawing similar conclusions from her seminal study of preschool provision in working class black and middle class white communities (Lubeck, 1985). She demonstrated how the values and aspirations – in fact the weltanschauung, the whole way of viewing the world – of the local practitioners permeated the organizational structure and interactional style of the preschools where they worked. This provided children with culturally specific resources to meet the challenges of school life ahead. In the case of the Headstart nursery attended mainly by members of the local black community, this amounted to a strong sense of community support and in the case of the white nursery, a strong sense of individualism. Shirley Brice Heath also famously showed how the different process of enculturation in poor white and poor black communities, which did not include attendance at preschool, left children without a bridge into the very different cultures of their schools and set them at a disadvantage from which they would struggle to recover (Brice Heath, 1983). More recently Liz Brooker has described a similar mismatch between the within-family processes for preparing for schooling in Bangla Deshi and white communities which fed into one primary school adhering to a very 'child-centred' reception class (Brooker, 2002).

I have seen ample evidence of such local variation, imbued with culturally specific values, as I have worked across the diversity of preschool provision in the UK over the last 25 years. In one disadvantaged community, for example, I could see that preschool practitioners were finding it difficult to respond to the government's guidance on promoting child-initiated activities. Their pedagogical style inclined to direct instruction, pumping children full of things they thought they would need to know to survive in school. Survival in a hostile environment was a core aspect of these people's lives; their jobs were in jeopardy, housing uncertain and the neighbourhood dangerous. In more affluent suburbs, where life was more predictable, practitioners were more comfortable with offering children choice, but then subtly shaped understanding of what they viewed as culturally acceptable choices by selective praise and attention. The way in which practitioners supported children therefore varied between settings, in a way which was matched to how practitioners perceived children's needs.

Investigating differences in preschool culture

Such differences can make interesting anecdotes, but in order to describe them more systemically and so consider their implications for children's future school careers (and beyond), it is useful to apply a descriptive framework which can move between societal, institutional and individual levels. I have developed a descriptive framework to capture differences in the way preschool provision happens, using concepts from Bernstein's theory of the pedagogic device, which is described in detail in Chapter 1. This is the set of 'rules or procedures via which knowledge is converted into pedagogic communication' (Singh, 2002: p. 573, 576), taking a broad view of pedagogy to include all kinds of knowledge shared by more experienced members with less experienced members of a community. The crucial aspect of Bernstein's theory for the purposes of describing preschool difference lies in the distinction he makes between two aspects of pedagogic discourse; 'instructional discourse' (ID) and 'regulative discourse' (RD). Instructional discourse, the discourse of competence, refers to aims, activities, assessments and outcomes associated with school subject knowledge and skills. This is now encapsulated for most preschool settings in the early learning goals set out in the Practice Guidance for the Early Years Foundation Stage (EYFS) (DCSF, 2008). RD, the discourse of social order, refers to the often tacit understandings about relationships between actors in pedagogic institutions. Aspects of the EYFS documentation now seek to shape regulative discourse, with 'Positive Relationships' identified as one of the four themes of the EYFS along with a set of commitments which this entails. Previous documentation, current when this study was carried out, also described aspects of the kinds of relationship which should pertain between children and staff in early years settings. Both sets of guidelines, however, still leave room for considerable variation.

The balance of the two elements of pedagogic discourse, ID and RD, can vary so that one or other element is fore-grounded. The changes in early years provision since the introduction of government funding in 1997 can be seen as resulting in a shift in the structure of pedagogic discourse in preschool provision, particularly in the non-maintained sector. As elsewhere in the UK educational system (Daniels, 2001, p. 139–140), this has been prompted by increasing emphasis on curriculum content, assessment and outcomes. Describing settings in terms of the *balance* between instructional and regulative discourse can be used to distinguish between a differential emphasis on the 'acquisition of instructional (curricular content) and regulative (social conduct, character and manner)' outcomes (Singh, 2002, p. 573). In the UK preschool sector, this is reflected in differences in emphasis on educational outcomes (can children count, write their names, handle scissors?) or on social behaviours (can children separate from parents, manage turn-taking, accept guidance from staff?).

In the next sections I shall present findings from a study comparing four settings in the non-maintained sector in England which shared many functional and operational similarities but which differed in the balance between instructional and regulative discourse. Case studies were built up from observation, documentary analysis and interviews between September 2002 and July 2003 and are described in full elsewhere (Georgeson, 2006). The perceptions of staff were elicited during career biography interviews and parents' views on preschool provision were sought through questionnaires. In the third part of the project children aged three and four were encouraged to talk about preschool activities by looking at photographs of activities and shots of the exterior, interior and outside space in their own and the other three settings in the project. Their responses were coded in three components designed to capture what children were talking about (Content), how they adjusted their talk in response to who they were talking to (Interpersonal) and the extent to which they were acquiring the particular Ways of Speaking used in pedagogic exchanges. This third component was based partly on reading Clare Painter's study of the development of language use in the context of simple day-to-day talk within the family, and how this prepares children for the sort of thinking they will need when they start school (Painter, 1999). The analysis produced different patterns of codes – essentially profiles of interactional style – from the different settings and gave some insight into differences in the way children were learning how to take part in pedagogic exchanges.

The four settings

Setting 1. '**Village Hall**' was a community preschool, which operated as not-for-profit organization run by a committee of parents. It had adopted an organic, open, egalitarian staff structure and for the most part blurred the boundaries

Figure 10.1 Setting 1 (top left) Village Hall; Setting 2 (top right) Rocking Horse; Setting 3 (bottom left) Orchard House; Setting 4 (bottom right) Building Blocks

between staff and parents, preschool and home, older and younger children. Structurally, it could therefore be described as weakly classified. The preschool setting prioritized socialization for children before they start school, that is, regulative discourse dominated. It was located in the centre of the village and playgroup sessions took place in the large open space of the village hall, which it shared with other community organizations.

Setting 2. '**Rocking Horse**' was a private day nursery situated in semi-detached house at the end of a residential street in an urban location. It adopted a hierarchical staff structure but blurred the boundaries between home and school. This setting prioritized socialization in homely surroundings so again regulative discourse dominated. The routines were organized around the needs of the youngest children so the whole setting moved to the rhythm of their sleep and feeding times. Staff developed strong bonds with both children, parents and each other and felt rewarded by watching child develop and gain confidence.

Setting 3. '**Orchard House**' was a private nursery school which had extended its premises to offer full day care for children from 0–5. It was located between a city and a small town in a large house surrounded by extensive grounds. It adopted a strictly hierarchical staffing structure, a rigidly timetabled day and maintained clear boundaries between staff and parents, home and nursery and between different ages of children. Structurally it could therefore be described as strongly classified. Instructional discourse dominated as the setting had a strong educational emphasis and included many school-like practices. Staff felt their role was rewarding when children demonstrated that they had remembered something which they had been told the day before; parents used school-like terms when describing what they liked about the setting.

Setting 4. **'Building Blocks'** was another community preschool run by two Christian charities but heavily dependent on short-term finance initiatives from the local authority. This meant that it had a complex organizational structure; there was a hierarchical staffing structure but local authority stakeholders and service users were involved in shaping policy. It had an explicit aim to educate children, parents and the local teenagers who took part in work experience there; instructional discourse therefore dominated. It was located on the high street of an inner city area, and served a multi-ethnic population. Members of staff were drawn from the local population (not from the mainly white demographic of two Christian charities) and reported different motivations; some spoke of their love of children, others of their fascination with their development, especially those who were developing atypically.

The pattern of differences between the settings was complex and the following section will compare just some aspects to illustrate how the structural and motivational differences permeated the different interactional styles which were evident in the four settings. Subtle differences in children's talk were identified which could be interpreted as their recognition and adoption of the special features of their setting's interactional microclimate.

Category defence

Looking first at the content of children's talk, there were differences between settings in the extent to which children sought precision in their own choice of words, that is, the extent to which children defended category boundaries and corrected use of words as opposed to tolerating vagueness. This provided the most direct link between children's talk and the organizational structure of their settings. The children's talk in the two day nurseries showed more instances of strong categorization than did talk from the two playgroups.

This manifested itself in more instances of children in the day nurseries wanting to label things correctly; for example, they were concerned to identify which room was being shown in the photograph. This is in keeping with a tendency to establish and maintain boundaries between categories, in contrast to the way children talked in the playgroups. Building Blocks playgroup in particular showed not only fewest examples of strong classification but also notably more instances of weak classification. This pattern of results is consistent with the descriptions of organizational structure produced in the case studies, which showed overall more rigidity in use of categories in the two day nurseries in comparison with the playgroups.

The greater emphasis on correct categorization in the two day nurseries could be viewed in part as an incidental by-product of the pragmatics of organizing day care for young children with a wide range of ages in multi-roomed accommodation. In order to make the best use of time, space and human resources, everyone involved needs to know who is supposed to be where, when and doing what. This means that, for effective organization, staff and children need clear and consistent labels to apply to places, people, things and events. Such considerations are much less important in the two community groups, where all children have free access to the whole internal space throughout most of the session, and timing is flexible.

In Orchard House (the school-like day nursery), however, distinctions were made over and above those needed to arrange efficient use of staff and space. Rooms are given labels that reflect the fact that particular activities happen there, whereas in Rocking Horse (the homely day nursery) most rooms were multi-functional and labelled by colour. In Orchard House, activity sessions and free play were sharply distinguished and clearly labelled, but these merged into each other in Rocking Horse. In addition, distinctions between staff, parents and children in Orchard House are sharply drawn and maintained with different forms of address, whereas everyone was called by their first names or diminutives in Rocking Horse. Orchard House would therefore seem to embrace an ethos of rigid classification in addition to the pragmatic use of labelling for clarification and efficiency.

It is possible to make further connections between these differences in organizational structure and the differences in pedagogic discourse of the two day nurseries. In Orchard House, instructional discourse dominated and resembled school pedagogic discourse in many respects. This includes having a strict timetable with the separation of activities into identified subjects. Orchard House's strict categorization is therefore at least partly related to its adoption of a school-like pedagogic discourse. In Rocking Horse, where concern for relationships was so important, the dominant discourse was regulative discourse and elements of its instructional discourse (like counting and learning the days of the week) are not rigidly timetabled, but interwoven into care and social activities, such as meal times and bathroom queues, as well as into (the relatively few) planned activity sessions.

Differences in pedagogical emphasis (care/socialization versus education) also affect how regulative discourse is transmitted, and this has implications for how children are supported to learn about values and relationships. Children at Rocking Horse were given explicit instructions about how to behave, in other words, instruction about the regulative discourse. However, at Orchard House, although it was apparent that some kinds of behaviour were acceptable and some unacceptable, children were not explicitly taught about this. Many of the values and cultural associations were conveyed tacitly.

The two kinds of knowledge – curricular content and values/behaviour – were therefore treated differently; at Orchard House, content knowledge was transmitted as discreet subjects through explicit instruction in dedicated sessions, but children developed an understanding of the values, behaviours and identity through attending to what is praised, foregrounded or borrowed from elsewhere. At Rocking Horse, children were explicitly taught about how to behave, but picked up understanding about what knowledge they should be acquiring from incidental questions. Such differences have implications for how different children might read their way into the pedagogic discourse of their present or future settings. Children with communication difficulties who attended Rocking Horse benefited from its explicit instruction about how to behave, while the clear division of content into school subjects at Orchard House prepared children for distinctions which they would need to learn on transfer to school. During the study, one practitioner at Rocking Horse mentioned that children noticed the difference in the pedagogic style, by commenting 'the teacher doesn't talk to me like you do' when they retuned to the nursery for after-school care.

Children's talk in the photograph sessions in the two playgroups gave rise to fewer instances of children defending categories than did talk from sessions in the day nurseries. In particular, not only did children at Building Blocks playgroup produce the fewest instances of category defence, but also they produced by far the most instances of 'vague' terms (such as 'thingy'). This could be explained by their relative inexperience with English vocabulary but these two factors (fewer instances of category defence, higher incidence of vague terms) contributed to a more relaxed, permissive linguistic environment than that which pertained in Orchard House, where children were more ready to challenge incorrect choice of words. Although staff at Building Blocks did correct children's use of language, they did so more by providing correct models than by pointing out that the child was wrong. Prompted by a concern to develop children's familiarity with English vocabulary, they frequently extended or amplified children's comments and corrected by agreement, as demonstrated in the following extract from transcript of session at Building Blocks, as a child looks at photograph of her own setting with a member of staff:

Child: They make all the messy cover
Adult: Yes, they tipped all the things in the box out on the floor
Child: All the box stuff on the floor

This is in contrast with the interactional style of staff at Village Hall. This setting prioritized regulative over instructional outcomes, with staff showing most concern that children should settle and feel comfortable in their new surroundings. They seldom corrected children's use of language. Children did not often correct or self-correct and instances of concern for correct labelling per se were rare. The children's use of language at Village Hall therefore appeared to mirror the setting's more open and flexible organizational structure and the staff's informal approach. The combination of blurred boundaries between home and nursery, with greater emphasis on instructional outcomes, at Building Blocks, however, created a different interactional environment where children felt comfortable using vague terms and approximations to English but at the same time were gently guided towards more accurate use of words and syntax.

Use of personal pronouns

Differences in emphasis on regulative discourse were reflected in differences in interactional aspects of children's talk. As well as differences in emotional tone, there were also differences in pronoun use. Statistical analyses found a significant difference in the use of pronouns between the four settings, with the two day nurseries producing similar patterns to each other, and the two playgroups looking very dissimilar. The use of first person singular (I/me/my/mine) could be seen an indication of the extent to which children felt comfortable bringing their own experiences and opinions into the discussion. Children at Village Hall made relatively more use of the first person singular than did children in the other settings. This is in keeping with the way this setting blurred the distinction between home and playgroup. Children might therefore have been more ready to bring their home experiences into the conversation.

Use of the first person plural (we/us/our(s)/lets) suggests the extent to which children felt that they belonged to, or 'owned' their setting, for example by noticing that 'we've got one of those' when a familiar piece of preschool equipment appeared in a photograph of another setting. The main difference in use of the first person plural between the four settings was that children at Building Blocks almost never used it. One child, who had been attending Building Blocks for a year, looking at photograph of her own setting with a member of staff, showed that she still regarded it as belonging to the staff, not to her.

> Adult: whose nursery is that?
> Child: yours
> Adult: awh (indulgent tone) ours? (points to self)
> Child: yeah

Use of second person (you/your/yours) indicates engagement with a listener, as does the use of questions and commands. This was more common during the photograph sessions in the two playgroups than in the two day nurseries, with Building Blocks producing by far the most examples of second person/listener-aware usage. This was puzzling, as it could be argued that greater awareness of the listener is in keeping with the description of the interactional climate at Village Hall and Rocking Horse, where there was strong regulative discourse around concern for others and informal relationships between staff and children. However, it is less consistent a picture which has been building up for Building Blocks, where there was a more egocentric environment and children showed less awareness of each other's needs. It is however, consistent with a culture where young children feel able to make demands of others' attention, particularly that of adult females (who were most often the 'listeners' during the photograph sessions in this setting). Many children at Building Blocks came from different cultural backgrounds from the children at the other settings, with potentially different use of linguistic resources such as repetition or agreement in response to other children's comments, or direct address in the form of second person pronouns or questions.

Response to use of personal pronouns is underpinned by cultural differences in indexicality, or the 'context dependency of signs . . . those aspect of meaning which depend on the placement of the sign in the material world' (Scollon and Scollon, 2003). Some languages have developed more sophisticated systems to make fine grain distinctions about the person being addressed; some avoid use of second person (you/yours) for all except most familiar relations. This is not a grammatical feature of present day English, but English speakers do avoid use of you/yours when this might draw unwanted attentions to individuals (for example, when hurrying a reluctant eater who is late for school: 'someone isn't eating their porridge'; and of course the celebrated use of first person plural by old-fashioned teachers parodied by Joyce Grenfell; 'we never bite our friends'). Although we might be unaware of it, we are very sensitive to pronoun use as it orients us immediately to how a speaker positions themselves in relation to us. If children from Building Blocks were accustomed to using and hearing pronouns differently, this could have implications for how some teachers in school might respond to their rather direct and (to them,) demanding interactional style.

Ways of speaking

Differences between the Ways of Speaking used by children on the four settings also did not follow anticipated differences in emphasis in pedagogic discourse. In particular, children at Rocking Horse, which prioritized care and socialization, showed proportionally more instances of school-like Ways of Speaking than Orchard House, the setting which most prioritized educational outcomes. This could possibly be explained by thinking about the nature of the activity – chatting about photographs – and how the children in the two settings might have interpreted the expectations for this task. At Orchard House, there were strong distinctions made between directed activities and play; there the photograph activity took place at play time and so children might have been less inclined to use the more school-like ways of speaking which they demonstrated in activity times. At Rocking Horse, where distinctions between 'work' and 'play' were blurred and opportunities for discussions about instructional content were just as likely to happen at lunch time as during a number game, children's expectations of the activity were less likely to influence how they spoke about the photographs.

Looking at the results in more detail, the biggest difference between Rocking Horse and the other settings is in the proportion of instances of co-construction. This is consistent with the high number of collaborative supportive comments from children at Rocking Horse in the interpersonal analysis, and with findings from the case study which revealed an ethos of awareness and pragmatic consideration of the needs of other people. Co-construction did not feature as often during the photograph sessions at Orchard House; the interpersonal tone here included elements of challenge, countering and assertiveness. Children tended to speak out in opposition to, rather than build on what others had said. This is consistent with the maintenance of sharp boundaries between categories that follows from strong classification. Familiarity with countering style could, however, prove useful in future educational contexts with a similar style and offers opportunities to sharpen children's ability to assign things to categories and so help them to learn to generalize. While co-construction could be seen as requiring more sophisticated understanding of two points of view in comparison with countering exchanges (Georgeson, 2009a), Payler (2009) has shown that the kind of interactive space which co-construction requires is not often evident when children move into school.

Implications of differences between settings

Although complex, the patterns of differences across the four settings suggested how the interactional micro-climate of individual settings mirrored the needs of the children and the perceptions and inclinations of practitioners. All this took place in the context of very similar activities within the same regulative regime and curriculum framework and supports the argument for diversity in preschool provision. Different children respond to the experience of attending preschool provision differently. For some, the difference between their home culture and mainstream culture can be large, and the choice of preschool provision can have an effect on how well they manage to bridge the gap between home and setting. For a variety of reasons, other children find it difficult to read their way into any new situation, and again, the ease with which they learn how to operate in a preschool setting can depend on the culture of that setting. In addition, some children find moving into statutory schooling more difficult than others do, and their preschool experience can also have an effect on the ease of this transition.

The differences in culture between the settings in this study have implications for how different children might first learn to be preschool learners and in the future learn to be pupils in school. Children who experience difficulty working out what preschool provision is all about might find it easier to settle into a setting with sharp boundaries between categories, which show them what's what and who's who in the setting. Some flexibility of control can allow children to find their own way and make mistakes without loss of self-esteem. For children outside the mainstream culture, permeability of boundaries between home and school can help them to use their learning from home in the preschool context.

Two settings from this study demonstrate how their particular combination of features helped to make them well-suited to the particular children on roll. Children who attended Orchard House did not, in the main, have particular difficulties, such as language or learning difficulties, which might have hampered their learning about the way things worked in their setting. They were therefore able to read their way quickly into the setting's rigid routines and rules, even when this was not made explicit. Their parents also showed more orientation towards the pedagogic discourse of statutory phase schooling and so these children were likely to be well-equipped from their home experience to pick up on the school-like pedagogic discourse of the nursery.

Building Blocks playgroup, on the other hand, showed a variation between rigidity and flexibility that suited children with quite different needs from those at Orchard House. Although children made their own choices most of the time, there was strong guidance over the correct use of language, which helped those children learning English in addition to their home language. They also benefited from the blurred boundaries between playgroup and the outside world, because this allowed them to bring their home experiences to bear on their learning in playgroup.

The need for diversity runs counter to the homogenization of practice that can follow from the current pursuit of 'effectiveness' and 'excellence', when both are narrowly conceived as performance on readily measured outcomes (Georgeson, 2009b). This study demonstrated that differences between settings, which follow from their differences in history, pedagogical emphasis and ways of operating, can be adaptive, with respect to the needs of the particular children who attend. Encouraging the rich diversity of preschool provision towards one model of 'effectiveness' or 'excellence' risks compromising the integrity of individual settings that have evolved to meet the particular needs of the communities which they serve.

References

Brice Heath, S. (1983). Ways with Words: Language, Life and Work in Communities and Classrooms. Cambridge: Cambridge University Press.

Brooker, L. (2002). Starting School; Young Children Learning Cultures. Buckingham: Open University Press.

Daniels, H. (2001). Vygotsky and Pedagogy. London: Routledge Falmer.

Department for Children, Schools and Families (DCSF) (2008). Practice Guidance for the Early Years Foundation Stage. Nottingham: DCSF Publications.

Georgeson, J. (2006). Differences in Preschool Culture: Organization, Pedagogy and Interaction in Four Selected Settings (Unpublished EdD thesis, University of Birmingham)

—(2009a). 'Co-construction Meaning; Differences in the Interactional Microclimate', in Papatheodorou, T. and Moyles, J. (eds) Learning Together in the Early Years; Exploring Relational Pedagogy. London: Routledge, pp. 109–119.

—(2009b). 'The Professionalization of the Early Years Workforce', in Edwards, S. and Nuttall, J. (eds). Professional Learning in Early Childhood Settings. Netherlands: Sense Publications, pp. 115–130.

Lubeck, S. (1985). Sandbox Society: Early Education in Black and White America; A Comparative Ethnography. London: Falmer Press.

Painter, C. (1999). Learning through Language in Early Childhood. London: Cassell.

Payler, J. (2009). 'Co-Construction Meaning; Ways of Supporting Learning', in Papatheodorou, T. and Moyles, J. (eds) Learning Together in the Early Years; Exploring Relational Pedagogy. London: Routledge, pp. 120–128.

Scollon, R. and Scollon, S. W. (2003). Discourses in Place. London: Routledge.

Singh, P. (2002). 'Pedagogizing Knowledge: Bernstein's Theory of the Pedagogic Device'. *British Journal of Sociology of Education*, 23(4), 571–582.

Vincent, C. and Ball, S. J. (2001). 'A Market in Love? Choosing Pre-School Childcare'. *British Educational Research Journal*, 27(5), 633–651.

Young People Not in Education, Employment or Training

Geoff Hayward

Chapter Outline

This contribution is concerned to understand the experience of schooling of a category of increasing policy concern, young people Not in Education, Employment or Training (NEET). Such an understanding is grounded in a Vygotskian conception of experience, as a dynamic internal relationship between the developing child and their social situation of development: 'a relationship defined by the forms of social practice that "relate" the child to the objective environment and define what the environment means for the child' (Minick, 1996, p. 48). The focus is on schooling, rather than other social practices because of the salience of that institution within policy thinking in terms of supporting young people to make the transition to adulthood and to economic independence.

But for a significant minority of young people it seems to fail, at least partially, to fulfil this function. The correlates of a young person entering the NEET category are well known – poverty, poor behaviour in school, low academic attainment, school exclusion truanting – and so on, with many of these factors appearing to have an early impact on child development (cf. Bynner and Parsons, 2002; Gorard and Rees, 2002; Dex and Joshie, 2005; Hansen et al., 2010). What such analyses suggests, when combined with a more economic perspective, is that NEET status for most young people is best understood not as a failure of schooling per se but as a boundary phenomenon: the issue is about making successful transitions within different social institutions and across the multiple boundaries between them – schooling, the labour market, families and social welfare – with their own rules, mediating artefacts, communities, and divisions of labour, and their own historical development. The 'NEET' issue is then one that needs to be understood at multiple levels of analysis – from the macro-economic to the micro-level of ongoing pedagogic interaction between learners and teachers – and across institutional contexts. A socio-cultural perspective facilitates such an analysis, tracing young people's developmental trajectories across overlapping and interacting situations of social development. This analysis is informed by insights from the Engaging Youth Enquiry (EYE) undertaken as part of the Nuffield 14–19 Review (Hayward et al., 2008, Pring et al., 2009) and the wider literature.

The engaging youth enquiry

The Engaging Youth Enquiry was an 18-month investigation into the perspectives of young people who had experience of being 'NEET' and the practitioners who work with them on a daily basis (Hayward et al., 2008). Generating rich data with young people at risk of social exclusion is challenging. To facilitate the process Rathbone, a voluntary sector organization with a broad experience of working with socially disadvantaged young people at risk of becoming 'NEET', became an active research partner. They facilitated the organization of the young people's workshops, held in contexts familiar to the young people, with trusted adults as facilitators. This approach provided more direct access to the young people's viewpoints than would have been possible with a more formal research approach with researcher-led interviews or questionnaires.

Practitioner workshops

Rathbone drew on the network of voluntary sector organizations and other relevant bodies with which it collaborates, such as Connexions, the youth service, youth offending teams, employers, housing officers and magistrates, for the practitioner workshops, in order to ensure that the Engaging Youth Enquiry benefited from a rich blend of the voices of practitioners and researchers. Each of the one-day workshops with practitioners was run as an open dialogue, with a set of guiding questions to structure the day's interaction. Bringing together practitioners from various different fields of work and different agencies (such as Connexions, magistrates, voluntary sector organizations, representatives from schools and colleges, researchers, employers, youth offending teams, among others) with researchers brought to light issues of dissonance that emphasized the need for cross-organization work to support young people at risk of becoming 'NEET'. One example was given by a representative from the Foyer housing project in Manchester, who spoke of the need for consideration of the housing issues when the Connexions service advises on education and training opportunities, and the need for a holistic view of the needs of young people by, for example, not allocating training which is on the other side of a large city to their accommodation.

Young people's workshops

The 36 young people's workshops were also run as extended conversations with the young people that took place on their territory (such as a Rathbone centre or other familiar location), and were facilitated by trusted adults (such as Rathbone or Connexions staff). This avoided the danger of researchers 'parachuting' into the young people's environment to interview them in an unfamiliar situation with an unfamiliar person. The young people's workshops were run in groups of eight to ten young participants to allow for each person to speak as they wished, but without requiring specific input from each young person. The conversations were initiated through a set of guiding questions, rather than a formal instrument, and participation in activities ranging from drawing maps of their local neighbourhoods to joint reflection on the circumstances they found themselves in and their trajectories towards 'NEET' status. This produced rich exchanges about the issues the young people were dealing with in their day-to-day lives and personalized accounts that directly countered prevailing policy discourse and assumptions about the needs of such young people and how these could be met. The use of the familiar adults and familiar contexts meant that the young people were at ease in the situation and were, in most cases, keen to engage with the issues involved. These were very wide ranging, covering the wider social situation and their experiences of schooling.

The English patient

The category Not in Education, Employment or Training (NEET) was formally created by the Social Exclusion Unit in 1999 (SEU, 1999). This label refers to 16–18 year olds who – due to their 'NEET' status – are at risk of not making their future successful and sustainable transition to education, employment or training. Young people in this category had been a growing policy concern since the late 1970s and early 1980s, largely as a result of the collapse of the youth labour market, increasing rates of youth unemployment and crime, and disturbances in Inner City areas such as the Toxteth riots. This is a problem with a long history: the construct NEET links to a family of related concepts such as Howard Williamson's 'Status Zero', social inclusion and social exclusion, and the idea of an 'underclass' traced back to at least 1880 by Welshman (2006).

NEET is a statistical residual category that includes highly heterogeneous groups of young people (in the English context 16–19 year olds). One such group consists of those who have been successful in mainstream schooling and are taking a gap year before progressing to Higher Education. These individuals are not of concern here. The remainder arrive in the NEET category via a wide variety of developmental trajectories which may or may not involve school disengagement – young carers, young mothers, low levels of academic attainment, poor behavioural histories, drug and alcohol problems, learning disabilities and so on – which may interact with each other in complex ways (Hayward et al., 2008). Despite this multitude of pathways into the NEET category, in policy and practice terms these young people are often grouped as having identifiable special needs – poor self-esteem, a lack of self-confidence, poor motivation, weak aspiration and so on which impairs their ability to make the transition to adulthood.

Making the transition to adulthood and an economically viable life

> . . . can be considered a developmental process with at least two aspects. On the one hand, such a process necessitates a newly mature sense of one's own identity, which in turn entails a redefinition of the roles one plays socially, particularly with regards to new social groups. On the other hand, adulthood means acquiring new skills, knowledge and know-how, all of which the young adult will need in order to play new social and professional lives. (Zittoun, 2004, p. 153)

To place the issue in its historical context, only 40–50 years ago 80% of English young people not in grammar schools did not take any public examinations and left school at 15 with no qualifications, although a sizeable number then moved into apprenticeships with day release to study at a Technical College (Pring et al., 2009). The remainder moved into low and semi-skilled jobs, primarily in manufacturing, mining, office work and retail. Such work, which was in plentiful supply, was accessed primarily via community networks, especially relatives in employment. The resources needed by young people entering such work to form new adult identities and the skills and knowledge needed to access employment were appropriated largely from resources provided by the community and its social networks.

That world has gone. The manufacturing heartlands of Scotland, the north of England, the West Midlands and South Wales have lost huge numbers of jobs. New jobs in the service sector are not evenly distributed across the country. The result is localized structural unemployment, which has a disproportionate impact on the young people in these areas. This means competition for jobs is fierce even for low-skilled work – this is the genesis of the 'NEET' problem, poorly qualified young people have been squeezed out of the bottom end of the labour market. The 'NEET' problem is then a product of long-term structural, economic and social change, which is just as much about employment, or rather structural unemployment, as it is about education and training (Hayward et al., 2008; Pring et al, 2009).

A common feature, therefore, of the experience of many of the young people involved in EYE was living in workless families in considerable financial hardship. This made it difficult to sustain engagement with education, provided little if any access to the social networks needed to gain employment but also engendered strong feelings among the young people to be independent in order not to be a strain on their families. Far from the usual stereotype of 'feral youth' living indolent lives many of the young people who participated demonstrated a 'will to productivity . . . a hunger . . . for productive engagement in society' (Resnick and Perret-Clermont, 2004, p. 16). They wanted to do something that they viewed as worthwhile and, as one youth worker commented in a practitioner workshop, 'these young people work hard to maximize their economic resources'. By and large the young people wanted to earn their way but some at least were doing so in ways that would not win social approval. But in the absence of paid employment many were filling their time by engaging in risky activities which could include membership of gangs and low-level criminal activity. The use of drugs and alcohol was a daily occurrence in many of their lives.

An industrial policy that aimed at the long-term regeneration of areas such as the Welsh valleys and the old manufacturing heartlands of the West Midlands and the north-east of England flies in the face of political adherence to the ideals of a liberal market economy and the ideology of a flexible labour market (Hall and Soskice, 2001; Iversen, 2005). Governments feel increasingly restrained in acting on the demand side of the employment equation and therefore invest more in acting on the supply side: the reform of education and training (broadly conceived).

Consequently, for practically all states education has become a, if not the, central plank of social policy as identified by Blair (2007):

> New Labour was, in part, about releasing us from an old-fashioned view of the labour market. . . . In a sense, a whole economy has passed away. The central economic idea of New Labour – that economic efficiency and social justice ran together – was based on this fact. . . . Human capital was becoming the key determinant of corporate and country success. Education that for so long had been a social cause became an economic imperative. . . . The challenge today is to make the employee powerful, not in conflict with the employer but in terms of their marketability in the modern workforce. It is to reclaim flexibility for them, to make it about their empowerment, their ability to fulfil their aspirations. . . .
>
> What all this means is not that the role of Government, of the collective, of the services of the State is redundant; but changed. The rule now is not to interfere with the necessary flexibility an employer requires to operate successfully in a highly fluid changing economic market. It is to equip the employee to survive, prosper and develop in such a market, to give them the flexibility to be able to choose a wide range of jobs and to fit family and work/life together. (Blair, 2007)

The pay off for individuals from their investment in the education and training needed to acquire such qualifications will be enhanced wages thereby achieving income redistribution and social justice. Such a policy vision is predicated on young people committing more time and energy to their education and training, and in developing the identities needed to sustain a successful education career. However, most of the young people involved in the EYE had rejected this commitment and had clearly not formed the sorts of identities needed for successful learning careers in the current Education and Training system. What can be done about this?

Schooling as a thinking space

To make progress with answering this question first requires a perhaps rather idealistic perspective on what schooling should be about but which has instrumental and economic importance. Schooling as a social situation of development should be seen in socio-cultural terms as providing young people with the means to think, the formation of consciousness through participation in collective activities. Following Perret-Clermont (2004, p. 3)

> Thinking is considered here in the large sense of a dynamic mental activity, both cognitive and symbolic, an alternative to acting out or to reacting. Thinking has its roots in collective activities that permit or even provoke it. The child and the young person enter communities of practice that make more or less explicit . . . their thinking and the discursive fruits of it. In dialogue, the child and later the adolescent are called upon as co-thinkers or challenged with issues on which they have to take a stance. This constant confrontation with joint activities, with words and other symbolic mediations, with role-taking, but also with socially built situations, with set problems and their accepted solutions, with memories and expressed feelings, contributes to equipping the individuals with the means to think, which he or she in turn learns to use by reinvesting them in new contexts and also in facing new technologies. (Perret-Clermont, 2004, p. 3)

This growing capacity to think is not only about learning information but also includes the ability to adopt a broader perception of what is at stake, to decentre and understand the perspective of the other, to try out new skills and new ways of proceeding, and to reflect upon experiences (Perret-Clermont, 2004). Developing the capacity to think in order to face the challenges of an increasingly hostile world can be seen as a rearticulation of the vision for education set out by Tony Blair above: the capacity to think in complex ways and with a variety of mediational means is essential to produce the sort of flexibility that the modern employee is seen as requiring.

Economically, schooling matters if it provides the sort of cognitive skills and other attributes valued by employers. Possessing such skills and attributes is, in part, signalled by the possession of qualifications, which can be seen as boundary objects between the worlds of schooling and work. However, it is only certain qualifications in the English context that serve this signalling function. It is high levels of attainment in the academic curriculum of schooling and attainment of academic qualifications such as GCSEs, A levels and degrees that provide the best returns in the labour market and fuel social mobility (Pring et al., 2009).

Arguably it is also exposure and success within this sort of broad curriculum, with a variety of subjects, which also affords the best opportunities for young people to develop their capacity to think. In particular, learning within the humanities and the arts is key to developing that broader understanding of what is at stake and to decentre to understand the perspective of the other. Such a curriculum provides access to powerful knowledge that can be used to act on the world in order to increase the likelihood of a successful transition to adulthood (Young, 2008).

It would seem, then, that in terms of meeting the needs of young people at risk of becoming NEET, providing access to and success in this academic curriculum is essential and the young people themselves recognize this: they talked about getting GCSEs, doing A levels, going to University. Yet for many of those participating in the EYE there was no real equality of access to such a curriculum. They perceived themselves as failing dismally in most (though not all) academic subjects, often leading them to reject that in which they needed to be successful.

A standard policy prescription to overcome this problem is to provide opportunities for more practical, vocationally related learning for those deemed at risk of failing in the academic curriculum. This policy assumes that the problem lies in the instructional discourse of schooling, with the knowledge and skills to be learnt (Bernstein, 1996). The history of the upper secondary education system of England over the last 30 years is littered with such initiatives which emphasize the need to equip young people with the skills that would increase their 'employability' and prepare them for work. The strongly classified and framed academic curriculum is seen as being irrelevant for these young people. What they need access to, this policy discourse suggests, is a more relevant vocationally oriented curriculum: this is the instructional discourse of vocationalism (Grubb and Lazerson, 2004).

Vocationalism seeks to create new types of thinking spaces to develop new forms of consciousness that will equip young people with the knowledge and skills needed to make the transition into the labour market. In reality, such vocationally oriented curricula (which must be distinguished from other forms of vocational preparation such as apprenticeship) all too often have become a curriculum of the self whereby young people operate not on the formation of thinking as the object of activity, but on their own identity empowered by tools for 'self-reflection and self-realisation' (Power 2008, p. 31.). The primary function of such a curriculum is therapeutic, a new form of care and control, not primarily the formation of thinking (Ecclestone and Hayes, 2009). What can result is a pedagogy (Bathmaker, 2005; Ecclestone, 2007) that provides limited if any access to powerful knowledge in the sense of Young (2008) or the development of thinking argued for by Perret-Clermont (2004).

Furthermore, the qualifications that young people gain through participation in such vocationally related activities have little if any return in the labour market (Jenkins et al., 2007; McIntosh, 2007; Pring et al., 2009). They do not support transitions to sustainable employment that can produce the sort of living wage needed to break the cycle of poverty that lies at the root of the 'NEET' problem (Stanley, 2007). Young people participating in the EYE, while sometimes acknowledging the potential motivational benefits that might arise from such programmes, understood the qualifications they might obtain lacked of credibility and chose not to pursue such learning opportunities after the end of compulsory schooling.

For many of those participating in the EYE, the discourse of vocationalism fundamentally misunderstood the nature of the problem being experienced by young people with school. For them it was the regulative discourse of schooling, the rules, regulation and authority relationships that guide the functioning of schooling as an institution that constituted the problem not necessarily the instructional discourse. Leaving the school to participate in alternative provision, whether in a Pupil Referral Unit or with an Independent Training Provider, may be seen as part of the solution for these young people. But this can distance them even further from powerful forms of knowledge.

Can we dismantle the 'NEET' problem?

Young people at risk of becoming 'NEET' and those who work with them find themselves ultimately in a Batesonian double bind: whatever they do they are likely to fail. If they try to engage with the formal academic curriculum they all too often do not succeed; engaging with a more vocationally oriented curriculum with weaker classification and framing does not seem to produce positive outcomes in the labour market. Young people who are at risk of becoming 'NEET' often recognize this, disparaging such initiatives as not leading to 'proper jobs' (compared to say apprenticeships) or simply as a means of warehousing them in the education and training system rather than providing them with the means to live more independent lives. Consequently the incentives to participate in such programmes, and the social spaces of development they provide, are weak as are opportunities for progression. Young people often vote with their feet or fail to progress even though they may have successfully completed the programme. The outcome is that they fall back into the 'NEET' category.

Adopt a trajectory-based view

To make progress requires a more fundamental understanding of why schooling for young people at risk of becoming 'NEET' does not support the intermental functioning within collective activities needed to develop the capacity to think and then enable policy and practice that can change life opportunities. Adopting a view that sees progression into the NEET category as involving long-term trajectory spanning multiple institutions and social spaces for development is a good start. Given the low likelihood of changing the behaviour of employers in a flexible labour market the focus has to be on dismantling educational inequality (Portes, 2005) by affording better access to the academic curriculum of schools to the age of 16. Success in this curriculum affords progression both to other academic learning opportunities and to forms of vocational preparation, such as apprenticeship, that deliver real returns in the labour market. Crucially this curriculum, if well taught, develops the capacity to think. It is both liberal and liberating.

Welfare matters

Young people from disadvantaged backgrounds are statistically more likely to disengage from and be permanently excluded from schooling. (Bynner and Parsons, 2002). The reasons for school failure can be linked to problems that originate early in life, indeed before birth (Gorard and Rees, Dex and Joshi, 2005; Hansen et al., 2010). Recent research from the millennium cohort study indicates links between early gross motor development evident at nine months with poorer cognitive and social outcomes at age five years. These, in turn are linked in complex and as yet not fully understood ways to financial hardship and parental well-being (Schoon et al., 2010). This suggests that ongoing welfare support and poverty alleviation are going to be crucial to help young people make the most of the opportunities to learn from what school has to offer. Access to good pre- and post-natal care helps, but reducing long-term financial hardship, and the corrosive effect this can have on families, requires good welfare systems that support unemployed people back into work. Such provision has to go well beyond the current English arrangements for welfare-to-work through enacting programmes to improve the education of poorly qualified parents.

Constructing alternative thinking spaces

A sociological analysis derived from the work of Bernstein suggests that failure in the academic curriculum results from a lack of access to 'the distinctive recognition and realisation rules which the school context demands. Unless disadvantaged pupils have access to these rules as well [as middle class students] they will always be at least one step behind.' (Power, 2008, p. 31). It is certainly the case that some young people at risk of becoming long-term NEET have failed to develop the necessary mastery of key literacy and numeracy skills needed to succeed within the formal secondary school curriculum. Others seem to lack the necessary social behaviours needed to successfully navigate the socio-cognitive conflicts of schooling.

The EPPE research demonstrated the crucial role of the home learning environment for the development of cognitive skills and pro-social behaviour. If the home learning environment is impoverished, for whatever reason, then constructing substitute spaces for thinking for disadvantaged children seems to be important. High quality pre-school provision delivered by qualified teachers leads to significant improvements in both the cognitive skills and pro-social behaviour of young people from disadvantaged backgrounds. Whether such programmes afford access to 'the distinctive recognition and realization rules which the school context demands' is unclear but what is clear are the literacy and numeracy gains for young people participating in such programmes. However, these programmes have to be much more than providing child care to enable mothers to get back to work. They have to provide access to structured play and instruction for disadvantaged young people which clearly support the development of thinking.

Other research has demonstrated that effective primary and secondary schools improve learning gains for both advantaged and disadvantaged young people at similar rates. But a crucial difference between those from more and less disadvantaged backgrounds is access to out of school learning opportunities, particularly over the long school vacations. This points to the importance of developing other social situations of development where disadvantaged young people can learn outside of school. The young people participating in the engaging youth enquiry frequently cited the huge importance of youth workers and other significant adults, such as Connexions workers, in their lives. Some Local Authorities such as Wolverhampton, now actively seek to include and formally the work of youth workers in the education of young people but this requires the development of appropriate structures, systems and principles. This is an area that requires far more systematic investigation.

Feeling safe matters

To work successfully in the collective practices that support the development of thinking requires you to feel safe so that you can fail. A common aspect of the experience of young people who participated in the EYE was a lack of personal security within the social practices that constitute schooling. Such feelings can arise for seemingly trivial reasons, such as being separated from friends as young people are split up into form groups and set classes as they enter and progress in the early years of secondary schools. For others schools are a source of fear arising from bullying. Others speak of a lack of recognition from teachers, early experiences of being labelled as 'non-academic', and of being seen as troublesome or difficult (which many actually are in the sense that they fail to conform to formal school requirements and dominant social norms which can include teenage pregnancy). Such a lack of recognition is often reflected in young people's perceptions of themselves as being 'thick', a feeling reinforced by institutional processes of setting.

All of these are factors that schools can do something about by changing the nature of their collective activities. For example, even if there are huge political pressures to set pupils on the basis of prior attainment, this does not mean that lower attaining students cannot be given cognitively demanding activities led by the best teachers in a school. The achievement gap is further compounded by poorer educational opportunities for the most disadvantaged learners not ameliorated (Portes, 2005).

Constructing inclusive pedagogy

There can be no doubt that English schools are becoming more effective at helping those from disadvantaged backgrounds. More young people from such backgrounds now attain the crucial results in the GCSE examinations taken at age 16 that supports further progression in academic learning and to Higher Education (HEFCE, 2010). Effective schools really do help such young people to acquire the necessary knowledge and skills to be as academically successful as their more privileged peers. In part this is about systems and procedures, the use of data and targeted interventions to help disadvantaged learners perceived to have the 'ability' to be successful.

But for the young people who participated in the EYE what really made a school effective was the quality of the relationship with their teachers that made their teaching inclusive. Many of the young people who participated in the EYE report reacting poorly to the monological discourse of classrooms, subjected to a narrow pedagogy focussed primarily on the distribution of information to be acquired for examination success. This is not necessarily to criticize teachers, who are often striving to do their best for their students through maximizing the likelihood of examination success, a key performance indicator for English schools (Pring et al., 2009). However, such monologic scripts by representing dominant cultural values may stifle the dialogues essential for developing thinking and trying out ideas in a secure environment (Gutierrez et al., 1995, Gutierrez et al., 1999). The production of counterscripts to such monological discourses by those who did not act in accordance with the teachers' perception of acceptable behaviour is a clearly identifiable factor in the accounts provided by young people that lead to them disengaging from schooling (Hayward et al., 2008).

Insights from the research on vocational alternatives to the academic curriculum are useful here. Young people at risk of becoming NEET do report that such a curriculum offering can be motivating and engaging. They value the chance to work with adults other than teachers, for example through the Increased Flexibility Programme (Golden et al., 2005). The alternative social spaces of development offered by such activities do render actions meaningful for young people, engender feelings of competence not experienced within formal schooling, an experience of being a person who is recognized and valued by other through an enhanced capacity to act in a personally meaningful, active relational space (Zittoun, 2004).

Such activities could expand the pedagogic practice of schooling but only if alternative constructions of power between students and teachers are constructed that alter classroom scripts – the normative patterns of life within a classroom: an 'orientation that members come to expect after repeated interactions in contexts constructed both locally and over time.' (Gutierrez et al., 1995, p. 449). Where the scripts of the 'teachers' and the counterscripts of students intersect, as they seem to do in these vocational settings and in inclusive classrooms, new meanings can be created. The establishment of such a 'collective' third space, as a particular social situation of development where 'students begin to reconceive who they are and what they might be able to achieve academically and beyond' (Guttierez, 2008, p. 48) would seem essential to helping young people at risk of becoming NEET to re-engage with purposeful developmental trajectories that enable them to join society (Perret-Clermont et al., 2004). But while facilitating such intersection to produce new interactions and rich zones of collaboration and learning seems necessarily to require a weakening of the framing of the curriculum, it is not in the interest of the young people to necessarily weaken its classification, to provide an alternative to the academic curriculum. The more practical learning being offered through the vocational alternatives somehow has to be used to promote engagement with academic learning if it is to be in the interests of young people not merely interest them.

Conclusion

Schooling, as an activity, should provide a potent thinking space for young people and for many it does seem to fulfil this function including some young people who are temporarily 'NEET' as a result of some short-term event, personal misfortune, or poor guidance as to what to do next. Such young people can be successfully re-engaged in the education and training system given appropriate support structures.

However for young people at risk of becoming long term 'NEET', or of joining that portion of the NEET population that churns backwards and forwards between low wage, ephemeral employment, short-term training initiatives and 'NEET' status this is mostly not the case. Their experience of schooling is all too often as an activity in which their actions were not rendered meaningful. By and large it did not produce the sort of social relationships between these young people and adults, especially classroom teachers, which afford meaningful involvement, resources to enable the development of thinking, and reflection on prior and future experience. This is not to say that these young people never had positive social relationships with some teachers; many spoke in the EYE about favourite school subjects, for example. But as a systematic experience schooling did not work out for them and their feeling of alienation from the institution simply grew with time spent in secondary school. Such disengagement simply serves to reduce the capacity to think, widening further the attainment gap between more and less advantaged young people and reducing opportunities to make a successful transition to adult life.

Research and a more socio-cultural perspective on pedagogy have developed our understanding of how to make the social practices of schooling more inclusive and reduce educational inequality. However, many of these insights seem to founder when they meet the demands of a state exercising a huge degree of control over the curriculum and the social practices of schooling, through the assessment and performance management regimes. Young people are literally on a treadmill of assessment and teachers are held tightly accountable for their success: there is little room for risk taking and the opportunity to fail safely that seems crucial to the development of collaborative third spaces within such a performance management regime. The provision of vocational alternatives may interest young people but participation in such activity may not be in their long-term interests because there appears to be little in the way of a labour market dividend from participating in such programmes. Further it appears that it is the strong regulative discourse of schooling, which can unwittingly encourage some young people to reject schooling when it would seem so obviously in their interests not to do so.

The solution seems to lie partly in coordinated action to produce high quality pre and out of school learning activities, which can act as additional thinking spaces for disadvantaged young people. Helping young people to feel safe and valued in school and the development of more inclusive pedagogies is also crucial. But ultimately the solution to the NEET problem lies in recognizing the need to create more jobs. Educational success can change your relative provision in the job queue but success for all does not guarantee jobs for all.

References

Bathmaker, A. M. (2005). Hanging in or Shaping a Future? Defining a Role for Vocationally Related Learning in a 'Knowledge' Society. *Journal of Education Policy*, 20(1), 81–100.

Bernstein, B. (1996). Pedagogy, Symbolic Control and Identity. London: Taylor and Francis.

Blair, T. (2007). Our Nation's Future – the role of work. Available on line at http://www.number10.gov.uk/output/Page11405.asp. Last accessed February 2010.

Bynner, J. and Parsons, S. (2002). Social Exclusion and the Transition from School to Work: The Case of Young People Not in Education, Employment, or Training (NEET). *Journal of Vocational Behaviour*, 60(2) 289–309.

Callaghan, J. (1976). Towards a National Debate. Available on line at http://education.guardian.co.uk/thegreatdebate/story/0,,574645,00.html. Last accessed March 2010.

Dearden, L., McIntosh, S., Myck, M. and Vignoles, A. (2000). The Returns to Academic and Vocational Qualifications in Britain. London: Centre for the Economics of Education.

Descy, P. and Tessaring, M. (2007). Combating Labour Market Exclusion: Does Training Work? *European Journal of Vocational Training*, 41, 64–83.

Dex, S. and Joshi, H. (eds) (2005). *Children of the 21ˢᵗ Century: From Birth to Nine Months*. Bristol: Policy Press.

Ecclestone, K. (2007). Commitment, Compliance and Comfort Zones: The Effects of Formative Assessment on Vocational Students' Learning Careers. *Assessment in Education: Principles, Policy and Practice*, 14(3), 315–333.

Ecclestone, K. and Hayes, D. (2009). *The Dangerous Rise of Therapeutic Education*. London: Routledge.

Golden, S., O'Donnell, L. and Rudd, P. (2005). *Evaluation of Increased Flexibility for 14 to 16 Year Olds Programme: The Second Year*. Slough: NFER.

Gorard, S. and Rees, G. (2002). *Creating a Learning Society?: Learning Careers and Policies for Lifelong Learning* Bristol: Policy Press.

Grubb, W. N. and Lazerson, M. (2004). The Education Gospel: The Economic Power of Schooling. Harvard: Harvard University Press.

Gutierrez, K. D. (2002). Rethinking Critical Literacy in Hard Times: Critical Literacy as a Transformative Social Practice. *National Council of Teachers of English*. Atlanta: GA.

—(2008). Developing a Sociocritical Literacy in the Third Space. *Reading Research Quarterly*, 43(2), 148–164.

Gutierrez, K. D. and J. Larson (2007). Discussing Expanded Spaces for Learning [Profiles and Perspectives]. *Language Arts*, 85, 69–77.

Gutierrez, K. D., et al. (1995). Script, Counterscript, and Underlife in the Classroom: James Brown versus Brown v. Board of Education. *Harvard Educational Review*, 65, 445–471.

—(1999). Rethinking Diversity: Hybridity and Hybrid Language Practices in the Third Space. *Mind, Culture, and Activity*, 6(4), 286–303.

Hall, P. A. and Soskice, D. (eds) (2001). *Varieties of Capitalism: The Institutional Foundations of Comparative Advantage*. Oxford: Oxford University Press.

Hansen, K., Joshi, H. and Dex, S. (eds) (2010). *Children of the 21ˢᵗ Century: The First Five Years*. Bristol: Policy Press.

Hayward, G., Williams, R. and Wilde, S. (2008). *The Engaging Youth Enquiry: Final Report*. Available online at: http://ora.ouls.ox.ac.uk/objects/uuid%3A0df73fda-befd-431d-a1bf-cd53c2493531

HEFCE (2010). Trends in Young Participation in Higher Education: Core Results for England. Available online at: http://www.hefce.ac.uk/pubs/hefce/2010/10_03/. Last accessed March 2010.

Iversen, T. (2005). *Capitalism, Democracy and Welfare*. Cambridge: Cambridge University Press.

McIntosh, S. (2007). *A Cost-Benefit Analysis of Apprenticeship and Other Vocational Qualifications*. Department for Education and Skills Research Report 834. Nottingham: DfES.

Minick, N. J. (1996). 'The Development of Vygotsky's Thought: An Introduction to Thinking and Speech', in Daniels, H. (ed.) *An Introduction to Vygotsky*. London: Routledge, pp. 28–52.

Jenkins, A., Greenwood, C. and Vignoles, A. (2007). *The Return to Qualifications in England: Updating the Evidence Base on Level 2 and Level 3 Vocational Qualifications*. London: Centre for the Economics of Education.

Perret–Clermont, A. N. (2004). 'Thinking Spaces of the Young', in Perret–Clermont, A. N., Pontecorvo, C., Resnick, L. B., Zittoun, T. and Burge, B. (eds) *Joining Society: Social Interaction and Learning in Adolescence and Youth.* Cambridge: Cambridge University Press, pp. 3–10.

Perret–Clermont, A. N., Pontecorvo, C., Resnick, L. B., Zittoun, T. and Burge, B. (eds) (2004). *Joining Society: Social Interaction and Learning in Adolescence and Youth.* Cambridge: Cambridge University Press.

Portes, P. R. (2005). *Dismantling Educational Inequality: A Cultural-Historical Approach to Closing the Achievement gap.* New York: Peter Lang.

Power, S. (2008). How should We Respond to the Continuing Failure of Compensatory Education? *Orbis Scholae,* 2(2), 19–38.

Pring, R., Hayward, G., Hodgson, A., et al. (2009). *Education for All.* London: Routledge.

Resnick, L. B. and Perret–Clermont, A. N (2004). 'Prospects for Youth in Postindustrial Societies', in Perret–Clermont, A. N., Pontecorvo, C., Resnick, L. B., Zittoun, T. and Burge, B. (eds) *Joining Society: Social Interaction and Learning in Adolescence and Youth.* Cambridge: Cambridge University Press, pp. 11–25.

Schoon, I., Cheng, H. and Jones, E. (2010). 'Resilience in Children's Development', in Hansen, K., Joshi, H. and Dex, S. (eds) *Children of the 21st Century: The First Five Years.* Bristol: Policy Press, pp. 235–248.

Social Exclusion Unit (1999). *Bridging the Gap: New opportunities for 16-18 year-olds not in education, employment or training.* [online] http://www.cabinetoffice.gov.uk/~/media/assets/www.cabinetoffice.gov.uk/social_exclusion_task_force/publications_1997_to_2006/bridging_gap%20pdf.ashx.

Stanley, G. (2007). Education for Work: The Current Dilemma of Post-Compulsory Education. *The Australian Educational Researcher,* 34(3), 91–100.

Welshman, J. (2006). Underclass: A History of the Excluded, 1880-2000. London: Hambledon Continuum.

Young, M. F. D. (2008). *Bringing Knowledge Back in: From Social Constructivism to Social Realism in the Sociology of Education.* Abingdon: Routledge.

Zittoun, T. (2004). 'Preapprenticeship: A Transitional Space', in Perret–Clermont, A. N., Pontecorvo, C., Resnick, L. B., Zittoun, T. and Burge, B. (eds) *Joining Society: Social Interaction and Learning in Adolescence and Youth.* Cambridge: Cambridge University Press, pp. 153–176.

Index